THE

ROAD

TO

POWER

SUNY Series in Israeli Studies
Russell Stone, Editor

A publication from the Center for the Study and Documentation of Israeli Society,
The Hebrew University, Jerusalem.

THE ROAD

TO

POWER

Herut Party in Israel

Yonathan Shapiro

Translated from the Hebrew by Ralph Mandel

State University of New York Press

Published by
State University of New York Press, Albany

©1991 State University of New York

For information, address the State University of New York Press,
State University Plaza, Albany, NY 12246

Production by Christine Lynch
Marketing by Fran Keneston

Library of Congress Cataloging-in-Publication Data

Shapiro, Yonathan.
    [La-shilton behartanu.   English]
    The road to power : Herut Party in Israel / Yonathan Shapiro :
translated from the Hebrew by Ralph Mandel.
      p. cm. — (SUNY series in Israeli studies)
    Translation of: La-shilton behartanu.
    Includes bibliographical references and index.
    ISBN 0-7914-0606-7 (alk. paper), — ISBN 0-7014-0607-5 (pbk. :
alk. paper)
    1. Tenu' sy ha-herut (Israel)   2. Israel—Political and government.
I. Title. II. Series.
JQ1825.P373T473713   1991   90-9887
324.25694'083—dc20   CIP

10 9 8 7 8 6 5 4 3 2 1

Contents

Acknowledgments

During the course of my work on this project, I conducted many useful discussions. I am grateful to my colleagues and students who helped me clarify and come to grips with many problems that intrigued me in the process of composing this work.

Professors Amos Funkenstein and Yoav Peled read an earlier draft and made many insightful comments. Aliza Lewenberg and Dani Levi had useful suggestions in the course of my writing.

Mr. Pesah Gani and his associates in the Jabotinsky Institute in Tel Aviv were very helpful during my collection of the data for this study. Mr. Yehoshua Ofir gave me access to the files of the National Workers Federation.

I received assistance in preparing this manuscript from the management and staff of the Wissenschaftskolleg zu Berlin (The Institute of Advanced Study in Berlin) where I spent the academic year 1986-87. I express my gratitude to everyone.

Introduction

The political parties have been my principal interest in my studies of Israeli politics.

My three previous books focused on the Israel Labor Party (until 1968, known as Mapai: Hebrew acronym for Eretz-Israel Workers Party).[1] The central research questions posed in these studies were: Who rules in the State of Israel, and how is that rule implemented? My underlying thesis was that political parties constitute the most important political organizations in a democratic state, therefore, a knowledge of their structure and composition is an essential prerequisite for understanding the power structure in such a state. This is manifestly the case in Israel, which was established by parties that shaped not only its political system but also its economy, its administrative apparatus, and its educational and cultural institutions.

My focus was on Mapai as the dominant party in Israel since the state's establishment. A party is dominant, Maurice Duverger contends, when its spiritual advantage enables it to obtain, over a lengthy period, votes far in excess of any other party. According to Duverger, a party attains this status "when its doctrines, ideas, methods, its style, so to speak, coincide with those of the epoch . . . domination is a question of influence rather than of strength; it is also linked with belief. A dominant party is that which public opinion *believes* to be dominant. . . . Even the enemies of the dominant party, even citizens who refuse to give it their vote, acknowlege its superior status and its influence; they deplore it but admit it."[2] This definition takes note of both the spiritual dominance of the central party and the spiritual inferiority of opponents and their consequent self-effacement.

The Herut Party, the subject of the present study, did not acquiesce in Mapai's spiritual dominance and refused to accept the values and political rules of the game that placed Mapai at the center of the party system, thus, relegating other parties to the periphery as partners or potential partners in a Mapai-led government. Herut, even though it took part in all the election campaigns, refused to acknowledge this dominance and thereby became a party that spurned the existing political structure, the system of values, and the political order within which

1

it operated. Herut did not reject the democratic system itself but the dominant party structure in Israel, at the center of which was a party possessing spiritual dominance—Mapai and then its successor, the Labor Party.

The upshot was that Herut remained isolated and without influence in the Israel polity.

In the 1970s, the Labor Party's spiritual dominance came to an end and with it the entire dominant party system.[3] In 1977, Herut attained power and its leader, Menachem Begin, became prime minister. Since then Israel has had a multi-party system with two major parties competing for power: the Labor Party and its allies (the Alignment), and the Herut Party and its allies (the Likud).

The present study deals with the structure of Herut and the course it followed from its establishment until it achieved power. A study of this kind, it seems to me, can enhance understanding of the theme that was the focus of my previous studies, namely, who rules in the State of Israel and how the rule is implemented.

Herut differed in its organizational structure from Mapai and other Israeli parties. Mapai was led by an elite that had at its disposal a bureaucracy staffed by a group of functionaries who helped the leadership garner support. The proficiency demonstrated by the bureaucratic machine in enlisting the support of members and voters derived from its ability to mediate between the party's leaders and its supporters with the aid of material inducements at its disposal.[4] The bodies that decided on party policy were staffed by the heads of the party machinery, and decisions were taken through a constant dialogue between the leadership and those who ran the party apparatus. I termed a party of this kind a "machine party."

The Herut leadership, claiming to represent the national interest and not any sectorial interests, whether economic or social, did not create machinery to mediate between the party leadership and specific interest groups. The leadership operated without the aid of a bureaucratic structure staffed by groups of functionaries who mobilized support for the party's leaders and took part in the articulation of party policy. Instead, Herut was headed by a leader who exercised one-man rule. His strengh emanated from his being perceived as the symbol and the embodiment of myths with which party members and voters identified. I term a party of this kind a "leader party."

Herut's different structure is attributed to the political socialization undergone by the party's founders and leaders during their formative years in Poland, and to their standing in the social and political structure of Israel during the years after the establishment of the state— when they founded and led their organization.

The Herut leadership was a "generation unit" whose members reached maturity in the 1930s and acquired their political socialization and formative political experience in the Betar youth movement in Poland. They continued to exist as a generation unit in Palestine within common organizational frameworks; in the military underground, they organized against the British Mandate authorities, in the Irgun Zvai Leumi (National Military Organization, or Irgun for short) and in the Herut movement, they transferred the political culture they acquired in Poland to the new country. Back in Poland, their reference groups were the European radical right and the ruling groups in the country, who also belonged to that political camp, particularly after the death of their leader, Jozef Pilsudski, in 1935.

The radical right in Europe was composed of many groups and organizations differing from one another. Nevertheless, they shared certain principles:

1. Nationalism is a supreme and total interest. Therefore politics is a total pursuit, and social, economic, educational, and cultural activity must serve this supreme interest.

2. All people can change and direct their destiny if they only so desire. The main thing is self-determination, and no undue consideration need be given to political, economic, and social constraints liable to impede this desire.

3. Political power is attainable by convincing the masses to vote for one's party or through a coup. Both options are legitimate. This principle has a further implication for radical-right movements. Such movements consist of a mass organization that operates to enlist the support of the masses and alongside it an elite military organization capable of staging a coup.

4. Heading the party is a leader who symbolizes the supreme national interest. He is therefore also the source of the ideological and organizational authority within the party and, when it achieves power, in the country.

Betar embraced these principles, but Herut, which was founded in Israel after the establishment of the state, functioned in a political and social system different from the Polish experience, and adapted itself to the new reality. Its most important deviation lay in its acceptance of the rules of the democratic game, which required both an organizational change and a modification of the attitude toward the leader. The change in the status of the leader, as I will try to show, was not great even though democratic procedures were introduced into the party.

This historical and cultural association with the European radical right has encouraged me to draw on the many studies published in the past 10-15 years concerning this political movement in explaining the Herut movement.[5] Many of the members and supporters of radical-right movements in Europe, researchers explain, came from middle class groups whose prestige had declined or who felt they were not receiving their due esteem in a changing society that had undergone rapid processes of industrialization, urbanization, and secularization. It was mainly peasants and townspeople who owned small and medium businesses that were pushed to the fringes in the new society. They developed a sense of frustration and hatred that was directed at the groups, which gained strength in the society; they were exploited by political leaders seeking their support. To help mobilize that support, politicians evoked cultural myths and symbols that were shared by all members of the society. These were national myths that concerned the nation's glorious past and future destiny. Such myths helped to cultivate the national pride of these groups, imbuing them with the sense that they were the loyal members of the nation and not the groups that had achieved power and prestige in the modern society. A good deal of pretense was entailed in this concoction of a mythical world through which the actual social reality, in which such groups found themselves on the margins, was ignored.

The leaders transmitted these myths—suffused with hatred for the ruling establishment—in emotional speeches, which they delivered at mass rallies, huge demonstrations, and large-scale ceremonies. Thus the crowd was made to feel that they were participating in a meaningful political act. Their participation in such assemblies effected no change in their situation in the polity, but was an outcry against the existing order.

Another category of professional literature I drew on is comprised of the many studies of populist movements in South America, particularly Peronism in Argentina. The Italian sociologist Gino Germani, who emigrated from Fascist Italy to Argentina and found himself under the regime of Juan Peron, has compared the two regimes.[6] Germani argues that the differences between them are largely a function of the differences in the social structure prevalent on the two continents. Support for the European radical right emanated chiefly from middle-class groups adversely affected by changes in the society, the concentration of power in the economic-industrial sector, and the growing strength of the organized working class. Support for Peron came mainly from migrants who moved from villages to the big cities, where they became workers and found themselves on the margins of the urban society.

Peron's movement, the studies maintained, arose at the point of convergence of the two populations. Elite groups, who had been stripped of their power and shunted aside by ruling groups or had been prevented from gaining access to the new centers of power, became the leaders of the movement. Their support came from the masses who migrated from Argentina's rural agricultural regions to the big cities, particularly Buenos Aires. They were less grieved by their economic situation than by their inability to integrate themselves socially into the new reality. They found work as laborers and gradually improved their economic situation but still failed to be absorbed culturally, socially, and politically in the urban society. They were not absorbed by the trade unions and the socialist parties that had a European tradition; they were controlled by second-generation European immigrants who had no common language with the former villagers. The alienation that subsequently developed among the urbanized villagers was exploited by politicians from the displaced elite groups, using means similar to those employed by the radical right in Europe. Here, too, hatred for the establishment was cultivated with the aid of national myths geared to convince the villagers that they were the true Argentinians and not the others who were under the sway of foreign ideas and accepted the dominance of foreign powers, such as the United States and Britain. The populist style of Peron and his aides resembled that of the European radical right. The leaders spoke at mass rallies in which they tried to give the masses the feeling they were participating in a political act. Many researchers argue that were it not for Peron's success in exploiting the alienation of the villagers and cultivating their national pride, he would not have achieved power; and, were it not for the Peronist movement, an authentic leadership would gradually have emerged among the villagers and helped them find their niche in the urban society.

In my analysis of Herut, I have also made use of anthropological literature dealing with myths and symbols. Students of the radical right emphasize the ability of leaders to enlist mass support through the manipulation of myths, which originate in the shared culture of leaders and their supporters, and thus wield such inordinate influence.[7] This emphasis on the manipulation of cultural myths is accounted for in the fact that many leaders and intellectuals of the radical right have admitted that their political behavior was influenced by the writings of Georges

Sorel and Gustave Le Bon, who believed in the power of myths to spur the masses to action. Many anthropologists have preferred to offer a sociological explanation for the influence of myths and symbols in the social and political system. They have examined the connection between the use of myths by different groups and the social system within which they operate.[8] In their view, the use of myths is aimed at strengthening the claim of various groups to status in the social system. In every society, competition exists among different groups for status and prestige, and one form of its expression is in a struggle over myths. Groups engaged in this struggle identify with myths through which they lay claim to a respectable status in the system, and denigrate myths of the groups competing with them for status.

An additional theoretical approach that has influenced my work sprang up in the 1950s and 1960s among American sociologists and historians who were studying radical movements in the United States, from the populists at the end of the last century, to present-day extra-parliamentary groups. A particularly important work is the study by the political sociologist Joseph Gusfield on the Prohibition movement that was launched in the mid-nineteenth century and won its brief triumph after World War I, when it brought about an amendment to the U.S. Constitution barring the sale of alcoholic beverages.[9]

Gusfield and other researchers, who have studied American extreme right-wing movements within certain states, have tried to develop an all-embracing theory that would also explain the European radical right and perhaps the populist movements in South America as well. They draw a distinction between "Class Politics," in which political parties and movements see to the material interests of population groups, and "Status Politics," which is a struggle for group prestige that preoccupies groups on the extreme right.

Status Politics involves two types of groups or social categories: (a) those that lose status and prestige in the wake of changes in the social system, and (b) those that feel they are not getting due recognition and prestige within the system. Democratic politics based on a distribution of resources and on compromises finds it difficult to satisfy groups fighting for prestige. In a political debate concerned with the distribution of myths and symbols of status rather than the attainment of material or other tangible accomplishments, it is more difficult to reach a compromise. Politics occupied with status may often lead, instead, to radicalization, in both the content and the style of the struggle between the groups involved.

In a struggle for status waged in the arena of politics through a dispute over myths and symbols, political activity loses its pragmatic character. Instead of looking for practical answers to burning issues, leaders deal in symbols and in the pretense that the reality is different from what it actually is. They engage in stirring up the crowd instead of attempting to solve its problems. The yearning for status, researchers say, is at times unconscious or only partly conscious in the crowd. This facilitates the emergence of a dramatic political style that solves nothing but gives its supporters a good feeling that they are important and central actors in the society.

The political interchange on myths that takes place between leaders with rhetorical ability and stage presence, and the masses, creates what anthropologists call "symbolic discourse."[10] Instead of a bureaucratic politics of committees and arrangements and practical compromises, the researchers contend, politics is transformed into a "politics of the piazza," made up of emotional speeches at rallies and efforts to enflame passions by enlisting the aid of good and just myths and symbols hurled against an establishment that upholds bad and unjust myths and symbols.[11]

In this book, I argue that the politics practiced by the Herut movement was Status Politics and not Class Politics. In the 1950s, its members were former Betar and Irgun members whose advance in the social and economic system and participation in the political system was blocked. As a result, they responded to a politics that gave them, with the help of myths, a feeling of value and importance in the system that rejectecd them, and fostered hatred for the ruling groups holding them back. This Status Politics succeeded in retaining its grip in Herut despite the movement's electoral defeats during nearly thirty years. A key factor in the success of the 1970s was the encounter between Irgun veterans in Herut and recent immigrants from the Oriental communities who had emigrated from Asian and African countries and who also yearned for status and for participation in a system that blocked their way. They, too, were responsive to the political style of the Herut leaders and adopted their myths and symbols.

When Herut became a ruling party, the Status Politics it espoused began to seep through the entire political system.

The first three chapters deal with the Betar youth movement in Poland and in Palestine. The book's main focus is on the Herut movement from its founding in 1948 until it achieved power in 1977. Chapters 4–6 are devoted to an analysis of the party's distinctive structure as it was forged in its first decade of existence. In those years, it was a party that accepted the rules of the democratic game but spurned Mapai's spiritual dominance. Chapter 7 discusses the party's failed attempts in the 1960s to escape its political isolation. The eighth chapter considers the ten years after the Six Day War in the wake of which Herut was extricated from its political isolation until its victory in the 1977 elections.

1

The Inception of a Political Movement

Ze'ev Jabotinsky, Liberal Nationalist

The founders of the Herut movement, which forms the subject of this book were, in the pre-state period, leaders of a military underground called the *"Irgun Zvai Leumi."* The Irgun existed as a military organization from 1937 until the establishment of the state of Israel in 1948. Its dissolution followed a series of dramatic events that are discussed in another chapter. Immediately thereafter a group of Irgun commanders headed by Menachem Begin, the organization's commander-in-chief since 1943, organized themselves and set up a party called the "Herut movement."

The party's founders were united by the bond of their shared experience in the underground period. However, an understanding of their political thinking and political behavior requires the examination of an antecedent stage in their history. Most of them began their political activity in the Betar youth movement. It was in Betar that the political ideas and practices of Herut leaders were shaped. The Irgun also evolved in Betar. Ideas that originated in Betar were later transferred by its members to Herut. I will therefore not examine the Irgun in this book but rather concentrate, in the first chapters, on an analysis of Betar. This must begin with an examination of Ze'ev Jabotinsky, the founder and leader of the Revisionist movement. Betar was affiliated with the Revisionist party, and both organizations were led by Jabotinsky until his death in 1940.

Much has been written about Jabotinsky, a controversial personality. The admiration he generated in some was equalled only by the antipathy, even the hatred, he aroused in others. These conflicting emotions are perceptible to this day in the attempts to assess his thinking and his activity as a Zionist leader.

The large number of speeches he delivered and his writings in the Jewish and general press enable Jabotinsky's partisans and detractors alike to deal with those aspects of his work that are consistent with their

9

perception of the man. The bulk of his writing was journalistic: reactions, published in dailies and weeklies, to current events, rather than a systematic political doctrine. The accessibility of this material has tempted researchers to analyze it and not to deal with its author as the founder and leader of a political party and a youth movement.[1]

It is not my intention in this study to examine either Jabotinsky's doctrine or the entire scope of his activity as a political leader, a subject that merits a separate study. Yet it is impossible to discuss the Betar youth movement without considering Jabotinsky's cardinal role in shaping it, particularly in its early years.

Ze'ev Jabotinsky was born in Odessa in 1880 to an assimilated, middle-class Jewish family. He became a Zionist nationalist Jew following his return to Russia after some years of study in Europe, mainly in Italy. Jabotinsky, then in his early twenties, already espoused a liberal world view and worked as a journalist in the Russian Press.

In these first years in the Zionist movement he displayed his independent thinking. Although socialism was the dominant ideology among his Jewish and Zionist peers in Russia, Jabotinsky remained loyal to liberalism and spurned socialism. As a result, he found himself more closely aligned with an older generation of Zionist leaders who also had a liberal orientation. This probably accounts for the relatively young age at which he became a member of the Zionist Executive (the body that headed the World Zionist Organization—WZO—after World War I).

Many Zionists of Jabotinsky's generation, seeking to fuse the national idea with the socialism that was then making inroads among the Russian intelligentsia, adopted a socialist-Zionist outlook.[2] Jabotinsky, in contrast, was a devotee of liberalism and believed that liberalism and socialism were incompatible. An article he published in 1912 described an imaginary encounter between one of the leaders of the Italian national movement, Giuseppe Garibaldi, who headed a group of Italian freedom fighters in the second half of the nineteenth century, and socialist contemporaries of Jabotinsky. Garibaldi is described as operating in a society "full of nationalist fervor, pervaded by enmity toward foreigners, an atmosphere incessantly rife with the unbearable declamation of patriotic slogans." In that period of a national liberation struggle, Jabotinsky explained, all other ideals were forgotten and neglected. "One's whole strength was consumed solely by national questions and *amor patriae*," it was an atmosphere of "true chauvinism." Today's socialists would undoubtedly look on these people as "obscurantists and opponents of culture. They are deceivers leading astray the ignorant masses." Garibaldi and his comrades demanded that the masses expel the Germans instead of saying to them: All men are brothers. "They tell them to establish states instead of telling them to introduce democratic procedures in the states. " They—Garibaldi and his friends—today's socialists would say, "are distancing the heart of youth from universal human ideals and inflaming their minds through the inordinate worship of the national past and the national tongue. They want all problems to be thrust aside, and the people to expend its best strength on building a gilded cage in which it can separate itself from its brethren who speak a foreign language."[3]

By means of this imaginary encounter between nineteenth-century nationalism and the universalist democratic socialism that engulfed Russia in the early twentieth century, Jabotinsky illustrated the unbridgeable gaps separating him from his fiercest opponents in the World Zionist Organization, the socialist-Zionists.

His denigration of socialism became still more acute after the Bolshevik Revolution in Russia. The revolution, he believed, was a disaster for humanity but most of all for the Jewish people.[4] He did not abandon his liberalism when he became a Zionist, and even though he admitted that nationalism as he understood it was not entirely compatible with the liberal idea, he tried hard to find a common denominator between the collective national idea and the concept of individual rights, which was at the core of liberalism. This contradiction between the two viewpoints he espoused distressed him all his life. Every so often he sought ways to bridge the two concepts. Thus, for example, in one of the first articles he wrote after becoming a Zionist, he argued that the purpose of national existence was the creation of a distinctive spiritual nationality. To this end a nation needed a state in which it would constitute an overwhelming majority, since only separateness and insularity would enable it to forge a distinctive system of values. But once that culture had emerged, the nation "will not set it aside for itself but will bring it to the joint international community for the general good." In other words, the distinctive culture of a people is created for the benefit of all humankind.[5] This was clearly an attempt to bridge the gap between his nationalism and his liberal-universal world view.

One element in the liberal world view, which he wished to preserve above all else, was rationalism. For many years he rejected the mystical, romantic version of nationalism and defined himself as a rational nationalist. The policy he preached was the outgrowth of a sober appraisal of the international reality. To survive in this reality, he explained, every nation must constantly defend itself against its neighbors. In relations between nations the rule was *homo homini lupus*. Hence, his conclusion "that isolation, distrust, a stand of 'being on watch' always, stern treat-ment at all times is the only means to hold one's own in this wolfish confrontation."[6]

Despite his best efforts, however, Jabotinsky was unsuccessful in reconciling this aggressive nationalism with a liberal outlook. When he first embarked on the liberal road, he coined the phrase: "In the begin-ning God created the individual." After adopting the extreme version of the nationalist outlook, he pronounced that: "In the beginning God created the nation." Pursuing his attempts to resolve the contradiction between these two conflicting slogans, he stated in his autobiography, written in the 1930s, that the two were not mutually contradictory because man's natural aspiration to serve the nation comes of his own volition. It is a voluntary act impelled by inner conviction and therefore does not contradict the belief in the centrality, desire, and aspirations of the individual, which is a fundamental tenet of liberal thought.[7] Jabotinsky accepted this argument in the years when he was influenced by the radical-right doctrine that spread rapidly through Europe in the inter-war period. His argument was consistent with the notion of these circles that true freedom is inner freedom and that the superiority of the nation is merely an expression of inner awareness of self-realization.[8]

No immanent internal contradiction exists between nationalism and liberalism. Liberal nationalism was a feasible concept. John Plamenatz contends that illiberal nationalism is more characteristic of eastern Eu-rope than of western European countries. The Russian and Austro-Hungarian Empires that ruled in eastern Europe until the termination of World War I were composed of many nationalities.

When the process of industrialization and urbanization began in these regions in the mid-nineteenth century, the dominant nations were able to control the governmental bureaucracies that were at the center of this activity, and, through them, broad areas of life. Other national groups found it difficult to achieve positions of influence in these orga-nizations and in some cases were completely excluded. These develop-ments affected mainly the intelligentsia, and it was the intelligentsia that became the standard bearer of modern nationalism. Cultural nationl-ism—an attempt to advance the culture of their people and adapt it to modern life—was a frequent recourse in these groups. Since these were for the most part peasant communities, lacking a developed language suitable for modern urban-industrial life, a prodigious effort was in-volved. Particularly difficult, Plamenatz says, was the desperate attempt by the intelligentsia from these national minorities to emulate the cul-tures of the dominant nations while simultaneously spotlighting their own cultural distinctiveness in competition with those cultures. The tension created by this contradiction was what pushed many of them into illiberal nationalism, ethnocentrism, and xenophobia.[9] The result, says another researcher, was the emergence of an ethnic nationalism in eastern Europe, as contrasted with a nationalism in western Europe that identified nationality with citizenship in the state and not with ethnic origin.[10] Within a generation or two, Poles, who immigrated even to Germany, were full-fledged Germans. Whereas Germans in Poland remained members of the German nation, an ethnic minority among the dominant Polish nation, and were excluded from influence bearing positions in the administration and the governmental bureaucracy.

This illiberal nationalism was linked to a deep sense of national inferiority, resulting from a constant comparison with the dominant nationality whose culture was emulated. This can be seen in Jabotinsky and other Zionists, too. The difference was that socialist and humanist values adopted by many Zionists curbed and moderated the illiberal element in their ethnic nationalism. The humanistic and unversalistic element in their world view drew them close to the Western European Enlightenment, which was the source of humanistic and rationalist nationalism. Futhermore, many of the Zionists in the socialist-progressive camp were still immersed in Jewish culture and tradition, and were therefore spared in part the difficult process of emulating the dominant culture attempted by the intelligentsia of ethnic peasant communities that lacked a rich cultural tradition comparable to that of the Jewish group. Jabotinsky, though, came from an assimilationist background and was cut off from this tradition. Ultimately he was attracted by the aggressive and emotional nationalism of the radical right.

The intellectual appeal of the radical-right ideas, which influenced him in the 1920s, is, I believe, also related to his political standing in the Zionist national movement at this time. It was in this period that he decided to head a Zionist party in opposition to the Zionist leadership, which he considered excessively moderate and compromising. He wanted a proud and aggressive nationalism.

Jabotinsky and the Radical Right

From the time he became a Zionist, Jabotinsky devoted his public activity to Zionist propagandizing—"agitation," as it was then called—as a speaker who criss-crossed Europe and in numerous articles in the Jewish Press. He excelled at both. He was a gifted and dazzling orator, and had a clear and lucid prose style in many languages. He gained fame as a

Zionist leader during World War I when he convinced the British government to set up Jewish army units as part of the British forces who took part in the conquest of Palestine. His attempts to maintain these units in Palestine after the war failed, but his activity in this regard made his name known throughout the Jewish world and helped get him appointed to the Zionist Executive after the war. Although he held a central position on the Executive, his differences with the majority led to his resignation in 1923.

Many of the disagreements between Jabotinsky and others on the Executive revolved around the relations between the WZO and the British government, which was given a Mandate by the League of Nations to help the Jews establish their own state in Palestine. Jabotinsky urged Zionists to pressure London to declare its support for the establishment of a Jewish state. Such pressures could prove fruitful, Jabotinsky believed, if Zionist propagandists like himself mobilized the support of English and world public opinion. With this goal in mind, he also demanded that the Zionist Executive explicitly define its objective as the establishment of an independent Jewish state.

These tactics were rejected by the majority. They countered that as long as the Jewish community in Palestine was small in number—there were then about 100,000 Jews in Palestine—preference should go to settling the country. Every new settlement, every Jewish school, and every Jewish-owned factory was a step on the road to the goal. Therefore the majority refused to issue proclamations that were liable to generate tension and contentiousness with the Arab majority in Palestine and England itself.They did not accept Jabotinsky's activist tactics. They advocated quiet diplomacy, with the brunt of the efforts devoted to getting Jews to come to Palestine and ensuring their absorption.

Jabotinsky sought international recognition for Jewish sovereignty in Palestine.He believed this was attainable by enlisting the support of sympathetic liberal public opinion in Britain and by convincing leading figures that the establishment of a Jewish state would serve British interests.

When the British government decided unilaterally in 1922 to sever the territory of Palestine east of the Jordan River from the rest of Palestine and transform it into an Arab emirate under Prince Abdullah, Jabotinsky wanted to protest by mobilizing Jewish and world public opinion. However, other Zionist leaders were apprehensive about straining relations with Britain beyond the breaking point while they still needed its help in settling Palestine.

Following his resignation from the Zionist Executive, Jabotinsky pursued his public activity, publishing articles in the Jewish press and appearing before Jewish audiences to vent his dissident views. Zionists who supported his activist ideas asked him to establish and head a Zionist party based on these principles. Among his supporters were liberal nationalist Zionists with whom he had ties dating back to pre-revolutionary Russia, along with a number of well-known personalities in the Zionist movement and the Jewish public in central Europe. These included Richard Lichtheim, a reputable German Zionist leader, and Robert Stricker, a member of the Austrian Senate. Jabotinsky's ideas also gained the ardent backing of a group of high school students in Riga, Latvia, who wanted to set up a youth movement grounded on these principles.

A new Zionist party, the Revisionist Party, headed by Jabotinsky, was organized shortly before the Zionist Congress of 1925. The party's late formation was apparently one of the reasons for its limited success in the elections against the veteran and established Zionist parties. But it was in this period, when the party was being organized, that Jabotinsky fell under the sway of a new political and intellectual movement with growing influence in Europe.

This movement, known as the radical right, was comprised of a large number of groups, organizations, and parties. What they all had in common was an awareness that they constituted a political and conceptual current in conflict with the socialist and communist left, on the one hand, and the conservative, liberal bourgeoisie, on the other hand. Thus, some of them dubbed themselves the Third Europe or the New Europe. The German Nazis and the Italian Fascists were only two of a large number of organizations associated with this ideological and political movement. In later years, they attracted far more attention because they attained power in their countries and came close to world domination. But there were many other groups, and there is no doubt that the Nazis in Germany were a particulary extreme group in this camp. Some leaders of the radical right in Europe considered them an aberration, especially after they transformed Germany into a country seeking to impose the German race throughout Europe.

All these movements shared an opposition to the status quo in their countries and a disposition toward extreme nationalism. The national outlook assumed a different content in each nation, related to its own distinctive history and culture. Since each of the movements was also struggling against the prevailing establishment in its country, each of them possessed its own special coloring as an opposition element. Every nationalism is unique. Therefore, as Richard Hamilton notes, in contrast to socialists who espouse a universal world view and who could be incorporated in a single international organization under the slogan, Workers of all countries, unite; it is inconceivable for nationalist movements to come together under the slogan, Nationalists of the world, unite.[11]

Each of these nationalist movements believed in the superiority of its nation and underscored the difference and conflicts of interest between their nation and others; this was felt most strongly in countries that suffered from unstable relations with their neighbors. A central problem in most of these movements concerned the borders of their country, resulting from historical developments, mainly in eastern Europe where different nations were geographically intermixed. Many radical-right movements aspired to change their state borders so as to incorporate all the members of their nation in their own nation-state. For many of them, the border issue preoccupied them to the point of obsession.

Another element uniting all the movements was their activism, which is better characterized as an orientation than as an ideology. They were convinced that it was within their power to change the course of their people's history and its standing in the world, if only they willed it. This activism and its attendant ambition were what first appealed to Jabotinsky—now the leader of an opposition party in the World Zionist Organization.

In his first years of opposition, Jabotinsky defined himself as Theodor Herzl's successor. Like Herzl—the founder of the World Zionist Organization—he believed that the goal must be international recognition of the Jewish people's right to an independent state, and that this should be secured even before the Jews constituted the majority in Palestine. Like Herzl, he was convinced that the Jews' exodus from Europe and the creation of a Jewish state were consistent with the self-interest of every nation-state harboring a Jewish minority. This self-interest could be explained to liberal and enlightened opinion in Europe. To succeed in such campaign, Jabotinsky argued, Zionism must pursue a more assertive policy. Over the years he became increasingly impatient with the cautious policy of the Zionist Executive, and came to adopt viewpoints of the activist radical right. He accepted the principle that the national idea was the one single and exclusive idea. All efforts must be devoted to political activity aimed at achieving the national idea. Economic and cultural interests that did not directly serve this objective would have to wait until it was realized.[12] This was a central idea of the radical right.[13] But what were the national goals?

All movements of the radical right posited the uplifting of national pride as their primary purpose. Germany's defeat in World War I and Italy's failure to reap the fruits of its allies' victory, and the insecurity of many of the states created in Europe after the war, nourished this need to ameliorate wounded national pride. Even during the severe economic crisis that afflicted Germany in the years from 1929–1933, Nazi propaganda continued to focus chiefly not on the crisis itself but on the injury done by the victorious powers and the German establishment to the honor of Germany in the aftermath of World War I. While the economic crisis helped the Nazis gain growing support among the electorate, Hitler's promises even during the period of the crisis dealt mainly with German national honor that had been trampled by the Treaty of Versailles and the behavior of the victorious powers.[14]

The Revisionist Party also held the defense of national honor to be a supreme value. "Jabotinsky's Jewish state . . . was intended to exalt Jewish honor," Kalman Katznelson, one of the party's intellectuals, wrote, "to reduce the gap between the Jews and the other civilized peoples, and thus to advance the equality of rights which Jews saw as the be-all and end-all." Jabotinsky's Jewish state was to be the central showpiece for the Gentiles: "You said we were incapable of establishing a state, yet here before your eyes is a truly magnificent Jewish State."[15]

Jabotinsky believed that to regain the esteem of Gentiles, Jews must alter their way of life. This was a major educational task of the youth movement he created. A central educational principle of Betar was the value he called "hadar" (a Hebrew word signifying, in this context, "grace" and "decorum"). Jabotinsky elucidated this concept in Ra'ayon Betar (The Idea of Betar) published by the Betar High Commission in 1934. Hadar, Jabotinsky wrote, is comprised of many actions in everyday life which, while perhaps individually unimportant, taken together constitute the very content of one's life. "Eat noiselessly and slowly," Jabotinsky wrote, "do not protrude your elbows at meals, do not sip your soup loudly . . . walking upstairs at night, do not talk—you awaken the neighbors . . . in the streets give right of way to a lady, to an elderly person," and so on and so forth. Particulary illuminating is his assessment the results of such behavior by Jews might have: "Were all Jews to act properly, the anti-Semites probably would hate us anyhow but it would be a hate mixed with respect, and our situation in the world would have been quite different than it is."[16] This argument exemplifies Plamenatz's description of the tension that gripped the intelligentsia of national minority groups in eastern Europe. It bespeaks the emulation and desire for integration into the majority civilization and the belief that in this manner the Jews would be recognized as civilized people. This aspiration united many leaders of the Jewish intelligentsia in eastern Europe. On the other hand, there was Jabotinsky's repeated demand that the Jews develop a distinctive culture and value-system and not emulate alien ideas of personages such as "Marx, Lenin, Gandhi, tomorrow perhaps Mussolini," as he wrote in 1934.[17] When Abba Achimeir, a member of the Revisionist Party, began publishing a column in the official party paper called "From the Notebook of a Fascist," what especially irked Jabotinsky was more Achimeir's use of a term culled "from alien worlds"[18] and not so much the extreme positions he advanced. The effort to preserve the Jews' cultural distinctiveness found unexpected expression in 1935 when Jabotinsky presented a new constitution for his organization after leaving the WZO and setting up the New Zionist Organization (NZO). One of the regulations required members to observe the Sabbath and study the tenets of the Jewish faith. This demand surprised many of his followers—like him, secular Jews. In later years, when his opponents cited this approach as proof of his political opportunism, his disciples retorted in his defense that it was a legitimate political act stemming from his desire to satisfy the requests of a religious faction that had been set up in the NZO and of other religious groups whose support he required.[19] It is difficult to accept this interpretation. Its weakness is pronounced when Jabotinsky's approach is found to parallel the adoption of religious values by secular leaders in other parties of the radical right.[20]

Like many of the leaders of these movements, Jabotinsky also arrived at the conclusion—which many of his associates did not share—that nationalism and religion were two world views that had in common support for tradition in the face of ideas that preached progress and change. Modern nationalism sprang up as an expression of the aspiration to conserve venerable traditions against those who wanted to break with them and to maintain social frameworks that curbed the impulse to social change. Radical-right nationalism was the refuge of many who feared such change. Futhermore, in the contest against universal and humanist socialism, which advocated equality and social justice, nationalism lacked a comparable moral dimension. Jabotinsky, like other leaders of the radical right, reached the conclusion that without this kind of moral dimension the national idea would be hard pressed to compete with the socialist idea, particularly among more idealistic youth. Speaking at the NZO's founding convention in 1935, after explaining that he had become convinced that it was wrong to separate state and religion, he added that the religious idea should be adopted in order to ensure that youth was not swept up "in the whirlpool of infinite influences that seize the youth of our day and poison them." To this end it was also important "that in the arena place be made for its fighters and in the pulpit for its preachers."[21]

In 1939 his consciousness of religion's importance as a positive educational factor among youth was reinforced. In a message to Betar published in the movement's paper in Poland in March of that year, Jabotinsky wrote that Betar's first task was to establish an army. Yet because the contemporary era was marked by religious wars, it was impossible to believe in the rifle without faith, and to that end a social doctrine was required. However, "there is no need to invent it because it already exists in the Biblical and Talmudic tradition"—all that remains is to systematize it, and this is what Betar was now called upon to do.[22] Against the socialist idea he pitted not liberalism but Judaism, since the two, nationalism and religion, were mutually complementary. Religion, too, produced Jewish distinctiveness and pride in the Jewish tradition.

Nonetheless, a perusal of Jabotinsky's writings on social and economic questions reveals that they were hardly grounded in the Jewish faith. An interesting example is a series of articles written in 1927–28 on the socioeconomic structure of the future Jewish state. Harmonious relations must prevail between workers and employers, Jabotinsky writes, who will be guided by the principle that the national interest supersedes every class or sectoral interest. This kind of harmony in labor relations can be guaranteed by compulsory arbitration. The state will compel arbitration through an institution geared to supervise worker-employer relations. A minimum wage will be set, but the institution responsible for arbitration will be empowered to raise wages when employers' profits increase and to lower them when profits decline. In this way the state will not only maintain a correct balance between the two groups in the economy for the good of the national interest, which strives for continuous economic activity in industry, but also avert the danger of factories closing and resultant unemployment.

A reader of Jabotinsky's articles may well come away with the impression that they show original thought. There is nothing in them to indicate that these social and economic viewpoints were actually a copy of the corporatist ideas of the Italian Fascists, which were adopted by many radical-right groups. Like them, Jabotinsky, too, adduced this economic plan as an alternative to socialist ideas. The claim of the socialists, Jabotinsky explained on another occasion, was that they wanted to change the whole structure of the economy. However, what should be striven for is not a change of the economic regime but only the elimination of poverty, and the way to achieve this was through corporatism.[23]

Similarly, most radical-right movements did not wish to change their countries' economic and social structure. We should not be misled by the revolutionary rhetoric, say students of Italy's Fascist regime. Even those who spoke of social revolution were not revolutionaries. As a result, when they attained power they did not change the existing structure and did not even raise up a new elite to replace the previous one. Thus, Renzo de Felice explains, when they lost the war and in its wake lost power, they simply disappeared and not a trace remained of them or their government.[24] The Revisionists and their successors in Israel, too, were not a revolutionary force and made absolutely no attempt to change the country's socioeconomic structure. One should not expect a leadership preoccupied with one theme exclusively—nationalism—to deliberately set about changing the status quo in the social and economic domains. Such changes may ensue, but only as an unanticipated result of political decisions.

If any doubts remain as to the source of inspiration of Jabotinsky's ideas, the series of articles mentioned contain an additional proposal regarding the future state's political structure. The parliament will be bicameral, Jabotinsky says. One chamber will consist of a parliament of professions. The associations of employers and laborers will elect their representatives, and in matters of labor relations this will be the determining institution. No mathematical counting of heads will thus be necessary, and the representation will be compatible "with the true task which these [heads] fulfill . . . in the country's collective experience."[25] "I abhor the class idea," Jabotinsky declared on another occasion, in terms that evoke the style and not just the content of the radical right.[26]

Under the influence of radical-right ideas, he deviated even from the rational bases of his political thought. Thus, he proclaimed at the party's 1930 convention in Prague that Revisionists were differentiated from other Zionists by more than ideological outlook. Revisionists were "a soulful race possessing a clear mentality, and that mentality cannot be transmitted to those not intrinsically raised in it." Therefore, it was pointless to try to convince a Zionist audience that had a different frame of mind. Instead, the party would do better to seek out people from "its own special race."[27] This emphasis on mentality and not on ideas also has its origins in the thought of the European radical right, influenced by the mass psychology of Gustave Le Bon. Inspired by his writings, certain leaders hoped to win the support of the masses not through rational persuasion but by enflaming their passions.

But Jabotinsky also aspired to change the mentality of the Jews. He ascribed considerable importance to effecting such a change in the Jewish people, to dispose them to fight for the nation's rights. Tilling the soil in Palestine, building houses, learning the Hebrew language, and studying its literature—all Zionist tenets—would not lead to the establishment of a Jewish state. What was important was the readiness to fight, and to that end a "psychology of gunshots, a longing for gunshots" had to be created, and the people's healthy instincts had to be developed.[28] Since the nation's future depended on its desire to fight, and since this stance could be expected only in young people, who were ready to sacrifice their lives for their nation, it followed that the future of the nation lay in the hands of its youth. "Long live Jewish youth!" Jabotinsky declared at a festive gathering to mark his fiftieth birthday—again, a sentiment expressed in a style characteristic of the radical right.[29] Readiness for war, though not war itself, was in Jabotinsky's view essential for a people aspiring to national independence. Not the strength of the troops but their willingness to fight was of the essence. This readiness would help achieve the goal through political means under the political leader.

Jabotinsky the Leader

Following some vacillations, Jabotinsky defined his role and authority as a leader in a manner identical with the heads of other radical-right movements. In such movements, the leader possessed an exalted status and exercised absolute authority over followers who were expected to obey his orders without question.

The first to expect this kind of total leadership were the rank and file themselves. Even parties of the radical right that did not formally accept the idea of the leader's centrality tended to exalt him and view him as the pinnacle of the hierarchy, with all others duty bound to abide by his word. These organizations, too, accepted the idea that the leader is the source of the organization's authority and ideology.[30] This is the most significant elitist element in radical-right organizations.

The leader's standing, Noel O'Sullivan explains, is based on the assumption that he understands intuitively the true will of the masses and is able to articulate it, "even if the people themselves are too confused or too stupid to be able to recognize their 'real' will in the decrees in which the leader formulates it." This outlook derives from the nationalist orientation of such organizations. In contrast to socialism, which formulates its goals with reference to rational models of a classless future society; nationalism is a doctrine incapable of adducing a rational basis for its goals.[31]

The leader's centrality in these parties also has a structural explanation. It results from the disinclination of nationalist parties to represent the interests of any particular groups in the population. Unlike other parties, which represent interests of groups, sectors or social classes, radical-right parties contend that they stand for the whole nation. Parties of this kind, whose world view is confined to the national idea, spurn the bureaucratic party structure, which is based on rational goals that the party organization is supposed to fulfill. Many of them find it difficult to define such goals. The absence in these parties of a consistent and logical ideology, of sectorial interests and of a bureaucratic structure, make the leader a far more central figure than he is in parties possessing an ideology and a bureaucratic organization. In such organizations the leader is empowered to articulate the goals: he expresses the will of the whole nation, incarnates the will of the masses, and is expected to lead them.

As the founder and leader of the party, it is not surprising that Jabotinsky devoted considerable thought to the problem of leadership and how to exercise his authority. For a long time he did not accept the radical right's ideas on this subject. The attitude toward the leader as "God's chosen" was, he believed, a "malignant disease" that was spreading throughout Europe. The idea that someone else should decide for you with regard to the fundamentals of morality and politics conflicted with the principle of freedom of choice. This kind of "leaderism" was a flight from the freedom that underlay the liberal idea.[32] So frequently and so vehemently did Jabotinsky reiterate his opposition to the idea of the omnipotent leader that one wonders what motivated him to do so.

One explanation is that many of his supporters in the Revisionist Party yearned for an all-poweful leader and saw Jabotinsky as the exalted leader whom they would follow. For years he rebuffed such expectations. At the party's convention in early 1932, when one of the delegates urged explicitly that Jabotinsky become dictator of the party, Jabotinsky rejected the idea in a sharply worded speech. But the speech seems to have made no impression whatsoever on the audience. At the council meeting that followed the convention, all those present rose when he entered the hall, a widespread custom in parties of the radical right but one that was certainly alien to other Zionist parties.[33] The admiration of the rank and file for their leader also found expression in the 1930 convention: when Meir Grossman, the party's secretary-general, made some remarks critical of the leader, the audience interrupted with outcries and would not let him continue. Only the intervention of Jabotinsky himself allowed Grossman to complete his speech.[34]

Although Jabotinsky seemed to reject his supporters' demands that he assume the role of an autocratic leader in the party, a gradual change was perceptible in his stand. Since 1929, growing differences had arisen with his close associates on the party executive over his proposal to secede from the WZO and establish a new Zionist organization. Initially he yeilded to the will of those who opposed the idea, even taking pride in it. If he were a leader "in the blind sense," he wrote, the party would have long since embarked on a different course. True, in that article he also maintained that the Revisionist Party Executive should resign because it opposed an idea accepted by the party majority. Nonetheless, he gave in to the majority on the executive.[35] He believed that through influence and persuasion he would eventually obtain their support. It was a method that had worked on previous occasions, but this time the executive was obdurate.[36]

Jabotinsky soon found himself at an impasse. He could not rely on ideological principles to bolster his standing, as leaders in other parties could in similar situations, because his party lacked a cohesive ideology. Nor could he enlist the support of the party machinery: no such apparatus existed, and the little that did exist was controlled by the secretary-general Meir Grossman.

In this situation, Jabotinsky began to behave increasingly like an autocratic leader. When members of the Party Executive tried to form a coalition with other Zionist parties against the Zionist Executive—a move that would undoubtedly have strengthened his party—Jabotinsky made himself inaccessible in order to foil the attempt. Grossman subsequently explained that this coalition did not appeal to Jabotinsky because he aspired to be a single leader and did not want his freedom of maneuver impeded by coalition partners.[37] A more serious episode is related by Jabotinsky's biographer and former assistent, Joseph Schechtmann. In August 1931, Jabotinsky published articles in the party paper to which he added the signature of his colleagues on the leadership without their agreement and even without their knowledge. When Schechtmann complained that his name, too, had appeared beneath one of his articles, Jabotinsky asked him with astonishment what he had found improper in an article written by him.[38]

But it was not until March 1932 that Jabotinsky took action that made him the party's absolute leader. Following yet another party council meeting in which he failed to convince his colleagues to leave the WZO, he astonished everyone by announcing to the press that he had dismissed the party Executive. Immediately he appointed a new Executive comprising people who accepted his opinions and did not question his leadership. He then declared that a referendum would be held in the party.

The need to hold a referendum after seizing power in the party stemmed from a desire to present his move as a democratic act. Like many leaders in the radical right of those days, Jabotinsky insisted he was a democratic leader, and what could be more democratic than a referendum? Thus, he wrote to a veteran party member:

> One can indeed argue about whether the method of the *putsch* is a good one; but it cannot be denied that I fought for the right of the majority, namely, for the basic principle of democracy. And if tomorrow I receive one vote less than my colleague, without any sense of insult I will join the ranks of the simple soldiers. You cannot believe that in my old age I will abandon the principles on which we were raised and that I will be dragged after the title of leader which I despise to the point of nausea.[39]

However, the referendum did not ask for a decision on the controversial issue that had split the Revisionist Party executive. Instead, party members were asked to support or reject the statement that "until the Sixth Convention of the party [scheduled for about a year and a half after the referendum] all the operational tasks of the entire Revisionist movement will be placed in the hands of Ze'ev Jabotinsky, president of the Union of Revisionist Zionists." The intention, Schechtmann explains, was to sidestep a discussion of the substantive issue, since the decision meant that Jabotinsky would direct the election campaign for the World Zionist Congress scheduled to convene within a year.[40] In effect, he asked the party to express its confidence in him as leader without reference to the issue in dispute.

Use of a referendum to consolidate autocratic leadership is characteristic of the radical right. It is one of the populist elements favored by this political camp. Leaders are thus enabled to present themselves as doing the will of the people whom they represent. At the same time, they do not make the people privy to their decisions. It is not viewpoints and opinions that are up for decision but the degree of the leader's personal popularity. Jabotinsky's behavior recalled that of Jozef Pilsudski who, a few years before Jabotinsky's *putsch*, forced the elected government of Poland to resign with the help of the army. He then insisted that this had been a democratic act because he had enjoyed majority backing. Pursuing this logic, he demanded, after seizing power, that lawful elections be held for president, and placed himself in candidacy. He took this course even though he had no intention of becoming president but only to prove that the majority was with him.[41] Mussolini also created unrest in the country with the help of his people until the intimidated parliamentary majority chose him as prime minister. He then held elections in which he exploited his standing as premier. Jabotinsky did exactly the same thing, staffing the party posts with his own followers, and with their help and the active help of Betar, assuring himself of an overwhelming majority in the referendum. His opponents, who realized what the result would be, boycotted the poll. Thus, Jabotinsky became a single leader in the style of the radical right.

Jabotinsky, like Jozef Pilsudski, had become an autocratic leader who exploited a formal democratic procedure as the basis to legitimitize his leadership. The literature terms this kind of leadership "Bonapartism," after Louis Bonaparte, who was elected emperor of France for life in a referendum.

In his efforts to show himself a democratic leader, Jabotinsky returned to the leadership issue time after time. Sometimes he claimed not to be a leader at all. "Those elected," he wrote in 1934, "are merely the dischargers of the program. We the masses will follow them and head them not because they are leaders but expressly because they are our servants. If of your own free will you have chosen a group of people and commanded them to work for you, you are obliged to assist them—or remove them."[42]

This is a transparent attempt to cast a different color over the putsch he carried out in the party. Similar claims—that they were not leaders but merely servants of the masses—were voiced by many figures of the radical right in Europe. But declarations were one thing and actions another. In 1932 Jabotinsky became the one-man ruler of the Revisionist Party, which continued to hold elections to its conventions, in which Jabotinsky was consistently re-elected party leader. Even his disciples admitted that after the *putsch* a new relationship was created between the leader and the other party members, "unlike other leaders of Zionism."[43] Many party members who had an independent standing in Jewish and general society left the party, including Richard Lichtheim, Robert Stricker, Meir Grossman, Ya'akov Klinov, and others. Jabotinsky was left not with colleagues and associates but with followers who revered him. It was from among these admirers that he selected the party's office holders, who reported directly to him on their activity.[44] Yohanan Bader, at that time a Betar activist in Poland, relates that all contacts with party headquarters in Paris were with Jabotinsky alone, to the point where he began to doubt that there was anyone else at the party headquarters.[45]

It is not suprising that around the same time that Jabotinsky consolidated his absolute leadership, he also began to express publicly doubts about whether a democratic regime was the most desirable form of government or was even attainable. True, Jabotinsky had been raised in the belief that a regime built on a universal franchise and the responsibility of government toward the electorate was the proper and best form of administration, and was convinced for many years that it merited support. But now—the article was written in 1934—the defects of democracy could no longer be ignored. The Jews, indeed, who still had no state of their own, need not be in the vanguard on this issue. But he had reached the conclusion not to recoil from a revision of his faith in the democratic system.[46]

In this period, however, particularly after Hitler's assumption of power, the European political situation began to undergo rapid change. Two political camps began to emerge: a liberal-democratic camp, and an anti-democratic, anti-liberal camp. The latter also espoused anti-Semitism as a central tenet. It was difficult for Jabotinsky to identify with the anti-democratic camp, but evidently such doubts and uncertainties were not shared by the younger generation in Betar.

His decision in 1931 to coopt the Betar youth movement into the Revisionist Party, place himself at the head of the movement, and imbue it with more overt radical-right coloring, was taken when the influence of this camp on his thinking was at its height. The Betar movement, as it was formed in those years, was the clearest organizational and ideological expression of this influence.

The radical right had two types of organizations, which at times were actually two wings of the same organization. The role of the party organization was to mobilize the masses to devote themselves to the national idea, oppose the establishment, and magnify the name of the leader. The second organization was quasi-military in nature, and through it violent means could be employed to destroy the status quo and seize power in the state. Both modes of taking power, the democratic and the violent, were legitimate in the eyes of the majority of the radical right movements. The Revisionist movement was the party organization charged with the task of mobilizing the support of the masses for the leader and his views. Its central role was to enable the leader to appear externally as being empowered to speak in the name of the masses. "Without Jabotinsky," Katznelson wrote, "it [the Revisionist Party] had nothing."[47] Pilsudksi's political organization, which he set up after the *putsch*, was similar. Its whole task was to drum up support for the leader and ensure that his backers were elected to the parliament.[48] Other radical-right movements set up alongside this open organization a second organization with a military or semi-military character. This second organization was capable of seizing a propitious moment and taking power by undemocratic means. The Betar youth movement was comparable to this kind of military organization. Even though it was established as a youth movement, it soon became, thanks to its military structure, the dominant organization in the Revisionist movement itself. Because it was in this organization that the future leaders of Herut underwent their political socialization and initial political experience, the next two chapters will be devoted to Betar.

2

Betar in Poland

The Betar Generation Unit

In 1931, Ze'ev Jabotinsky was elected head of Betar at its founding convention in Danzig. Jabotinsky determined the organization's structure, wrote its constitution and until his death in 1940 appointed its office holders.

Yet Jabotinsky's central role was matched in importance by the group of youngsters in Betar who were born between 1910–1920 and reached maturity, the majority of them in Poland, in the interwar period. During these years, they became followers of the European radical right and of the ruling group in Poland, the latter becoming the reference group for these politically aware young people. This was also their common ideological denominator with Jabotinsky, who was fifty-one when he became head of Betar.

The initiators of Betar were not from Poland. They were a group of youngsters in Riga, Latvia, swayed by Jabotinsky's ideas in the years after his resignation from the Zionist Executive. Although accepting his activist notions, they established the movement virtually on their own after being convinced by him of the need to undergo military training so that they could take part in the struggle to establish an independent Jewish state. It was here that the difference lay between their movement and other Zionist movements that prepared their members for a life as *halutzim* (pioneers)—manual laborers—in Palestine kibbutzim. In its first years, Betar also readied its members for agricultural settlement, but the movement viewed military training as a central facet of their activity and organized itself in a military structure, with battalions and companies led by commanders who gave orders. Initially Betar wanted to maintain its independent existence and not identify itself with the Revisionist movement, which had started out as a non-Socialist party but within a few years had become anti-Socialist. Betar's founders in Riga preferred not to associate themselves with any party, and looked for a way by which they could avoid defining themselves as right or left.

29

Their military orientation was revolutionary enough among East European Jewry in this period, which was dominated by Jewish organizations espousing left-wing and progressive viewpoints. It soon became apparent to the center in Riga that the branches, particularly in Poland, were disposed to identify with the right. This kind of affiliation—a circular sent from Riga to the branches by the worried leadership warned in early 1928—was liable to cause large-scale resignations from the movement.[1] But developments in Betar were beyond Riga's control. The Polish wing quickly became the movement's largest and leading branch. Already by 1930 its members outnumbered those in all other branches combined.[2] The movement's center was transferred to Poland and it was there that it was built up as a world body when a meeting was held in Warsaw in 1929 with the participation of members from various countries, followed by the founding convention in Danzig in 1931. The convention resolved that Betar was an organization based on a military structure and linked organizationally with the Revisionist movement, though preserving a measure of autonomy. As mentioned, Ze'ev Jabotinsky, the leader of the Revisionist Party, was elected head of Betar at the founding convention.

Betar in Poland aspired to set up an organization with the task of preparing its members to be soldiers in the service of the homeland. They were convinced that a military struggle was the one and only road to political independence. This outlook converged with that of Jozef Pilsudski, who, as the country's leader, was convinced that its independence had been achieved thanks to the military strength of the Polish liberation movement, and that only a powerful military force would assure the preservation of that independence. After Betar had organized itself along military lines, a commander was required whose word would be law. A leader of this stature could not be drawn from their own age group. Jabotinsky was an ideal candidate. He had organized Jewish military units in the British Army in World War I and then led the Jewish defense in Jerusalem against attacks by Arab marauders. For this he had been jailed by the British, adding luster to his reputation. In those first years, the Betar youngsters pressured him to assume command of the organization. They needed a commander-in-chief who would be looked on as "heaven-sent," and for this they had no candidate of their own. He only was accepted "as a supremely gifted commander requiring no external authorization."[3]

Their ardent desire for a leader was influenced by ideas gleaned from the radical right. As we saw, these ideas also appealed to Jabotinsky, but he hesitated for a long time about becoming the leader of a youth movement at his age. Only after the 1929 meeting in Warsaw, when the movement's rapid expansion was obvious, did he consent to assume the leadership. He set up Betar in the same format that existed in other radical-right paramilitary organizations. It was he who delineated the movement's hierarchical structure, determined their authority, designated names and symbols for the different ranks, and even designed the movement's uniform—brown shirt and black tie—as well as preparing an educational program for the various age groups.[4] Finally he also agreed to become the movement's supreme commander.

Naturally the Betar youngsters were aware that the ideological sources of their movement were totally different from those of other Zionist and Jewish organizations. This is evident from a document prepared by the Betar leadership for a school for movement *madrichim* (counsellors) in Poland, in the mid-1930s, which surveyed the organization's history. Whereas all the other Jewish movements were influenced by social democracy, the document stated, Betar was influenced by "the chauvinism that visited Eastern Europe, particularly Poland."[5] Nationalism was a supreme value in the Poland of this period. So pervasive was its influence in the Polish society, according to the historian Norman Davies, that it became the source of prestige and the touchstone of respectability in every walk of life.[6] It was not a nationalism with a liberal coloring. From the outset it was the extreme-right model that held sway. The illiberal and intolerant element in Polish nationalism was the result of the protracted suppression of the Polish nation during the country's lengthy conquest by its neighbors, combined with the fact that some 30 percent of the population of independent Poland were members of other nations. This was the fire that fueled Polish nationalism, Davies argues, and accounts for its extremism and intolerance.[7] While the majority of Jewish organizations, Zionist and non-Zionist, kept their distance from Polish nationalist groups that exuded xenophobia and anti-Semitism, and leaned instead toward groups bearing a progressive and cosmopolitan orientation, Betar emulated precisely the groups espousing nationalism, chauvinism, and anti-Semitism. Aware of their distinctive identity, they insisted at the Danzig convention, over the objections of Jabotinsky himself, that their organization be granted a large degree of autonomy within the Revisionist movement.[8]

The Formative Experience of the Betar Youngsters

To understand the spiritual and political world of the Betar youngsters, it is necessary to follow the political developments in Poland and the disputes within the Polish national camp. This camp was marked by a debate dating from the beginning of the century between Jozef Pilsudski and Roman Dmowski. On the eve of World War I, Pilsudski reached the conclusion that a European war between the great powers was inevitable and that it was essential to prepare a Polish military force that could seize the opportunity afforded by the war in order to liberate Poland from the foreign yoke. Dmowski, in contrast, did not believe that a military struggle would serve the goal and preferred instead political and diplomatic activity.

Pilsudski's ambition was for Poland to be a sovereign state within the boundaries that had existed before the first partition in 1772. These borders would ensure Poland's return to its days of glory and would best enable it to preserve its independence in the face of its two powerful neighbors, Germany and Russia, which were liable to put its liberty in jeopardy. Dmowski, for his part, preferred a smaller country but one containing a homogeneous national population as a guarantee of Polish sovereignty and cultural autonomy.

In 1914, Pilsudski set up the Polish Military Organization that launched guerilla warfare against the country's Russian rulers. During World War I, he was able to acquire legal status for his organization within the framework of the Austro-Hungarian Army. He now commanded the Polish Legion. Toward the end of the war, he was imprisoned by the Germans but was soon released; he immediately became the leader of the nascent Polish state. Polish miliatry forces under his command fought against the Russians in 1920–21 and extended Polish territory beyond what the Allies had originally agreed on. But even after these developments Poland had still not recovered the boundaries it possessed before the first partition. This objective remained the fervent desire of many nationalist circles in the Polish Republic during the interwar period.[9]

Pilsudski was regarded by the Poles as the country's liberator. The fact that his military struggle against the Russians had brought about the enlargement of Polish territory enhanced his popularity and lent credence to the notion that it was his military struggle that had brought Poland independence. This military success also fostered the ambition to expand the country's boundaries still further until the 1772 borders were restored, and fueled the belief that this was attainable by force of arms.[10] For many Poles, Pilsudski, who was identified with this goal, came to embody this national aspiration.

The dispute between Pilsudski and Dmowski continued after independence. Historians know it as the debate between Federalists and Centralists. These terms are somewhat misleading. Pilsudski the Federalist was convinced that in order to preserve its independence, Poland must be a great power and maintain a large army, while integrating the minorities into the Polish state and in the collective effort to safeguard its independence. However, autonomy for the minority groups was restricted within the federation framework, and even Pilsudski held that the hegemony of the Polish nation and its culture must be upheld. Dmowski, on the other hand, was unwilling to rely on the loyalty of the minorities to the Polish state. Only members of the Polish nation, and not the minorities resident in the country, should be entrusted with the defense of Poland against its neighbor-enemies, Dmowski maintained. These ideas drew him ever closer to the European radical right.

Pilsudski was the stronger and more influential politician of the two, particularly after his military *putsch* in 1926. He then became an autocratic ruler notwithstanding the continuing party activity and the holding of parliamentary elections. In these years, Dmowski turned largely to educational activity among the youth. Following Pilsudski's death in 1935, his successors embraced many of Dmowski's ideas and thereby they, too, were increasingly identified with the radical right. Pilsudski's Greater Poland idea blended with Dmowski's extreme nationalism and his distrust of the loyalty of ethnic groups to the Polish state.[11]

This was the political climate as Betar members were reaching maturity and which impacted on their Jewish-national world view when they became active in the youth movement. So dominant was the influence of the political situation in Poland and its ruling groups on the Betari's political thought, that in my estimation it is impossible to comprehend their political outlook and political behavior after establishing Herut without reference to their formative experience in Poland.

I call this age group of Betar activists a "generation unit" following Karl Mannheim's definition. It is an age group that, under the influence of conditions and events that occur during their adolescence, which constitutes their formative period—the years between seventeen and twenty-three, in Mannheim's estimation—adopt a world view conflicting with or differing from that of the older generation. Significant historical events that occur in the formative period may undermine the world view prevalent among older people, and spur youngsters to seek new meanings for the social reality and solutions to unanticipated problems.[12] A new world view that develops among young people may influence the generation unit thus formed even after they attain maturity. This is particularly so in cases when the collective framework forged by a group during adolescence is preserved, as was the case with Betar members, who remained in the movement after adolescence, and subsequently joined the Irgun and Herut.

In Betar's first years of existence, there seemed to be agreement between Jabotinsky and the movement's young people on ideology and organization. On the eve of the founding convention, Jabotinsky explained the considerations that had guided him in drawing up Betar's constitution and planning its organizational structure. The new movement, he noted must adopt a "cautious attitude" toward the democratic principle of elections. Taking a cautious attitude did not mean "as yet to definitely eliminate this entire principle." But one should "avoid going overboard." The new organization would be built on two foundations, Jabotinsky explained, a school "and something along Legion lines, an institution that will teach order and discipline," and of course elections were not customary in either establishment. These arguments recall notions espoused in the radical-right camp. One is especially struck by his contention that democratic procedure is inefficient and that the "election fever" in democratic organizations disrupts their smooth operation. Many in the radical right preferred to adduce practical arguments such as these against democratic procedures rather than cast doubt on the system itself. Jabotinsky ruled that the question of which procedures should be done away with and which preserved would be examined in the light of how effective they were in assuring members' loyalty, and the concern to preserve order and discipline in the organization. He therefore sought a way to enable members not appointed by him to positions of command in the organization, to voice their opinion in conventions, but without letting this interfere with the organization's functioning.[13]

The constitution Jabotinsky brought for the approval of Betar's founding convention in Danzig called for the movement to be organized in a military hierarchy, with all office holders appointed from above. The head of Betar appoints the executive, and the executive, in turn, with the sanction of the leader, appoints the commanders in the various countries. Only the head of Betar is elected by the whole convention and stands for reelection at every convention, held biennially. (Actually, the convention was held triennially in 1931, 1935, and 1938.) Between conventions, another official document stated, "there is no trace of elections in Betar. Everything is based on appointment and discipline." A commander who is appointed by the body above him does not represent his unit in the organization's supreme institutions. On the contrary, "he represents the head of Betar, the whole movement vis-à-vis his people who follow his instructions." (The identification of the movement with the head of Betar is a characteristic radical-right formulation.) *"This is the main difference* between Betar and the other Zionist organizations," the document asserts. [emphasis in the original] Again the explanation cited is efficiency. But appended to this explanation is the comment that centralization infuses the organization with strength. "The special Betar structure is a tremendous force because it concentrates the will of the movement in one person who deserves the nation's unlimited trust, and empowers him to use the movement, as an artist uses his tools, to revive the nation and build the state."[14] The idea that the leader expresses the will of the entire movement, and is also its source of authority, is a central element in the principle of the leader *(Führerprinzip)* found in all parties of the radical right.

In a letter Jabotinsky sent to all Betar members prior to the second convention, in 1935, he commended the limited democracy that existed in the movement. "Between one convention and the next the Betari is not alone but a highly disciplined soldier submitting to the orders of his commanders and their commands. But at the world convention—once every two years—the Betari becomes the possessor of his Betari state. It is he who levels criticism about the results of past work and determines the line for the future. He selects the Supreme Institution from whom derives in the coming two years all the authority of the chain of representatives and commanders throughout our movement."[15] (Supreme Institution, too, was a typical radical-right formulation; it actually refers to the head of Betar, Jabotinsky himself.)

On the face of it, the election of the leader as laid down in the constitution constitutes the democratic element in the military organization. But this is a symbolic act. In an organization built on military discipline like Betar, it is not surprising that Jabotinsky was always unanimously reelected until the day of his death. Even in 1938 when, as will be seen below, the majority of delegates supported a policy against his wishes, he was unanimously elected movement leader. The desire to preserve democratic overtones but to ensure that these were merely ceremonial and devoid of practical significance, was also widespread in many radical-right organizations. The world of symbols and the concomitant disregard of reality, and the ability to live with the contradiction between symbolic activity and political reality, typified this political camp.

The Betar Organization in Poland

From the outset Betar emphasized military education. For the young activists, this was the outgrowth of a belief that a military struggle was the road to political independence in Palestine. It was this stance of the young generation in Poland that attracted a large influx of young people to the movement's ranks. The identity of outlook they shared on this question with the ruling group in Poland brought them encouragement from the Polish government, which even helped Betar in the military training of its members.[16] In the course of time, this success led the Betar leadership to make military education the centerpiece of its activity. As one of Betar's leaders explained in 1938: "Today Betar's goal is a military one. Betar is not culture and it is not the Hebrew language, today it is only a military school or an army. Cultural training has to be restricted to the learning of one small book."[17] Even to the degree that cultural activity existed, it was geared to training Betaris to be soldiers. The guidelines to *madrichim* for teaching history to the youngest age group (12–15) instructed them not to concentrate on a specific historical period "but around a historical hero. The discussion should be appealing and filled with legends and acts of heroism. In particular the link between the content of the discussion and the present should be played up. Underscore all national aspects and moments of sacrifice, and so forth." Another document, dealing with the cultural work plan, instructed counselors to pay considerable attention to liberation movements and the role of youth movements within them, "and to the doctrine of war in the past, present and future."[18]

Jabotinsky encouraged this emphasis on military education. In Betar he saw the military arm of his movement. Betar was for him an elite group of soldiers totally devoted to the national idea and to the leader who expressed that will. A Betar member, Jabotinsky explained, is not a worker or an employer exploiting economic opportunities, but rather a monk devoting his whole life to the realization of the national idea. Every Betari who settled in Palestine, Jabotinsky declared, must serve at least two years in a military unit. These new immigrants would live in camps that would be like military barracks and spend all their time in military training and in any task assigned them by the movement, meaning by Ze'ev Jabotinsky, the leader of Betar.[19]

The highest expression of the military idea was the absolute discipline required vis-à-vis the leader. When it emerged, for example, that Betar was being discriminated against in the Jewish Agency's allocation of immigration certificates, Jabotinsky decided that as a protest, Betar would refuse to accept even the few certificates available to the movement. This put Betar members in extremely difficult straits. But Jabotinsky did not give in and demanded that anyone who disobeyed him be explelled from the movement.[20] He also insisted on the expulsion of those who reached Palestine after receiving entry certificates via Betar but who then refused to join the military units in the barracks. "It is better for us if not a single Betari goes to Eretz-Israel than to bring in people who shirk conscription," he pronounced.[21]

Many of Betar's young leaders looked askance at Jabotinsky's attitude toward Betar as an elite group submitting to his absolute authority. They preferred an organization that could expand its influence and its membership among the Jewish population. So they had no wish to obligate their members to be "monks." They did not declare that it was their members' absolute duty to settle in Palestine for fear the older members would leave the movement, and in practice they did not even compel new immigrants to join the mobilized battalions.

The military wing's desire for greater influence was characteristic of radical-right organizations that were composed of both an elitist military organization, and a civilian organization whose task was to mobilize mass support. Betar leaders believed that the military organization took precedence and did not assent to their members leaving Betar and joining the Revisionist Party at age eighteen. This stand sparked an ongoing dispute between Jabotinsky and Betar leaders. Jabotinsky's position was that every Betari should join the Revisionist Party upon turning eighteen.[22] Betar disagreed. The founding convention in Danzig decided that after turning eighteen, Betaris—the future soldiers—would become lifelong members of a reserve unit called "otzaron." Disagreements about whether Betaris should join the Revisionist Party persisted at the 1935 convention, when it was decided that the move would only occur at age twenty-three. Menachem Begin and others objected to this arrangement, too, and in practice it was not carried out. The Betar commander in Poland admitted openly in the movement's paper in 1936 that Betaris were members of the movement for life. Naturally, he wrote, we could order them to join the Revisionist Party, which would only prove that they still belong to us, so that the demand to join the Revisionist Party was pointless.[23] Betar, then, was an autonomous body that aggrandized its organizational strength and became a far more powerful organization than the Revisionist mother-party. But in the first years this autonomy was rarely exercised. The heads of Betar accepted Jabotinsky's leadership on all issues even when they dissented from his views. For them he was the supreme commander.

The majority of the Betar leadership objected to his proposal in the early 1930s to leave the WZO and set up an alternative Zionist organization, but decided to follow him despite their demurrers.[24] A similar affair played itself out in 1934–35 when Jabotinsky signed an agreement with David Ben-Gurion, then still the general-secretary of the Histadrut Federation of Labor in Palestine. Under the terms of this agreement, the Histadrut recognized the independent existence of the National Workers' Federation, the labor union of the Revisionist Party in Palestine, which was controlled by Betar. Jabotinsky for his part pledged "to refrain from all party modes of combat that go beyond ideological and political debate." The agreement was signed against the background of violent disputes between the Histadrut and the National Workers' Federation, with the Histadrut striving to maintain a comprehensive closed shop system. Some clashes, however, were wholly politically motivated. Betaris, for example, were attacked by an organized group of workers during a parade they held in the streets of Tel Aviv. These developments worried the leaders of both movements. Ben-Gurion understood that in the voluntary society of the Yishuv, in which his party had now become the central force, the only means to obtain control over the whole society was by bringing about consensus and agreement between the various political parties. Jabotinsky, who at this time began to have reservations about the terror and violence of the European radical right, sought ways to restrain the young people in Betar, who found the radical right and its methods appealing. These radical youngsters naturally objected to the agreement with Ben-Gurion; one of the leading dissenters was the twenty-one-year-old Menachem Begin. But on this occasion, too, Betar accepted the leader's authority.[25] Ultimately the agreement was rejected in a referendum held among the Histadrut rank and file.

The Betar leadership found itself in a trap. The moment they accepted the idea of the leader as a basic ideological and organizational tenet, and Jabotinsky as that revered leader, they had no choice but to do his bidding. In an organization like Betar, it was inconceivable to even think about questioning the leader's authority, let alone about deposing him. As Binyamin Eliav, a Betar commander, explained in an interview years later, when he was long since a member of Mapai, to him it had always been clear that in Betar he had to accept the leader's authority even on issues on which he disagreed with the leader's position.

In that interview, held in 1967, Eliav maintained that the Revisionist Party did not accept the principle of the omnipotent leader. It was by force of personality that Jabotinsky had been their revered leader. The interviewer pressed Eliav and reminded him that in a previous interview he had related that once he had not accepted Jabotinsky's opinion but nevertheless responded, "At your order." Was there not a contradiction here? No contradiction was involved, Eliav replied, as the case in question had occurred in Betar, and there Jabotinsky was his commander.[26]

The tension between Betar's young activists and their leader Jabotinsky intensified in the second half of the 1930s. At that time, as already mentioned, Pilsudski's successors took stands ever closer in spirit to the radical right. The movement they set up in 1936, the National Unity camp, "accepted the doctrines that were prevalent in those days in Germany, Romania, and particularly in (Fascist) Italy."[27] A comparable development was discernible in Betar. But in Betar the upshot was a crisis in relations with Jabotinsky, who in these years began to distance himself from the Fascist camp, after Germany under Nazi rule had become a dictatorship. Being more prudent and more rational, Jabotinsky was unwilling to break with the Western democracies, particularly not with Great Britain who ruled Palestine. He believed that Britain's cooperation was essential for the achievement of the Zionist goal of the creation of a Jewish state in Palestine. Furthermore, the Nazis unleashed a regime of terror and detention camps, pursued a policy of anti-Semitism and promulgated discriminatory anti-Jewish legislation, all of which made life for Germany's Jews insupportable. This did not stop Betar's continued drift to the radical right, along with the ruling clique in Poland, which was its reference group. This, as the next chapter will show, helped undermine Jabotinsky's authority in Betar.

There are some who ascribe the radical course followed by Betar to the petit bourgeois background of the Betaris that heightened their economic and social insecurity and caused them, in this view, to identify with developments among the non-Jewish members of their class, who formed the radical right's base of support. It is argued that other Jewish organizations, which supported the left and the liberals and considered the radical right their enemies, originated from higher strata of the middle classes. However, we lack sufficient data to examine this conjecture.[28]

On the other hand, data are available regarding my assessment that the generation factor informed the political thinking of the Betar group. The Betaris were for the most part born in Poland between 1910-1920, reached maturity in the 1930s, and were influenced by Polish nationalism, which was most pervasive in their age group. In previous books, I dealt with generation units whose members reached maturity in pre-revolutionary Russia or in the first years after the revolution, and in Palestine created left-wing parties and the Histadrut. They, too, were deeply influenced by social processes in the Russian society of which they were a part. They arrived in Palestine at a young age and succeeded in transforming their earlier experience in a manner commensurate with the new reality they found. Abetting this ability was their exposure to the rich and diversified political tradition of the Russian and European workers' socialist movement, combined with the fact that they had reached maturity in a revolutionary period, in which people are more daring in breaking out of conventional moulds and trying out new ideas.

Jabotinsky, too, was a product of the revolutionary period in Russia, even though he spurned socialism and lived most of his life in Europe. For Betar he played a role that Mannheim terms "forerunner." This is a person of some standing in the adult generation who, by breaking the conventions of his own generation encourages youngsters to form a new independent unit. Within his own generation he is a deviate, but he helps youngsters sever themselves from the conventions of the adult genera-tion.[29] However, after the initial years, when Jabotinsky played such a crucial part in the group's generational cohesion, the ruling group in Poland—which was an equal influence on them—seems to have become a sufficiently strong reference group to enable them to cut themselves off from the revered leader and guide.

One example of this developoment was their attitude toward the Jewish religion, which differed from Jabotinsky's. As I explained earlier, Jabotinsky reached the conclusion that the Jewish religious tradition should be cultivated as part of the Jewish national idea. (See pp. 18–19.) Yet Jabotinsky took an instrumental approach to religion, and therefore it is unlikely that as a secular Jew he was ready to accept the manner in which Betar implemented this instruction. An article in the Betar regu-lations stated that anyone found violating the Sabbath in public would be expelled from the movement.[30] The Betar training camps in Poland carried out the Sabbath eve ceremonies and observed the Sabbath itself punctiliously. The Betar commander in Poland, who supported these customs, explained that Bar-Kochba's fighters had also observed them: they, too, had prayed before battle and had observed the Sabbath.[31] (Bar-Kochba was a legendary leader of the Jewish rebellion against the Roman Empire in the Second century A.D.) As national extremism inten-sified at the end of the 1930s, we witness an attitude toward religion that was surely far from what Jabotinsky had in mind. Thus, for example, the Betar newspaper in Poland bitterly attacked Jews who had celebrated the New Year on the night of December 31, 1938, the so-called Sylvester holiday with its Christian religious roots. When Herbert Samuel, a British Jew and a senior figure in his country's Liberal Party, expressed himself on the situation in Palestine in a manner that displeased the Betaris, their paper denounced him fiercely in an article entitled "Why Doesn't He Convert." Around this time Betar leaders also embraced religious notions such as the advent of the Messiah and the vision of complete redemption, which they used to help formulate their movement's political purpose.[32] The military issue was another subject on which differences cropped up between Jabotinsky and the young Betaris. As far as Jabotinsky was concerned, military education had as its aim to arouse collective loyalty and national pride. The "ceremonial" side was of importance to him in forging the collective spirit. Jabotinsky explained what he meant in a 1933 article entitled "On Militarism":

> You can fire up (for one minute, at least) the worst assimilator with Jewish-national enthusiasm by a simple method: Take a few hundred Jewish youth, dress them in uniform, and have them march past him in unison, but with perfect timing so that each step of the two hundred boys rings out in a single thunderclap "like a machine." There is nothing else in the world that makes such a great impression on us as the ability of the mass at certain moments to feel and also to act as one group with one will operating at the same pace. This is the whole difference between a "mass" or a "rabble" and a "nation."[33]

Jabotinsky was also willing to view the very existence of a military force as a factor that would induce the British to give the Jews a state; he did not expect Betar to create a military force that would fight to conquer Palestine. Yet precisely this was the outlook of the Betaris. They took literally the idea that Pilsudski had brought about the establishment of the Polish state through underground military activity. It was in these terms that one of the Revisionist intelligentsia explained the difference between them and Jabotinsky. Jabotinsky wanted a military force as a means to shape a people, to be like all other nations. Whereas for the Betaris their movement's transformation into an armed force that would fight to liberate the homeland was "the determining factor."[34] They would not accomplish this by a political battle, Menachem Begin explained, but by guerilla warfare as Pilsudski had done. "We must shoot," Begin wrote in 1938. "The hit is not important.... They will throw us into prison, condemn us to death."[35] The world of the Betar activists who reached maturity in Poland in the interwar period was less complex than the world of Jabotinsky and his generation, and more closely resembled the world of the ruling group in the Poland of the late 1930s.

But in the paramilitary organization called Betar, Jabotinsky was the leader and supreme commander, and the duty of discipline toward him was absolute. His disagreements with his subordinates created a growing difficulty toward the end of the 1930s, when Betar organized its own military underground in Palestine that fought against the British. These developments, which centered on Palestine, form the subject of the next chapter.

3

Betar in Eretz-Israel

Brit Habiryonim

Among various Zionist circles, the idea prevailed that a violent military struggle was sine qua non for establishing a Jewish state in Palestine. This was also saliently the orientation of a small group of Russian Zionists who settled in the country in the early 1920s. They were convinced of the need to do battle with the indigenous Arabs and with the British authorities who had ruled the country since 1918. It was already clear that the British government was in no rush to set up a Jewish state, notwithstanding its commitment to the League of Nations when it was awarded the Mandate for Palestine.

The nucleus of this fascinating and unique group consisted of three intellectuals, all born in Russia around the turn of the century: Uri Zvi Greenberg, a poet, Abba Achimeir, a brilliant journalist, and Heschel Yevin, a writer and journalist. They were joined by Yosef Katznelson, who unlike the other three was not a thinker but a man of action. All four reached maturity during the Russian Revolution; hence, their formative experience was identical to that of the Zionist Socialists who also settled in Palestine around the same time and created the Mapai machine. Indeed, like the Socialists, their initial political activity in Eretz-Israel was also carried out within the framework of left-wing parties and the Histadrut Labor Federation. Soon, however, they embraced views akin to the radical right in Europe. In this they followed the pattern of other radical-right leaders, who began their political careers as Socialists. Abba Achimeir wrote his first articles in Eretz-Israel for *Hapoel Hatza'ir*, the journal of a party of the same name that was the more moderate of the two major parties in the Histadrut. Achimeir also worked for the Histadrut's cultural department. Uri Zvi Greenberg and Heschel Yevin were members of Ahdut Ha'avodah, at the time one of the more doctrinaire of the two major Histadrut parties, to the point where orthodox Marxists felt at home in it. The fourth member of the group, Yosef

Katznelson, was a clerk in Solel Boneh, a Histadrut-affiliated construction company.

Their deviation from the dominant political outlook in these left-wing parties was evident from the first articles they published—Abba Achimeir, as mentioned, in *Hapoel Hatza'ir*, and Uri Zvi Greenberg in Ahdut Ha'avodah's *Kuntress*. Both men admired Lenin: not because they shared his Bolshevik world view, but for his ability to translate ideas into practice. In Achimeir's interpretation, Lenin had convinced the Bolshevik wing of the Russian intelligentsia not only that it was necessary to draw a distinction between morality and politics, but that morality must also be subordinated to politics. In this idea lay the secret of Lenin's success. In contrast, Achimeir said, Aleksandr Kerensky, the moderate Socialist who was premier until the Bolsheviks' October Revolution, failed to grasp that the transformation of a society requires that people be imbued with so powerful a belief in the goal that they are willing to sacrifice themselves to achieve it. Because no one was committed to sacrifice and devotion under Kerensky's democratic regime, neither was anyone willing to lay down his life for it. As a result, Lenin was able to seize power.[1]

Another Zionist group that settled in Eretz-Israel around this time and joined Ahdut Ha'avodah had a different interpretation of events in the Soviet Union. Like Lenin, they, too, aspired to create a Socialist society, but even though they were impressed with the boldness and imagination he evinced as a leader, they spurned the dictatorship he established.

In these first post-revolutionary years not many Socialists in Europe or Palestine grasped the significance of the Soviet Union's transformation into a one party dictatorship in which all opposition was suppressed. It was precisely this perception that the Socialist-Zionist newcomers tried to get across to their veteran comrades in the Yishuv (the pre-state Jewish community in Palestine). After a group of these new arrivals set up the machinery of the Ahdut Ha'avodah party, beginning in 1927 (followed by Mapai in 1930), they endeavored to impose their political outlook on the emerging Jewish community. This group rejected dictatorship in favor of other methods of control and supervision, while preserving the formal trappings of democracy that enabled free association in parties and regular elections.[2] Once this group had consolidated itself in power, it was obvious that the labor parties' press could no longer be a vehicle for ideas supporting dictatorship and repudiating democracy, such as Achimeir and Greenberg espoused in the years

1925–27. It was in this period that they, along with Yevin, parted company with the left and joined the new Revisionist party.

In his articles at this time, Achimeir noted that in a democratic regime control always resides with the conservatives, thus precluding the possibility of generating social change. Benito Mussolini, who Achimeir saw as the true heir of the nationalist ideology espoused by Giuseppe Mazzini and Giuseppe Garibaldi—and who indeed also began his political career as a Socialist—had understood the frailties of democracy and had therefore revived Bonapartism. In other words, like Louis Bonaparte before him, Mussolini, by threatening violence, was able to intimidate the liberal democratic parties and receive their assent to his rule. Achimeir also had words of praise for another former Socialist, Jozef Pilsudski, who in this same period seized power in Poland in a military *putsch*.[3]

Uri Zvi Greenberg took a similar line in *Kuntress*. Zionism, he declared, could be realized only through a "spiritual dictatorship" on the Soviet model. In the Soviet Union, the rulers had mobilized the entire educational and cultural machinery in order to instill their ideas in the masses and thereby ensure their loyalty and devotion to the revolution. While rejecting Communist doctrine, Greenberg ardently admired the Communists' modes of operation. The Histadrut leadership, he wrote, should "bow their heads to the pyschology of the masses" and not think that they could bring off the Zionist revolution by means of the organizational structure they had erected.[4]

Greenberg likewise drew on the Bolshevik experience in his repudiation of bureaucracy, which in this period was perceived as a means to preserve the domination of the bourgeoisie and the capitalist system. Greenberg's interpretation of "spiritual dictatorship" emerges from another piece he published in *Kuntress* in which he assailed the paper for accepting an article advocating views that deviated from the Zionist consensus of those days. "Freedom of speech turns into anarchy of speech," he asserted, and cited as an example for emulation the Soviet Union, where anything inconsonant with the regime's idea of the state "is stifled—and rightly so."[5]

The trouble was that the social-democracy of Ahdut Ha'avodah and Mapai did enable freedom of speech and debate, and spurned the idea of a dictatorship. Disappointed, the intellectuals whose articles we have been quoting left the workers' parties and joined the Revisionists. Now they devoted themselves to attacking the social democracy that had gained dominance in the Yishuv.

They rejected the notions of universalism and humanism and the idea of democracy espoused by Zionist Socialists. Their allegiance was to one exclusive ideal: the national idea. Achimeir wrote that before the Yishuv could channel all its material and spiritual resources into the achievement of the national goal—establishing an independent Jewish state—it must first rid itself of all ideas based on Socialism and democracy. "The attempt to foist on Zionism a Russian revolutionary vehicle . . . cost us dear." Instead of taking as a model "the cosmopolitan revolutionary movement of Eastern Europe . . . we must learn from the national revolutionary movements of Central Europe"; and not from the Jews in western Europe, who were for the most part Socialists and progressives, but from "Western gentiles"—meaning the radical right.[6] These ideas, Achimeir explained, were in harmony with the modern world of the twentieth century, whereas the Socialist outlook "is wholly rooted in the Europe of the old regime."[7]

Achimeir's sympathy for Nazism disappeared following Hitler's rise to power and his persecution of Jews. However, he still clung to the radical right. In 1936, he declared his support for Francisco Franco in his fight against the Republicans in the Spanish Civil War. The Yishuv, he now urged, should take an example from the devotion and sacrifice evinced by Franco's forces. What was needed was a "Zionist Alcazar," he wrote, referring to the horrific episode in the Spanish Civil War in which Republican forces surrounded the Alcazar fortress in Toledo and threatened to kill the son of its commander, a Franco loyalist. The father refused to yield and his son was executed before his eyes. For the Franco camp the event became a symbol of sacrifice and devotion. It was this model of fanaticism that Achimeir wished to adopt as a symbol for the Zionist movement.[8]

In short order, the group of intellectuals who abandoned the left and joined the Revisionist party became the leaders of its maximalist wing. In the years 1930–32, when Jabotinsky labored unsucessfully to convince his colleagues on the Executive to leave the WZO, the militants could not abide the leader's hesitation in wielding his decision-making authority. Privately, Achimeir likened Jabotinsky to the deposed Kerensky in Russia. He preferred a Lenin to a leader like Jabotinsky,[9] and on another occasion wrote that he was looking for a Jewish Mussolini.[10]

The four Russian Jews whose coming of age coincided with the Revolution yearned for action. They soon found allies in the many youngsters from Russia who joined left-wing parties in Eretz-Israel but grew impatient at the cautious approach displayed by those parties in relations with the local Arab inhabitants and the British authorities.

Some of them joined Achimeir and his friends when they founded Brit Habiryonim (Association of Brigands).

The Achimeir group also dubbed themselves *Sikarikin*, after a sect of knife-wielding extremists in the period of the first Jewish revolt against the Romans, in the first century A.D. The name caught their fancy because of the sect's terrorist character and its readiness to fight not only external enemies but also those among their own people whom they accused of collusion with the enemy. The negative attitude toward the *Sikarikin* expressed by historians of the period, including Zionist historians, reinforced their decision to adopt the name.

Brit Habiryonim preached a violent struggle against the Arabs, the English—who were seen as reneging on their pledge to establish a Jewish state—and Jewish leaders from the Zionist left who in their estimation were reluctant to fight and favored compromise as long as Jewish immigration and settlement activity continued. Such people were considered traitors.

Although adducing some substantive arguments in support of their policy, their basic appeal was to the emotions, particularly national pride. They abhorred what they called "deference to the *goyim*" (gentiles), a humiliating stance for a proud national movement.

To awaken feelings of national pride they demonstratively evoked national myths and symbols. One of their first illegal actions was to blow the *shofar* (ram's horn) on Yom Kippur at the Wailing Wall—the remnant of the Temple—in Jerusalem. This custom had been banned by the authorities for fear it would provoke the Arabs and generate unrest. Brit Habiryonim chose this form of demonstration as a symbolic expression of resistance to those who sought to harm the Jewish nation and uproot its traditions.

In early 1933, they pulled down the Nazi flag that flew over the German consulate in Jerusalem—another symbolic act, this time against the anti-Jewish policy of the newly installed Hitler government. Achimeir, who just the previous year had described the members of his group as Jewish Nazis, now added the Nazis to the list of the enemies of the Jewish people.[11]

When, around the same time, the Jewish Agency decided to conduct negotiations with the German government on the transfer of Jewish property to Palestine, the wrath of Brit Habiryonim knew no bounds. In their eyes, as in the eyes of other Revisionist party circles, this was another demeaning act that undercut Jewish national pride—a supreme value.

The property-transfer dispute exemplifies the disparity between the outlook of Zionist Socialists and their liberal partners, on the one hand, and proponents of radical-right nationalism, on the other hand. The former were pragmatic politicians who sought simultaneously to help Jews wishing to leave Germany with at least part of their property, and to finance the building of the Jewish homeland. Such pragmatic considerations were alien to the radical right. The totality of the principle of national pride left no room for such deliberate activity as finding material resources to achieve self-set goals. The abyss between these two world views—the mystical and emotional vs. pragmatic and calculated—would prove unbridgeable.

The vituperative style employed by Brit Habiryonim in their paper against the leadership of Mapai and the Jewish Agency was all but indistinguishable from the inflammatory rhetoric utilized by many groups of the radical right, including the Nazis themselves, now despised by Brit Habiryonim. Some of their most vicious *ad hominem* tirades were directed against Chaim Arlosoroff, a Mapai leader who tried to negotiate with the German government on the transfer of Jewish property. The unbridled language of these pieces could be read as a call to wreak physical violence on Arlosoroff. This is indeed how they were read by Yishuv circles who were unaccustomed to this style of imagery and were not cognizant of the gap that existed in these movements between symbolic discourse and practical action.[12]

Thus, when Arlosoroff was murdered in June 1933 on the Tel Aviv beach while on home leave between visits to Germany, it was widely believed that Brit Habiryonim had committed the crime. Achimeir and another member of the organization were arrested, tried, and acquitted for lack of evidence. Nevertheless many remained convinced of their guilt, and the storm of emotions in both camps in the Yishuv did not soon abate. The Revisionist party itself, after some hesitation, due apparently to its uncertainty that Brit Habiryonim was not in fact behind the murder, came out in defense of the group, who continued to insist that their hands were clean.

The conventional explanation for the organization's cessation of activity following the trial is that Abba Achimeir came out of prison a broken man, due in no small measure to his ostracism by broad circles of the Jewish public who continued to believe him guilty. In this climate, and without Achimeir's presence as leader, the group languished and fell apart.

Structural weakness would also seem to have played a part. Brit Habiryonim had a small membership and built no organizational apparatus that would enable it to absorb Betaris who were arriving in the country and wished to join. Brit Habiryonim enjoyed great popularity in Betar-Poland. Theirs were the kind of actions Betar aspired to, this was the type of activity they trained for. The Betar movement in the Yishuv expanded rapidly. The new arrivals brought with them a predilection for organized underground military activity, and within a few years they would continue the chain by founding the Irgun, for whom Brit Habiryonim was a paradigm.[13]

A further stumbling block for Brit Habiryonim was the opposition of the official Betar leadership in the Yishuv, whose authority in the legal youth movement they headed was jeopardized by the group's actions. Jabotinsky, too, was troubled by the problem of authority in his relations with the group. He was said to hold an "ambivalent"attitude.[14] He looked favorably on Brit Habiryonim because its actions helped alter the Jewish mentality in the direction he advocated. Under its inspiration Jews grew proud, ready to risk their lives in violent deeds for the sake of the nation. He believed, moreover, that a demonstration of Jewish strength would help convince Britain to support the Jews' national aspirations in Eretz-Israel. When Betaris who arrived via the illegal immigration route were arrested, Jabotinsky encouraged movement members worldwide to demonstrate against the British government and even "to break windows" in British consulates. This indeed was done by fervent Betaris. But Jabotinsky wanted controlled violence in support of the political and diplomatic activity which he regared as paramount, not in place of diplomacy, as Brit Habiryonim urged. Thus, he backed the Brit but also tried to restrain its activists, believing he could accomplish this by exercising his authority as head of Betar.[15]

The activity of Brit Habiryonim was extremely short-lived and did not put to the test Jabotinsky's authority as leader, as the Irgun would do a few years later. Following the group's disintegration, Jabotinsky recruited its leaders for his movement's educational and propaganda activity. To this end, in 1936 he invited Uri Zvi Greenberg to come to Poland as editor of a new party paper. He also asked Achimeir to serve on the presidium of the New Zionist Organization that he had established in 1935.[16] With their aid he hoped to forge in the Jewish people what he called "the psychology of shooting" to supersede their *galut* (exile) mentality. But he seems to have preferred the psychology of shooting to real shooting.

Betar Activity in Eretz-Israel

As already mentioned, Jabotinsky intended Betar to be his movement's elite unit. As such, its test came when Betar members who arrived in

Eretz-Israel were required to live in barracks for two years, continue their military training, and execute any mission demanded by their leader. To Binyamin Eliav, who in 1934 was appointed the "commissar" of these groups, this total mobilization was proof that Betar was an elite movement, demanding of its members an "entry tax" consisting of two years of their lives. In the training camps, the idea was to make every Betari a soldier: this indeed was the primary goal the organization set itself.[17]

It was no easy task to convince the Betaris who arrived in the country to remain in the barracks. Readiness for self-sacrifice was not lacking—as would be demonstrated in 1937 when the majority joined the Irgun. But for many the idea of languishing under a regime of strict military discipline and doing constant military drills was not a very appealing prospect. The more so when it became obvious that Jabotinsky had no intention of actually sending these battalions into battle to conquer the land.

In the meantime, the sheer economic maintenance of the units became an insupportable burden. Efforts were made to locate them close to Jewish settlements where the cadets might be able to earn a living while continuing to train. One idea raised in the course of the many discussions about the future of the units was to emulate the kibbutz movement, but this conflicted with Betar ideology. How would they be different from the leftist settlements they despised? Seemingly, a Socialist ethos was a sine qua non for establishing agricultural cooperatives, whereas the Betaris were bent on launching a violent struggle for national independence.[18]

But under the existing conditions, it was not surprising that many Betaris evaded induction into the units, while many of those who did join the camps soon looked for ways to leave. The archives of the mobilized units contain numberless requests of members to be released so that they could move to the city. Of the diverse personal reasons cited for the requests, the most frequently adduced was the need to support family members who had just arrived in the country. The fact that the majority of the requests were denied did not prevent people from leaving the units, even though this was considered desertion, punishable by expulsion from Betar. By the end of 1934, 300 evaders or deserters had been expelled. What is especially interesting is that two-thirds of them did not even take the trouble to lodge an appeal. At their height the mobilized groups numbered no more than 200 members.[19]

These developments were a grievous disappointment to the Betar leadership. The movement's new commander in Eretz-Israel wrote in 1934: "A Betari who flees from one of the services, however justified his reason, is not a Betari, and all his vows are as nothing and all his dreams are empty. This kind of Betari must be expelled from our ranks without mercy because he is of no use."[20] Such exhortations and threats, however, proved totally ineffectual.

Those who completed two years of service also found themselves in difficult straits: because no one bothered about their absorption during this period, they literally had no place to go and nothing to do.[21] The Betar organization, unable to backtrack from its demand for mobilization without undermining its credibility, had reached a total impasse in Eretz-Israel. Their only hope, as someone remarked perceptively during one of the discussions about the situation, was that "political events" would imbue the mobilized units with a rationale for existence and fire the movement with purpose.[22] This indeed is what seems to have happened following the eruption of the Arab Revolt in 1936. The violent campaign launched by the Arab national movement against the Yishuv furnished Betar with an opportunity for military action, and the movement's fading fortunes were revived.

Until then, however, the new immigrant Betaris and their families had to be absorbed and provided for. To meet these needs, a more practical group was formed in the movement and a trade union set up. This activity had its beginnings as early as 1930, when a growing number of Betaris, who arrived from Poland, burning with the anti-Socialist zeal they had assimilated in the world of the radical right, convinced older groups of Revisionists to leave the Socialist Histadrut Labor Federation and establish an independent organization—the National Workers' Federation, created in 1933. They had hoped to enlist all non-Socialist workers in the Yishuv, but soon discovered that only Betaris were willing to join the militantly anti-Socialist organization. The result was that the NWF became an integral part of the Betar movement.[23]

At the head of the new organization was a cohesive group whose members espoused corporatism, the socioeconomic world view of the radical right. This ideology was adopted by the Italian Fascists, and had also gained a foothold in various Eastern European radical-right movements.

Corporatism favored the continued existence of the capitalist system but sought relations of understanding and harmony between workers and employers, unity based on a common national interest. Corporatists disdained the idea of the class struggle and demanded that the state create structures that would ensure class cooperation. For this reason, for example, they supported compulsory state-supervised labor arbitration. As mentioned, Jabotinsky also believed in corporatist ideas (pp. 19–20).

These concepts, and their new independant labor organization, encouraged the corporatist Betaris to mount a struggle against the left-wing Histadrut. Their opposition to anything smacking of the left, a posture they brought with them from Poland, was integral to their world view. In the eyes of the European radical right, socialism was the most implacable foe of the national movement. The NWF opened labor exchanges and introduced medical services that competed with the Histadrut. But by doing so they outraged the members of Betar's mobilized units. These men, who took little interest in the socioeconomic questions that preoccupied the NWF activists, objected to the new organization because it "totally emulates the leftist Histadrut." Moreover, as far as the mobilized battalions were concerned, anything that diverted energy from the main cause—a military struggle to bring the Jewish state into being—was anathema. They were particularly angered by the NWF's willingness to offer work to Betaris who left the military units and moved to the city.[24]

Nevertheless, the NWF's pragmatic approach appealed to many Betaris. Of the approximately 4,400 persons, who participated in the election of delegates to the organization's founding conference in 1934, the majority were Betar members. The NWF became the most powerful organized body in the Betar Revisionist camp in Eretz-Israel. As will be seen, this state of affairs persisted in Herut as well, until they left the movement in 1967.

Moreover, until the creation of the Irgun, the NWF was the one organization that engaged the Socialist establishment in a violent confrontation; this clash with the Socialist establishment worked like a magnet on many Betaris.

In the first years, Jabotinsky gave his backing to the confrontation with the left and the Histadrut. However, following the Nazis' rise to power, Jabotinsky began looking for a way to back down from his total and uncompromising opposition to the Zionist leadership. The purpose of the agreement he signed in 1934 with David Ben-Gurion, the general-secretary of the Histadrut, was to terminate the violent disputes between the Histadrut and the NWF (See chapter 2.). Under the terms of the pact, the Histadrut would recognize the NWF's autonomous existence, its right to run its own labor exchanges, and its prerogative to request pre-strike arbitration in any plant where NWF members constituted a certain percentage of the workers (no exact percentage was specified in the draft agreement, but the proposed figure was between 15 and 25 percent). The NWF really had no desire for an accord with the Histadrut, preferring to carry on the struggle, even if it entailed violence, against the Socialist organization. In this period, however, they were not yet audacious enough to disobey their leader, and therefore they ratified the pact with a heavy heart; they saw no cause for regret when the Histadrut itself withheld approval.[25]

As the NWF consolidated itself organizationally, its leaders began to depart somewhat from their original corporatist ideology. As the heads of a workers' organization, they became convinced that the workers constituted the linchpin of the national revolution and that the working class must therefore form the basis for the Revisionists' party activity. The worker is the revolutionary element, one NWF leader explained: "It is he and not the middle classes whom we must win over."[26] Ultimately the NWF's commitment to the economic well being of its members produced an agreement with the Histadrut. This occurred in 1937, in the midst of an economic depression. The agreement was less advantageous for the NWF than the 1934 text they had signed only under Jabotinsky's prodding. The earlier pact had provided for an independent labor exchange, whereas in 1937 they were forced to accept the monopoly of the Histadrut's labor exchange and agreed to job quotas for their members.

Although it was concern for the welfare of their members that forced them to adopt a pragmatic approach, the compromise was made possible because their energies were now directed principally into the Irgun's military struggle. As one NWF official put it, concessions were acceptable because it was right to ensure subsistence for those who were devoting themselves to the supreme cause: the struggle to establish a sovereign Jewish state.[27] This same pragmatic attitude continued to characterize the NWF in the period of the state and caused ceaseless friction with the Herut leader, Menachem Begin. Although NWF leaders remained loyal to the basic ideas they had absorbed in Poland, their sense of responsibility toward their members led them to adopt a more pragmatic approach and to take exception to the politics practiced by Menachem Begin and his associates, which ignored the material interests of the movement's members. However, these differences with Begin and his aides were obscured in the years when they all rallied to the military campaign of the Irgun.

The National Military Organization (Irgun)

The Irgun was established as an autonomous underground organization following a series of events that began already in 1931. It was then that non Socialist Zionist parties that were fed up with the control exercised by Mapai and the Histadrut over the Haganah (the underground self defense organization of the Jewish community) set up a separate organization known as "Haganah B." Initially the organization was run by a coalition of non-Histadrut middle class parties, but it was soon dominated by a majority of new immigrant Betaris. They maintained independent organizational ties even as members of Haganah B and constituted "an underground within an underground."[28] As a result, the authority of the organization's command hierarchy, which was not entirely comprised of Betaris, was undermined.

The organized and sustained assault of Arab national groups on Jewish settlements beginning in 1936 spurred Zionist parties to try to heal the rift between the two military organizations. An agreement reached between the two headquarters was rejected by Betar; it proceeded to set up its own military organization that launched guerilla operations against the Arab population and subsequently against the British, too. The new organization drew its inspiration largely from the model of Pilsudski, whose creation of a similar organization had heralded the start of his military struggle for Polish independence. Indeed, the very name of the new group was a Hebrew rendering of Pilsudski's Polish Military Organization.[29] However, not all Irgun members were also Betar members. The Irgun attracted a number of youngsters who had been born or brought up in Eretz-Israel, including David Raziel, who within a short time, became the organization's commander-in-chief. These youngsters supported the Betaris who wanted to mobilize the entire Yishuv, not in self-defense against Arab raids, but in a deliberate military struggle against both Arabs and British with the aim of forging an independent Jewish State.

To those born in Eretz-Israel, the idea of achieving political goals through military means was not new. There had been the "Nili" group, for example, which during World War I carried out espionage missions for the British when they invaded Palestine and fought to oust the Turks, who at that time ruled the country. In this way, Nili believed, they could convince the British that the Jews were a trustworthy and valuable ally, and thus induce London to commit itself politically on behalf of the Yishuv. Nili, too, had acted against the advice of the Yishuv leadership and the workers' parties, which viewed the affair as an adventure from which no political benefit could accrue, but which could jeopardize the Yishuv's very existence.[30]

As I pointed out in my book, *An Elite Without Successors*, the militancy of the native-born generation, their belief that only by force of arms could a state be brought into being, and their decision to undertake this mission, were influenced by a combination of the national education they received in the Hebrew schools and the Eretz-Israel reality of incessant violent disputes between Jewish settlers and the local Arab population, all of which impinged powerfully on their formative years. The schools taught them to identify with their ancient Israelite ancestors, who had warred to preserve their independence. Their teachers, ardent Zionists, preached the rejection of the Diaspora. The whole exilic period was perceived as a melancholy episode in the history of the Jewish people from which Zionism would now release them. They, the proud Jews, unlike their forebears who languished in ghettos, preferred to call themselves *Ivriim* (Hebrews), to distinguish themselves from Diaspora Jews. The Irgun, too, embraced this stance.[31]

For the Irgun, the national aim of establishing a state was the supreme and exclusive goal. As David Raziel—one of the non-Betaris who was brought up in Palestine and joined the Irgun, later becoming its commander—explained: "From the standpoint of national morality, everything which has the good of the nation at heart will be considered good, even if it brings misfortune to an individual or to many individuals; and everything which is detrimental to the nation will be considered bad, even if it brings happiness to a multitude of individuals. National military morality stands at a far higher level than private morality." Raziel added that "exile has obscured our national visage and national honor which must stand above moral imperatives such as honoring one's parents and love of family." Pursuing this line of thought, Raziel argued that it was necessary to fight against those in the nation "who deny the supreme national duty, or at least evade it." Indeed, against these people even measures considered unsuitable for conventional morality should be employed. "The nation must be liberated despite itself," Raziel quoted Napoleon approvingly.[32]

Again, these ideas were not alien to the many native-born youngsters who were members of Histadrut-affiliated youth movements or had joined the Haganah. Now, however, they ran up against stiff opposition from the adult leadership that had been educated abroad and were graduates of Zionist-Socialist movements. As they saw it, a military struggle waged by the small Jewish community against their Arab neighbors and against British rule was devoid of political logic and was liable to terminate any prospect of establishing a Jewish state. Besides pragmatic political considerations, the liberal and Socialist Zionists adduced, in support of their position, universal humanistic principles and the moral stricture against killing innocent people. How this leadership was able to prevent the majority of the native-born young generation from taking up arms at this time is not germane to this book.[33] Some youngsters, at any rate, were able to overcome the influence of the Zionists' progressive-Socialist leadership and the social stewardship of the Yishuv hierarchy, particularly after Betaris espousing a radical-right national outlook, arrived in the country in growing numbers. They brought with them the idea of a military struggle utilizing guerilla warfare along the lines of Jozef Pilsudski's Polish liberation movement.

The Irgun launched reprisal operations against the Arab population from which came the armed groups that attacked Jewish settlements. After the British government turned hostile to the Zionist movement, restricted Jewish immigration to Palestine, and then prohibited the sale of land to Jews in much of the country, the Irgun directed the brunt of its activity against the British authorities. Betar members in Eretz-Israel and in Poland were spurred to activity by the formation of a military underground. This was what they had trained for, and they threw themselves into operations with abandon. Among those who stood out as the Irgun's most loyal adherents in the country were Betaris who had remained in the movement's organizational frameworks—the mobilized battalions and the NWF. Support for the Irgun came also from Betar in Poland. Indeed, Irgun activity in Eretz-Israel at this time would have been unfeasible without the support the organization received from Betar in Poland prior to launching military operations. Secret Irgun cells formed in the branches predated the Haganah B split,[34] and within a short time Irgun supporters constituted the majority in Betar-Poland. They were active in drumming up public support, led the way in collecting arms and funds, and were even able to convince the Polish government to assist in the military training of Irgun members who arrived from Ertez-Israel for this purpose.[35]

The parallels between Pilsudski's struggle for Polish liberation and the Irgun's activity in Eretz-Israel helped win the sympathy of the Polish rulers. That sympathy was intensified by Jabotinsky's plan for the "evacuation" of Poland's Jews and their transfer to Eretz-Israel. The evacuation idea, which was embraced by most of the Polish political parties in this period, heightened support of the Revisionists and the Irgun. This, in turn, reinforced support for the Irgun among the Betaris and their sympathizers in Poland. These ties with the Polish establishment were forged precisely in the years of heightened anti-semitism and the growing influence of the radical right in the Polish ruling elite. A bizarre identity was forged between an anti-semitic and nationalist radical right, and a Jewish national movement.

The Betaris' rift with their leader, Jabotinsky, who looked askance at their mounting extremism and repudiated the idea of an armed struggle in Eretz-Israel, pushed them to identify even more strongly with the radical-right posture of the Polish rulers. In the absence of support from the movement's leader, the Polish hierarchy functioned as a significant reference group that accorded their actions legitimacy. Not even after Pilsudski's death did the Polish ruling group accept Nazi and Fascist ideas *en bloc*. Opposition parties were still permitted, and parliamentary elections were held. Of course, anti-democratic ideas were widespread in Poland. But Pilsudski's successors, while curtailing minority rights, freedom of speech, and the rule of law, did not support, at least not officially, the establishment of a dictatorial regime such as existed in Germany and Italy.

Jabotinsky and the Irgun

From the outset, the Irgun developed an independent policy that was not sanctioned by Jabotinsky and the official institutions of Betar and the Revisionist party. Menachem Begin offered a succinct summation of this policy: "A political struggle to be conducted by military means."[36] Not, then, diplomatic negotiations and the enlistment of public opinion such as Jabotinsky envisaged, but a military struggle with the aim of expelling the British from the country and establishing an independent state.

Jabotinsky did not despair of the political route to attain a Jewish state. He believed that it was possible to convince the British that an independent Jewish state was in their own best interests. Moreover, since he thought that without British aid the Jews would not be able to create a state of their own, he did not want to expel the British but only to induce them to revamp their policy. This, he was certain, could be effected by mobilizing British and world public opinion.[37]

It followed, then, that initially Jabotinsky also supported the policy of *havlagah* espoused by the Zionist leadership. *Havlagah* was the Hebrew term used to denote a policy of restraint in dealing with the Arab nationalists' attacks on Jewish settlements. This policy was severely criticized by the Irgun. Bolstered by his belief that the new conditions created by the Arab onslaught against the Yishuv would lead Britain to agree to the establishment of a Jewish defensive military force, Jabotinsky held that this option was preferable to the formation of an underground military organization.[38]

He soon found that the young Betar activists thought differently. Betar educated its members for war. It was only natural that the developments in Eretz-Israel since 1936, combined with the spread of radical-right ideas in Europe, and especially in Poland, should reinforce Betar's inclination to support a military struggle for the realization of Jewish national aspirations. Betar was no longer in Jabotinsky's control.

To maintain his authority in the organization and uphold his political line, Jabotinsky sought an agreement with Mapai on uniting the Irgun and the Haganah. His only request was that the Irgun retain a modicum of autonomy in the united body. At a certain stage of the talks the plan seemed feasible. It had the support of Eliahu Golomb, who oversaw the Haganah on behalf of the Mapai leadership, and some of his colleagues. The negotiations were protracted and fitful, and at times appeared on the verge of a breakthrough, but finally they broke down. Ben-Gurion was one of those who opposed granting the Irgun autonomy in a united organization.[39]

In September 1938, before the final collapse of the talks, Betar held a convention in Warsaw at which Menachem Begin presented the Irgun's plan to conquer Eretz-Israel. Begin was already then a leading figure in Betar-Poland; he headed the group that supported the Irgun in the movement's leadership. The formal draft resolution presented to the delegates called for amending the oath of allegiance that every Betari had to take. Until then Jabotinsky's wording was used: "I will lift my arm only in defense." Begin proposed adding "in defense of my people and the conquest of my homeland" in order to signal the new Betar-Irgun policy.

In a speech to the convention, Begin asserted that the world's conscience could no longer be relied on and that Irgun policy must be brought into line with current political reality. Political Zionism must give way to military Zionism. As an example, Begin cited Italy's war of liberation, explaining that without Garibaldi's armed struggle, Conte di Cavour's diplomatic efforts to achieve Italian independence would not have borne fruit. At this point, Jabotinsky intervened from his seat on the presidium, and the following exchange ensued:

JABOTINSKY: The gentleman should bear in mind the percentage of Italians and non-Italians in Italy. [An indirect allusion to the different situation in Eretz-Israel, where Jews were a small minority, facing a large Arab majority in the country and in the region.]
BEGIN: I will try to illustrate from the Irelanders' war of liberation. One can fight in another country for the homeland. [A reference to the activity of the Irish underground in England as part of the independence struggle.]

JABOTINSKY: Would the gentleman please tell me how he will get the Betari soldiers into the country without the support of foreigners. BEGIN: If the force is created, help will come also from the Diaspora . . . JABOTINSKY: Has the gentleman taken note of the proportions of the Jewish military force and the Arab force in Eretz-Israel? BEGIN: We will win by virtue of our own moral strength.

The ferocity of Jabotinsky's subsequent reply to Begin surprised even his supporters. He likened Begin's speech to "the squeaking of a door," by which he meant an unpleasant noise having no point or purpose, and called for such squeakings to be suppressed. According to Jabotinsky, the Irgun's plan to conquer Eretz-Israel was absurd and unworkable. Until we form the majority in the country, Jabotinsky said, someone must hold the doors open for us, and therefore we are dependent on the world's conscience. But to think that we could accomplish what Garibaldi and Eamon De Valera did "is mere prattle, and if you think there is no alternative to what Mr. Begin proposed and you have arms—you have as good as committed suicide. If there is no more conscience in the world, the only alternative is [jumping into] the Wisla [River] or [joining] Communism."[40]

Jabotinsky and the young Betaris in Poland now inhabited two different worlds. Unlike Jabotinsky, who never completely cast off liberalism, Betar activists were swept up by the radical-right nationalism then at its height in Europe. This is clearly shown, for example, in the Betar press in Poland. The Yiddish-language Betar-Irgun paper *Die Tat*, which appeared in Warsaw until the outbreak of the war, was sympathetic to these organizations; its reports on them showed a positive bias. A case in point is a series of articles the paper ran in late 1938 and early 1939 entitled "The Third Europe." This was the overall name given to radical-right movements such as the Nazis in Germany, the Fascists in Italy, the Iron Guard in Romania, and the Franco camp in Spain, and so forth. In an article devoted to the first years of Hitler's movement, the writer explained that Hitler's attempted *putsch* of 1923 in Munich had been carried out in order to derail the German leadership from its track of *havlagah*—the same term that Zionist leaders used for their policy of moderation in their dealings with the Arab nationalist movement in Palestine. As an example of such restraint in Weimar Germany, the article cited Berlin's agreeing to sign the ruinous Treaty of Versailles. Hitler's move had been successful, the writer concluded: Nazi propaganda and the *putsch*—even though it had resulted in Hitler's arrest and imprisonment—had been instrumental in breaking the government's policy of restraint.[41]

Another writer in *Die Tat* maintained that anti-semitism was not an integral part of Nazism, which in the final analysis was a version of Fascism. The democracies, according to this writer (who, incidentally, was based in Tel Aviv), were no better than Nazi Germany. As no democratic country had yet granted the Jews full rights, there was no reason to support those countries. The democracies worshipped power like everyone else, and there was no difference between detention camps in Germany and refugee camps in England. This article appeared in April 1939.[42]

A few weeks later, in an editorial entitled "Hitler and Judaism," the paper wrote that it did not reject Hitler's views, not even on the race issue. It objected only to the campaign that "in practice" he was waging against the Jewish people, and its desire to establish an independent state.[43]

Throughout this period Jabotinsky was still officially the autocratic head of Betar. At the time he delivered his impassioned denunciation of Begin in the Betar convention, he still harbored the hope that agreement could be reached with Mapai on unifying the Irgun and the Haganah. This, according to Eliav, who was then a confidant of Jabotinsky's, accounts for his sharp and unsparing attack on Begin.[44] Jabotinsky also refused to appoint Begin head of Betar in Poland, even though Begin's proposals had gained a large majority in the convention and he clearly enjoyed broad popular support among Betar activists. When the prospects for an agreement with Mapai collapsed, Jabotinsky yielded to the pressure and in early 1939 approved Begin's appointment.[45]

In the last phase of his leadership, Jabotinsky (who died in New York in 1940) tried to restore his waning authority in Betar. True, no one threatened his formal leadership: he was the revered leader of an organization that needed just such a leader. But the real strength had passed to the heads of Betar and the Irgun. They now constituted the strongest organized force in the Revisionist camp. In his efforts to uphold his leadership, Jabotinsky fluctuated between opposition to Irgun plans and submission to pressures even as he tried to moderate them.[46] In February 1939, Paris was the venue of one attempt to strike a compromise between the conflicting pressures. At this meeting, it was decided that David Raziel, the Irgun commander, would also be appointed head of Betar in Eretz-Israel. Formally, this put Raziel under the command of Jabotinsky, the leader of Betar. Jabotinsky continued to insist that every decision on an Irgun operation be brought to him for prior approval; when this was not done, the frictions intensified.[47] In August 1939, the Irgun decided to dispatch a delegation of its own to the Zionist Congress in Basel. Jabotinsky's assent was not sought: he was merely told about the decision. Jabotinsky was furious at this flaunting of his authority, but when he was informed that the delegation, which made a stopover in Paris on the way to Basel, would cancel the trip if he "forbade" them to proceed, Jabotinsky did not dare take this step. Thus, as Joseph Schectmann, his assistant in those days, relates, he was forced to yield to Betar's wishes and give his formal assent to a policy he opposed.[48]

Some observers believe that had it not been for the outbreak of the war, Jabotinsky finally would have been deprived of his leadership in Betar.[49] At all events, even though he maintained his formal leadership position, he was no longer the absolute leader he had been in the early 1930s. At the beginning of 1940, he was forced to agree to the removal of his people from the political committee responsible for the Irgun in Eretz-Israel. In practice, this meant a further significant weakening of his control. Another desperate attempt to preserve something of his authority followed. After Jabotinsky, in a letter to Raziel, agreed to the personnel switch, one of his aides dispatched another letter, expressing agreement that the majority on the new committee consist of people proposed by Raziel, but requesting, for continuity's sake, that some of Jabotinsky's loyalists remain on the committee.[50] Jabotinsky died not long afterward.

When Menachem Begin arrived in Eretz-Israel in 1942, it was only natural that he be offered command of the Irgun and leadership of Betar. Both Jabotinsky and Raziel were dead. Begin refused to accept the appointment as head of Betar. There is only one head of Betar, he declared, namely, Ze'ev Jabotinsky, an irreplaceable leader. Ze'ev Jabotinsky is, therefore, the head of Betar to this day.

Thus, Begin buttressed the idea of the leader. Jabotinsky, a distinguished and irreplaceable leader for Betar, came to symbolize the idea of the absolute leader. Begin pronounced himself Jabotinsky's pupil and successor in total disregard of the situation that had developed in the intervening years. He thus became leader of a movement that believed in the principle of the omnipotent leader. From 1943, when he was appointed commander of the Irgun and leader of Betar in Eretz-Israel, until his resignation as head of Herut in 1983, he ran the movement, intially as commander of the Irgun and from 1948 as chairman of the Herut movement.

In this book, I do not deal with the history of the Irgun, not even with the period when Begin headed the organization. This, notwithstanding the fact that the majority of the founders and leaders of Herut served in the underground military organization, and Begin became leader of Herut in large measure thanks to his standing as commander of the Irgun in the period antecedent to the party's establishment. As commander of the Irgun, Begin dealt mainly with the political aspects of the organization, formulating its political line and propaganda, and with financial and organizational problems, rather than becoming involved in actual military operations.[51] During the underground period, he came to symbolize the organization in the eyes of its members and supporters. This status facilitated his choice as leader of the new party.

The underground experience strengthened the solidarity of the members and their allegiance to their leader in the political party formed after the establishment of the state. Overall, though, I believe it was their formative political experience in Betar that shaped their world view, their political behavior, and the organizational-political structure they built. In the following chapters, I shall discuss the Herut movement since its inception in 1948.

4

A New Political Party Seeks Its Way

Establishing A Political Party

The establishment of the State of Israel on May 14, 1948, did not affect the Yishuv's internal political structure. Under the British, the Yishuv had enjoyed a large measure of domestic autonomy. The Jewish inhabitants were nearly all incorporated in *Knesset Israel*, which was organized as a democratic association of parties whose representatives were freely elected to *Asefat Hanivharim* (Elected Assembly). The latter, in turn, elected bodies that administered the Yishuv's autonomous institutions.

Since the 1930s, Mapai tried to form the broadest possible coalition and created what I have elsewhere called a "dominant-party regime." (See p. 1.) All the Zionist parties in the Yishuv associated themselves with this political structure. The party leaders espoused distinctive world views but learned to work together within the voluntary democratic frameworks that were formed. This entailed far-reaching compromises on their part, as well as acceptance of the spiritual and organizational hegemony of the dominant party. The Yishuv structure was emulated in the independent state. Upon its establishment, the parties comprising *Knesset Israel* set up the Provisional State Council that elected a provisional government. The Irgun, which was not part of this structure and had operated not as a political party but as an underground military organization, remained outside the political structure.

Agreement was reached that upon the termination of the War of Independence, elections would be held for a Constituent Assembly. The question confronting the Irgun was whether and in what form to maintain their organization in the nascent state. One option—which was finally adopted—was to form an independent political party.

The decision to establish a party that would undertake to abide by the rules of the democratic game was not a self-evident development. The political tradition that the Betar-Irgun activists had brought with them from Poland did not point clearly in this direction. While many radical-right parties in Europe took part in democratic elections, their underlying motive was not a belief in democracy but a desire to exploit democracy for their own purposes. In their eyes, a coup was an equally legitimate means to achieve power. Although formal democracy was preserved in Poland, in practice the regime became increasingly authoritarian, especially following Pilsudski's death. His successors were not over zealous in their allegiance to the democratic idea.

Betar had no agreed position on this subject, but the non-democratic frame of mind that prevailed within the ruling class in Poland struck a responsive chord among the Irgun-Betar members. Since the policy of the Zionist leadership was bankrupt, as one of their number wrote in the Betar paper in Poland on the eve of World War II, there was no doubt that ultimately the people would catapult them into power. Hence, he proposed that the Yishuv institutions and the Zionist movement transfer power to them in an orderly fashion even though they were a minority. Otherwise this would be effected via a "crueller and more brutal path of revolution" and civil war.[1]

Since 1937, Betar had devoted itself wholly to a military struggle and had given little thought to the political structure it wished to see in the future state. This was consonant with their belief that in the stage of the armed struggle all issues and ideas liable to deflect from the single goal—the establishment of an independent state—must be relegated to the sidelines. When the state arose, they were unprepared for the new situation.

Furthermore, the years when they were engaged in the military campaign had witnessed vast upheavals in the international political arena. The Allies' victory over Germany and Italy was hailed as the victory of democracy over fascism and over the whole radical right. In 1948, Betar graduates found themselves in a world dominated by ideas that were in total conflict with the principles—now anathema—they had been raised on in their formative years in Poland. Their decision to establish a party that would participate in democratic elections took into account also the democratic Zeitgeist that now reigned in the West and in Israel following the Holocaust and the defeat of Hitler.

At the same time, the decision seems to have been taken only after a series of events in the first years after the establishment of the Jewish state finally convinced them that this was the only practical option to survive within the political system of the fledgling state. Begin was among those who intended, even before the state's establishment, to form a party that would contest power democratically; but it was the events about to be described that probably ensured his success in convincing many Irgun leaders to join him.[2]

In 1947, even before the U.N. resolution on the creation of a Jewish state, it was clear to Begin that the British would soon leave the country. A captive of the political conceptions he had absorbed in Poland, he was convinced that because the Irgun was the national liberation movement, which had forced the British out of the country, the liberated population would turn to them as leaders even though they were a minority group. The precedent had been set in Poland following the Germans' withdrawal in 1918, when Pilsudski, the veteran freedom fighter, was released from prison and welcomed with open arms as the leader of free Poland. Begin's political thought was also influenced by the romantic approach and the unrealism that was also integral to the political climate in Poland in the years between the two world wars. Begin's fidelity to this approach led him to misjudge Mapai's political and economic strength.[3]

This miscomprehension of the power wielded by Mapai is readily discernible in an article in an early issue of *Herut*, the paper of the newly founded Herut movement, in October 1948. In the article, Heschel Yevin, a founder of Brit Habiryonim, tried to explain how Mapai's dominance of the new state had come about. In most cases, Yevin wrote, a liberation movement rules in a newly liberated country, even if it is a minority group. In Israel, however, the unexpected had happened because of the Arab invasion of the country following the British withdrawal. Only a leadership capable of mobilizing the entire resources of the Yishuv could have withstood the Arab armies, and this meant the dominant party, Mapai. Thus had Mapai been able to preserve its power.[4]

This is a peculiar explanation. It is not only the Irgun's absolute confidence about its having expelled the British that is peculiar—a belief that to this day is solidly entrenched in former Irgun people and their families (this is a subject we will return to), but also, at least as peculiar, is the disregard of Mapai's economic and organizational clout in the Yishuv. Mapai also had full control of a military organization, the Haganah, which on the eve of the War of Independence numbered 60,000 members. The Palmach alone—the Haganah's commando units—outnumbered the entire Irgun. It is inconceivable that Mapai, which dominated a system of this magnitude, would have been unable to consolidate its rule, irrespective of whether there was an invasion of Arab armies.

The Irgun was disappointed in the U.N. resolution that called for the establishment of a Jewish state in only part of Mandate Palestine and that relegated to Jerusalem the status of an international city outside the boundaries of the future state. The outcome of the War of Independence extended the country's borders, but Betar dreamt of a great Jewish state on both sides of the Jordan River within the original borders of the British Mandate. Betar refused to accept the new reality and sought ways to alter it.

One way was to continue the war and conquer additional territories. This was ruled out by the Government of Israel headed by Mapai and its leader, David Ben-Gurion, which reconciled itself to the borders of the new state. An attempt by the Irgun to continue prosecuting the war would be tantamount to a declaration of war against the Government of Israel as well. But even before the Irgun's leaders could decide on their policy in the new situation, a crisis erupted in their relations with the newly installed government. A ship carrying a large quantity of arms and hundreds of volunteers was dispatched by the Irgun from France. The intention was to have the ship reach the country before the formal establishment of the state, but it arrived only on June 20, during a U.N. declared respite in the fighting between Israel and the Arab states. During the respite, the introduction of arms into the war zone was prohibited. The cease-fire had been agreed to by both sides, but in practice both were arming for the next round of battle.

The arrival of the Irgun ship, called *Altalena*, placed the government on the horns of a severe dilemma. When first informed about the ship by the Irgun, the government sought ways to unload the cargo secretly in order to get its hands on the arms. The details of the negotiations are still cloudy, but it is clear that the Irgun demanded that its own people unload the ship and that 20 percent of the cargo be transferred to Irgun units in Jerusalem.[5] As an international city, Jerusalem was not formally part of Israel, and a large number of Irgun personnel were stationed there.

The Irgun's demands were rejected. When the ship arrived off Netanya and was boarded by Begin and others, the area was ringed by the Israel Defense Forces (IDF). Shots were exchanged and both forces sustained casualties. Begin ordered the ship to make for Tel Aviv in the hope that the IDF would not dare attack in full view of the city's inhabitants. This hope was soon shattered, and a shell fired by the IDF set the ship aflame. Begin and his people were taken from the ship and permitted to leave the site.

Many government ministers believed the Irgun had intended to make use of the arms and volunteers aboard the *Altalena* to execute a *putsch* against the democratic regime. Actually, no such *putsch* appears to have been planned, although vacillation by the Israeli government could have brought about cirumstances conducive to a coup attempt by Irgun commanders. According to one explanation, the government's decisiveness in ordering the IDF to open fire on the Irgun ship is related to the ministers' European political background. Their origins lay in the liberal-left culture in Europe which, in the 1930s, witnessed the collapse of democracies and, after the victory, partook of the consciousness of the democratic forces that democracy must never again succumb. They perceived the Irgun as part of the radical-right camp that had very nearly vanquished the democratic regime in Europe.

Begin's actions in the *Altalena* affair was criticized in Irgun circles. Some charged that his confused and indecisive behavior had placed his subordinates in an impossible situation.[6] My own view is that Begin failed to grasp that a sovereign state entails political behavior of a different order from the prestate period. The demand to receive 20 percent of the weapons was better suited to Yishuv politics, when Mapai controlled the voluntary community thanks to its ability to make meaningful concessions and engineer compromises with other actors. But Ben-Gurion's sovereign government behaved differently from the Jewish Agency Executive he had headed in the prestate period.[7] Ben-Gurion and his colleagues were prepared for the new situation, whereas Begin, the Irgun leader, needed more time to understand that the establishment of the state had brought into being a new political situation.

At all events, when the army of the new state was ordered to use force against the Irgun, Begin moved to prevent bloodshed. He recoiled at the idea of Jews shedding Jewish blood. Likewise, he was unwilling to take up arms against the government of the Jewish state, perceiving that such a step, coming on top of the ongoing total war with Israel's neighbors, would jeopardize the state's very existence. Like many on the radical right, he was bent on tilting against the establishment, but not at the price of endangering the survival of the state, which for him was a supreme value. Yet beyond all this, even if Begin and his colleagues had been willing to take the leap, the government's decisiveness in the *Altalena* affair, together with its control of the IDF, ruled out a successful coup attempt. Moreover, Begin, as will be seen, was not one to take inordinate political risks. Thus, the lesson he and his associates drew from these events was that the only way to survive in the new political constellation was to form a political party.

One veteran member of Betar-Poland, Israel Eldad, expressed his disappointment in Begin precisely because of his refusal to carry out a *putsch* in the newly created state. After the IDF's sinking of the *Altalena,* Eldad told Begin he should proceed to Jerusalem at the head of the Irgun and there declare a struggle for Free Judea, to encompass all of historic Eretz-Israel. Eldad ascribed Begin's reluctance to act to the flawed nature of his revolutionary doctrine, which led him to strike a posture of self-effacement "before the formal trappings of the state."[8]

The same political reality that convinced the leaders of Betar-Irgun to form a party also spurred them to expunge every memory of their connections with the European radical right, and instead to play up the liberal and democratic elements contained in the doctrine of Ze'ev Jabotinsky and the Revisionist movement. One of the first formulations of the new party's platform stated that "the Herut movement declares itself to be an anti-Fascist movement because Fascism is based on the principle of force." Herut was also a "non-Communist" party. It was, rather, a democratic party, "and the principle of democracy is liberty."[9] The party's constitution, adopted at its second convention in 1951, rejected both fascism and communism because both entailed a totalitarian regime.[10]

But Herut, notwithstanding its declared allegiance to democracy, differed from other Israeli political parties. The principal difference lay in its structure.

The Structure of Herut

A political party consists of three components: organization, ideology, and leadership. Organizationally, the Israeli parties were mass parties, that is, made up of members organized in branches, who elect their representatives to the party's highest institutions, which in turn determine policy and choose the party's leaders. This organizational model was developed in Europe in the second half of the nineteenth century by the Socialists following the enfranchisement of the working class. The Socialists utilized the new organizational concept to recruit the support of the workers, who had just acquired the right to vote. Their success in obtaining growing support from the workers, who constituted the majority of the electorate in these countries, led the bourgeois parties, who competed with the Socialists for the support of the new voters, to emulate this same party structure.[11]

In Israel, too, the first workers' parties were organized as mass parties along European lines. Other parties followed suit. (The exceptions were the centralist Communist party and the ultra-Orthodox Agudat Israel, which was controlled by the Council of Torah Sages.)

In addition to its formal organizational structure, a mass party sets up a bureaucratic apparatus. Its role is to enable the leaders to control the party organization. The apparatus "mediates between the party's leaders and its supporters by dispensing material rewards placed at its disposal."[12]

Another major role of the party apparatus is to mobilize support in election campaigns. It does this by responding to the needs of both individuals and groups. That response is reflected both in the party platform and, more concretely, in the form of a network of benefits that are made available as a quid pro quo for electoral support.

The officials who run the party machine are generally more loyal to the party's ideological principles than its principal leaders, who are more disposed to make ideological concessions and compromises as they go about consolidating political power. This pattern is discernible even in American political parties, which are generally considered less ideologically oriented than their European counterparts.[13] The pattern also held true in Mapai.[14]

As I noted in my studies of Mapai, the consequence of this complex organizational structure is that party policy is determined by two groups: the party leaders and the functionaries who control the party apparatus. Decisions in such parties are the result of never ending give-and-take between the leadership and the heads of the apparatus. But a party is more than an apparatus. It is also a voluntary organization whose members support a certain ideology and program. Ideology, too, is an instrument through which the leadership retains its dominance over the members, but at the same time it serves as a control mechanism regarding their own actions. Studies have shown that a party's ideology forms a basis for discussions and negotiations between the leading groups in the party that shape party policies. Ideology gives expression to interests and yearnings of the party's members and voters. Ideological revisions are often related to changes that occur in the party's electoral base and to attempts by the leadership to win the support of new groups. True, every party has a solid body of members and voters who are loyal to the party and its ideology. But parties in a democracy aspire to increase their strength by recruiting additional members and voters, and these efforts frequently entail ideological shifts.

Herut adopted the central organizational concept of a mass party. Immediately after the decision was taken to form a new party, Menachem Begin appointed a Central Committee to run the organization, and a broader Council that included a large number of former Irgun commanders. He also set up branches throughout the country that in 1949 elected representatives to a party convention at which Begin was elected party chairman.

Begin's purpose in establishing a mass party on the model of other Israeli parties was to accord Herut and its leaders legitimacy in the democratic political system of the young state. But by his actions he effectively discarded a major structural feature of a radical-right party. The military unit that existed in such organizations retained the option to achieve power even through violent means; whereas a democratic party organization composed of branches that vote for the party's institutions in general elections is not geared to seize power by violent means. In Herut's first years of existence, an internal debate raged as to whether the party should confine itself solely to democratic means. It was not until 1954, at the third party convention, that this debate was concluded when it was resolved that only through elections would power be attained. Recourse to violence would have meant a return to a paramilitary structure and underground activity.

Another contributing factor to Begin's decision to form a mass party patterned on other Israeli parties was his belief that in such an organization he could ensure his standing as party leader. To this end he brought with him from the Irgun a group of people who formed the apparatus that assured his leadership and his control over the organization. Here too, then, he did not depart from the structure of other Israeli parties.

At first, it seemed that the presence of this small group of followers would suffice to guarantee his leadership. How was the Herut list for the First Knesset drawn up, Yohanan Bader, a member of the group, asked rhetorically in his memoirs. "Simple," he replied: "Begin did the work and the Central Committee approved his proposal."[15]

According to Eri Jabotinsky, Jabotinsky's son and now active in Herut, two other people competed for the leadership of Herut in this early period. One was Hillel Kook, a leading Irgun commander, and the other Dr. Arye Altman, the leader of the Eretz-Israel Revisionist Party. But when the list of Herut candidates for the Constituent Assembly was revealed, the public was surprised to learn that Kook's name appeared in the fifth place, while the majority of the other realistic slots were occupied by Begin's loyalists from the Irgun.[16] (In the Israeli electoral system of proportional representation, each party compiles a list of candidates. The "realistic" places on the list are comprised of those who stand a good chance to win a Knesset seat.)

The leadership contest with Dr. Altman was more difficult, as the latter was backed by an organization—the Revisionist party. Indeed, Altman also had the support of the leaders of another organization, the National Workers Federation (NWF). They opposed Begin because of his desire to run the show himself. The NWF, as an organized body with vested interests, had need of a structure that would allow them to influence the decision-making process of the various committees and councils as was the case in other democratic political organizations.

Eliezer Shostak, the secretary of the NWF, was appointed by Begin to the Herut Council but did not attend its first meeting, convened by Begin, in October 1948. Shostak apologized, explaining that the invitation had reached him late, but this was patently an excuse.[17] Two separate lists ran in the general election of January 1949: the Herut movement, headed by Menachem Begin, and the Revisionist party, led by Dr. Altman and Eliezer Shostak. The leadership issue was thus left to the decision of the electorate. As things turned out, Herut received 11 percent of the vote, while the Revisionists did not obtain the minimum of 1 percent required to enter the Knesset. Although no study exists of voting patterns for the two parties, it is obvious that the majority of NWF members, as well as many Revisionists, cast their ballot for Herut. Kalman Katznelson, himself a Revisionist who now joined Herut, ascribes this result to the voters' belief that Begin was superior to the Revisionist functionaries "because he had carried off a tremendous historical enterprise and led the Revisionist community to its greatest victory." Faced with a choice between Altman and Begin, the voters opted for the commander of the Irgun.[18] Following this debacle the two parties united. The upshot was that the activists in the Revisionist party and the NWF, who wished to survive in the political system, accepted Begin's leadership on his terms. He became an absolute leader.

The origins of this one-man leadership, which was a departure from the norm in other mass parties, lay primarily in Begin's perception of political leadership as authoritarian leadership, a notion he acquired in his formative years prior to settling in Eretz-Israel when Jozef Pilsudski and Ze'ev Jabotinsky were his role models. Both were leaders who made decisions and expected their assistants to implement them without question.

This leadership style typifies all radical-right parties, even those that disdain the idea of the all-powerful leader and elect their leaders in democratically constituted conventions. In part, the reason for this lies in the distinctive structure of these parties. Democratic parties represent groups with different interests and ensure the loyalty of their members and voters by giving expression to economic or ideological interests of the different groups. Party policy results from the striking of a balance between the diverse interests, and the task of the leadership and the party machinery is to find the happy medium that will assure the allegiance of the various groups and the support of the voters.

In contrast, Begin's Herut, like radical-right parties, considered itself a national party and refused to seek the support on the basis of sectorial or other specific interests. Herut directed its appeal to all strata of the population and refused to address itself to particular groups. In election campaigns, Begin insisted that the emphasis be placed on national policy issues and not on economic or social questions.[19] This fundamental principle determined the character of the leadership in Herut, hence also the weakness of the party apparatus in contrast to the mass parties that operated on the social-democratic model.

Menachem Begin and the Intelligentsia

Begin consolidated his control in the party with the help of a number of followers who were personally loyal to him and accepted his leadership unreservedly. The result was to alienate the intelligentsia who joined Herut. These included journalists, lawyers, and other members of the liberal professions. Many of them had been politically active in the prestate period. Some wrote for the dailies, weeklies, and monthlies published by the Revisionist movement or held senior command positions in the Irgun. Widely educated, they now sought a place in the new party consonant with their abilities and education. They aspired to influence in the decision—and policy-making process of the new party, comparable to the status enjoyed by the intelligentsia in other Israeli political parties.[20]

The Revisionist, Betar and Irgun intelligentsia did not regard Begin as one of their own. In this attitude was reflected one of the differences between Begin and Jabotinsky. Both aspired to absolute leadership, but Jabotinsky, the intellectual and man of the world, succeeded in forming a cadre of loyal followers from the intelligentsia. These people were unwilling to accept Begin's leadership. Binyamin Eliav, for example, who bowed to Jabotinsky's authority even when he disagreed with him, was unwilling to accept Begin's leadership.[21]

Another intellectual who never joined Herut, Israel Eldad, says that Begin fit the category of what he called "semi-intelligentsia." This was a distinct social group in eastern European Jewish society. It was comprised of people who wished to emulate the intelligentsia by placing spiritual issues at the center of their life, but lacked the necessary conceptual and educational tools to realize their ambition. Begin's education and spiritual development had not gone beyond the high school level, Eldad noted derisively.[22]

These disparities between the intelligentsia and Begin produced friction, but the basic source of the conflict was their desire to have a hand in running the party and share in the decision-making process.

Begin, as mentioned, believed that as the leader of a national movement he must make decisions alone.

To enable him to manage Herut without intervention, he brought with him from the Irgun a group of deputies whose personal loyalty to him was absolute. Some had been his assistants as far back as the years of Betar-Poland; in the Irgun they dealt with propaganda, finances, and administration. The most outstanding members of this group were Arye Ben-Eliezer, Haim Landau, Yohanan Bader, Ya'akov Meridor, and Esther Raziel-Naor. They were totally unknown to the general public before Begin chose them to be Knesset Members on behalf of Herut[23]—a state of affairs that only increased their dependence on Begin. Their sole virtue, according to one journalist who followed their activity, was that they had endured many years of suffering in the underground.[24]

In a group that was called on to carry out the leader's orders without question, Katznelson wrote, "loyal members of the underground could not be absorbed." Only those "who are part underground activists and part functionaries" could find their niche in the party. This background determined the nature of their behavior in the political system, Katznelson added. They accepted Begin's leadership unreservedly, and instead of working to achieve public goals they gradually assumed the pose of *hauteur* and self-importance characteristic of a debased level of public activity.[25]

In my estimation, the disdain evinced by Katznelson and others in the intelligentsia for the personal and intellectual abilities of this group fails to take into account their situation in the organization. True, the need for self-effacement vis-a-vis the leader is not calculated to draw gifted people into a party, but this is not the main reason for the weakness of the group appointed by Begin to handle the organizational side. Begin did not consult with them in determining policy; they were called on to carry out his orders unquestioningly. Because Begin did not ask for their advice before making decisions, they could not understand the logic and motivation of his decisions. In this state of affairs, even gifted people could not have exercised leadership or administrative skills.

This structural explanation is reinforced from a comparison of the group who comprised Begin's assistants with the group of aides that Jozef Pilsudski gathered around him following his *putsch* in 1926. He, too, placed persons who had been with him in the underground, the Polish Military Organization, in administrative positions. His primary criterion for selecting them and assigning them key positions was their personal loyalty to him. For the most part, they, too, had not been combat commanders in the underground but had carried out political and propaganda missions, and were accustomed to obeying Pilsudski and not operating on their own initiative.[26] Pilsudski made his decisions alone and transmitted to his assistants guidelines for their implementation in the form of orders. Pilsudski's aides called him the "Commander" while they themselves were known as "colonels." It is well known that Begin's underlings also referred to him as the Commander, and the Betar veterans in Herut, cognizant of the great similarity between Pilsudski and his assistants and Begin and his assistants, dubbed the latter colonels. Pilsudski's aides were also said to be inexperienced and lacked the intelligence and ability needed to fulfill their task.[27] In both cases, their behavior seems to have been dictated by an absolute leader whose mode of rule precluded efficient administration. The upshot was that Begin's aides were unable to supervise either the party organization, consisting of thousands of members, or the internal elections for the party convention that was held every two or three years.[28]

But in the early 1950s, it was the intelligentsia who left Herut, while Begin maintained his grip on the party through this group of assistants lacking in administrative and leadership ability. These developments form the key to understanding Herut to this day.

Following the conclusion of the military struggle for independence, which had preoccupied them throughout the decade preceding the state's establishment, it emerged that the intelligentsia, the members of the Irgun, and the Irgun's supporters in Betar and the Revisionist party, did not always share the same views. Attitudes on social and economic issues ranged from the conservative to the progressive. Some believed that the paramount question that the new society must cope with was the religion-state relationship and the interconnection between religion and nationalism. They advocated separating the two. There were those who demanded a clear pro-American and anti-Communist foreign policy posture (in the first years of the state the Israeli government took a neutral stance in the inter-bloc rivalry). Some considered it vital to reform the electoral system by introducing a two-party instead of a multiparty regime. The leaders of the intelligentsia were also divided on how to go about achieving their goals. Some were democrats, others believed in extra-parliamentary activity, still others viewed both modes as equally legitimate. There were also those who opposed a stance of total opposition to the existing regime and urged Herut to join the Mapai-led government coalition in order to fight for the party's goals from within.[29]

Nevertheless, consensus prevailed on certain issues. First, everyone wished for a clear policy and an agreed plan of action to be articulated.

To this end, the party was called on to mobilize all factions of the Betar and Revisionist intelligentsia, from the extreme right to the moderates, including those who did not join Herut. The demand was voiced by all circles of the intelligentsia, radicals and moderates, conservatives and progressives.[30]

Second, there was a unanimous call for the creation of an efficient organization with a hierarchical bureaucratic structure at its core. Within these frameworks it would be possible to train a cadre of experts in the administration of large organizational apparatuses and with their help voters could be recruited and the party's strength augmented.[31]

The intelligentsia believed that it had a contribution to make to the party in both areas, ideology and organization. Hence, their demand that Begin hold discussions in the party institutions on the party's goals and on the running of the organization. It was Begin's refusal to consult with them and share in decision making that ultimately led many of them to abandon party activity, irrespective of their views and opinions on the various issues. As Katznelson explained in his letter of resignation from the party, he was leaving because of "the anti-democratic regime you [plural] have imposed within the said framework."[32]

One of the first to depart was Avraham Weinschel, who left the party in protest against Begin's autocratic leadership.[33] Shmuel Katz refused to be a candidate on the Herut list for the Second Knesset because Begin wanted only yes-men.[34] Two other Herut MKs, Hillel Kook and Eri Jabotinsky, broke away from the faction and set up an independent faction. Others, including former senior Irgun commanders, dropped out for similar reasons. They were unable to find scope for activity under Begin.[35] Yet although they accused Begin, they vented their anger primarily at his assistants, for creating what they said was a Byzantine-like atmosphere around him.[36]

Begin was concerned over these developments. Initially he sought to impose his authority over the intellectuals by assuming the role of movement ideologue. This, he hoped, would consolidate his leadership position. Begin began taking steps in this direction immediately after the general elections of January 1949. Herut received 11 percent of the vote, as compared with Mapai's 36 percent, enabling the latter to form a coalition with relative ease. This result disappointed many in Herut: they considered it an expression of the public's ingratitude to those who had freed them from British occupation. Begin was one of the first to recover from the defeat. He decided to make Herut a salient opposition party, but also a party loyal to the state, the democratic regime, and the principles of liberal democracy. Along with others in Herut, Begin believed that a Socialist party like Mapai would not be overly zealous in maintaining the rule of law, civil and minority rights, or a free economy. The other parties who aspired to join a Mapai-led coalition would undoubtedly make concessions in these spheres. Only Herut could assume the role of the guardian of liberal democracy.

The intention, Begin explained, was for Herut to be "a serious and sincere opposition. . . . Good government actions will be praised, ill-conceived actions will be condemned."[37] Begin considered his party an integral part of a democratic regime in which power periodically changed hands. In his assessment, his party's liberal-democratic thrust held out the prospect of obtaining broad electoral support that would bring it to power within a reasonable time.

The activity of the Herut Knesset faction centered on preserving civil rights and the rule of law. Herut opposed the extension of the Emergency Regulations from the Mandate period under which people could be imprisoned without trial for lengthy periods. The party protested the existence of press censorship and said the trial of civilians before military courts infringed "basic human and civil rights."[38] On the other hand, they supported the chief of staff's decision to prohibit soldiers from attending a gathering of former Haganah units. "Others, too, can organize thousands on a similar demonstration of strength," the party's daily, *Herut*, editorialized. It was strongly implied that the Irgun, too, would not be permitted to organize a rally of this kind.[39]

Herut charged that the government was politicizing the public service. Once in power, Herut would not follow Mapai's lead, but would leave all officials in place, for in a democracy, "governments come and go but the official remains forever."[40]

When the First Knesset, which had been elected as a Constitutent Assembly that had the task of drawing up a constitution, decided to defer the constitution to a later date, Begin was furious at this blow to democracy. He demanded that a constitution be written, because "if the Constituent Assembly promulgates a constitution, the government will not be able to do whatever strikes its fancy."[41]

In his keynote speech to the second Herut convention, in 1951, Begin set forth his liberal-democratic ideology. Begin believed that this speech, which was viewed as a major programmatic statement, would constitute a fundamental and comprehensive ideological document for his party. The speech was reprinted several times in the 1950s and 1960s under the title "A World View and a National Orientation."[42]

A significant part of the speech dealt with the liberation of the homeland. "The true goal of Jewish policy is to complete the liberation."

According to the Herut platform, the homeland then encompassed the area of the former British Mandate as well as Trans-Jordan (today the Kingdom of Jordan). To complete the liberation, readiness even for war was required: "The people have to be willing to fight for their land, for it is their land."

As mentioned, the speech concentrated on Herut's liberal world view, which comprised three principles: freedom of the individual, the amelioration of society, and the supremacy of the law. Basically, the text consisted of a random collection of ideas. A society, for example, "is formed within the organically integral framework called a nation." Or: the principal guarantee for the preservation of freedom is the education of the peoples. Begin cited approvingly Thomas Jefferson's notion that rebellion against a regime that denies freedom of thought and expression is not a right but a duty.

Marx was given short shrift. Marx had been mistaken on predicting polarization between the propertied and propertyless classes, because the establishment of public-share corporations and the progressive income tax had brought about the distribution of capital rather than its concentration. In contrast, Begin lauded Montesquieu's idea of the separation of powers, but explained that this principle was not applied, since the government constituting the political leadership possessed a majority in the House of Representatives and utilized that majority to impose its will on the House. Hence, he concluded that the law is "the last bastion of human liberty in our time."

Begin further declared that the state had the duty to protect economic freedom and free enterprise. The state was also obliged to ensure the basic needs of its citizens, and so on and so forth. The editor of the daily Ma'ariv, Azriel Carlebach, who was hardly an adversary of Begin or his party, summed up the speech in the following words: "It came out as a failed attempt to imbue the Herut movement with a doctrine, a doctrine composed of fragments of sublime universal ideas as they are formulated in simplistic juvenile literature, as lofty ideals per se, without conclusions, without showing how they might be achieved."[43] The Herut intelligentsia were even less enthusiastic.

A preference for vague generalizations and a reluctance to commit himself to a specific program would characterize Begin in the years to come as well, but in his 1951 speech his intellectual limitations were also on display. When all is said and done, his intention had been to vest his party with an ideology. Begin's limitations are even more striking when set against the proposals that were submitted to the convention by a cohesive group which called itself "Lamerhav."

Many members of the intelligentsia had either refrained from joining Herut in the first place, or had ceased their activity in the party before the convention. But there were others who organized themselves with a view to taking part in the convention. One such faction was the Lamerhav group, which presented its own plan of action at the convention. Its members added their voices to the call to bring back the Betar and Revisionist intellectuals who had left the party, with the aim of articulating, together with them, a world view and a program for the new party. They urged the adoption of a program that could deal with the economic and social problems facing the new state: civil rights, economic planning, the status of non-Jewish citizens in the Jewish state, the religion-state question, and the ties between Jews who were citizens of Israel and Jews in the Diaspora. The party, they argued, must take a position on Israel's standing in the world and on "the destiny and place of the Hebrew nation amid the clashing world views and ways of life."

The concrete operative proposals put forward by Lamerhav showed that it constituted the extreme radical right wing of the intelligentsia. Lamerhav wanted the power of the Histadrut reduced through the nationalization of public transportation, which was in the hands of Histadrut cooperatives. The group wanted land purchased in the past by the Jewish National Fund to be sold to private investors. Their radicalism showed itself most blatantly in their notion of not confining themselves to parliamentary activity alone, but on the contrary, placing the emphasis on vigorous extra-parliamentary activity. As one of the group's leaders declared, Herut must become "a dynamic political movement with revolutionary goals." Instead of waiting until the regime fell apart by itself, Herut must "bring about its fall through all the public means available to a dynamic and audacious movement."[44]

This extremism cost them the support of many moderate convention delegates, particularly the NWF leadership, whose aspirations and operational plans were the opposite of those espoused by Lamerhav. The moderates objected to Herut's becoming a total opposition, urging that it try to find its niche in the existing political system by joining a government coalition under Mapai in order to influence policy from within. Begin himself was adamantly opposed to joining a Mapai-led coalition, but objected equally to extra-parliamentary activity. He demanded that Herut restrict itself to activity consonant with an opposition party within a democratic parliamentary framework. Begin was saved from possible defeat at the convention by the spilt within the intelligentsia. Lamerhav's strength was estimated at 25 percent of the convention delegates.[45] The NWF group was also numerically strong, although they did not organize as a separate faction. They made known their views outside the convention, but decided not to broach them on the convention floor: thus, was Begin's continued rule in the movement assured for the time being.[46]

Still, his control was shaky. The strength of the opposition at the convention reflected the weakness of the group of Begin's assistants. Their inadequate supervision over the party branches left the way open for the opposition to organize and elect a large number of delegates to the convention. This weakness was never overcome, due to Begin's failure to create the kind of machinery that in other parties consolidates the leadership's control over the party organization. The intelligentsia, in all its parts, was superior to the Begin group in power of expression and organizational ability. The entire strength of the "colonels" was a function of the personal influence wielded by Begin over the party members, many of them former Irgun activists. This structural weakness jeopardized the party leadership. Especially when the ruling institutions of a mass party are chosen by election, it is difficult for the leadership to maintain its rule without an efficient bureaucratic apparatus. Herut's failure in the Knesset elections, which were held shortly after the convention, brought Begin's leadership to a crisis point.

The Fight Over the Reparations Agreement

A coalition crisis led to new elections in June 1951. Herut's Knesset strength was cut nearly in half, from fourteen to eight MKs.

No analysis of these election results is available, so that one can only conjecture the reasons for Herut's decline. One cause had to do with the large number of new immigrants who voted for the first time. Many of them supported the ruling parties because of their dependence on the coalition parties that had assisted them with housing and social welfare. Equally important, their desire to be assimilated in the new country turned them away from a salient opposition party like Herut. But Herut's support among the veteran population also fell. One explanation for this is the party's inordinate preoccupation with its glorious past as a liberation movement instead of focusing on the problems facing the new society, particularly the economic crisis generated by the unprecedented scale of immigration. The party's evocation of Irgun activity, and its hammering home of the fact that the leader of Herut was also the commander of the Irgun, seems to have assured the loyaliy of many Irgun members and supporters, but evidently had a boomerang effect on other voters.[47] Similarly, a large number of voters were frightened by

Herut's call for the renewal of the war in order to conquer those areas of Eretz-Israel still in Arab hands, and possibly also Trans-Jordan. In a speech that had wide reverberations, Begin spoke about the need to evacuate the women and children from the country during the war he envisaged with the Arab states.[48] Herut's decision to serve as a total opposition and its concomitant refusal to join the Mapai coalition was also anathema to many voters, who opted to cast their ballot for the General Zionists—a moderate rightist party—instead. Indeed, the latter party was the chief gainer in the June 1951 elections. It rejected the government's social and economic policy, but was ready to join a coalition led by Mapai in an effort to influence government policy.

More important for the purposes of the present study, which deals primarily with Herut's leaders and members and not with its electorate, are the internal developments that occurred in Herut as a result of the defeat. Begin immediately resigned as party chairman and as head of the Knesset faction. He told his stunned aides that he intended to withdraw from political life, resume his law studies (begun while he was still in Poland), and become a lawyer. All attempts to dissuade him from this course were futile. Although he did not formally resign from the Knesset, he no longer attended its sessions.

This state of affairs went on for about half a year, until publication of the Reparations Agreement between Germany and Israel in December 1951. Under the terms of the agreement, Israel was to receive economic aid as compensation for the Nazi government's murder of Jews. Begin, his follower's relate, could not sit idly by in the face of the blow to Jewish honor entailed in the government's signing of the agreement. He felt obligated to block the Knesset's ratification of the accord. It was in order to mobilize the party for a struggle against the Reparations Agreement, we are told, that he decided to resume his post as Herut chairman.[49]

The entire party rallied to the protests and demonstrations against the agreement. Party mobilization resembled a military operation. All party branches were ordered to have their members place themselves at the party's disposal and obey its directives. At Begin's instigation, the major event was a demonstration in front of the Knesset building during the debate on the agreement's ratification. Party members were ordered to absent themselves from work that day; chartered buses were available throughout the country to transport them to the big demonstration in Jerusalem. Begin delivered a fire-breathing speech to the mass rally. The Irgun would not allow the agreement to be ratified. When the IDF attacked the *Altalena*, Begin declared, I ordered that no response be made. Now I say yes, the time has come for action. He spoke about a civil revolt, about refusing to pay taxes, about disobeying the law, and going to prison *en masse*. "When we say we will sacrifice our life, we will give it at any cost, even if I am fated to die . . . Liberty or death!"[50]

Enflamed by this rhetoric, the Herut masses marched on the Knesset and tried to force their way in. They were driven back by the police, using tear gas. Begin himself entered the Knesset for the first time since the elections and disrupted the proceedings until he was ejected from the chamber by order of the Speaker. The debate went on and the agreement was ratified. Begin was suspended from the Knesset for three months, an extremely harsh and indeed unexampled punishment.

Things grew quiet in Herut following this big ruckus. Begin and his aides were behind this development as well. Writing in *Herut* in reaction to Begin's suspension from the Knesset, Yohanan Bader asserted that this was an insupportable blow to democracy. He added, however, that any decision on a response "will be made following a full weighing of the situation, or will be postponed for a time if we so decide. We will decide what to do tomorrow, then we will decide what to do the day after tomorrow, and we will make the decision when the time comes. We will retain the initiative."[51] Begin, for his part, wrote in *Herut* that the government's decision justified "rebellion using all means." But that step was not necessary: it was sufficent "to get the masses to sign a petition calling for a plebiscite on the subject."[52] This was of course meaningless. The Israeli constitutional system contained no provision for a plebiscite, and there was no way Begin could force the ruling parties to take this course. Nor indeed did he make any great effort to do so. When the first goods within the framework of the Reparations Agreement arrived in Israel about a year and a half later, Begin was not in the country. He was in the midst of a lengthy visit to South Africa, and some of his critics in Herut claimed that the trip had been timed so that he would not be compelled to act.[53]

This pattern of behavior—extreme and emotional verbal declarations, but failure to take the steps obligated by those declarations—became Begin's hallmark. His was a symbolic discourse informed by a world of symbols and myths but detached from reality. Politics of this kind was looked on askance by the intelligentsia. Both the moderates and the extremists were outraged by his behavior regarding the reparations: the moderates because of statements that they thought undercut the democratic regime, the extremists because he did not translate these statements into deeds. Both sides assessed the affair as a political failure, since Begin's declared objective—to prevent the agreement's ratification—was not attained.

Some ascribed this to his emotionalism and his confused thinking,[54] while others viewed it as part of his desperate search for issues his party could support. This, at all events, was the opinion of Eliahu Ben-Horin, a former Jabotinsky aide and Irgun activist. The objective remained unattained, he wrote, because a struggle against German reparations could not be a substitute for a socio-economic platform.[55] What Ben-Horin and his colleagues failed to grasp was that there had not even been an attempt to articulate a concrete plan of action, that it was all a symbolic surrogate for rational political action.

Begin was undoubtedly emotional and impulsive. But the Reparations Agreement had not come out of the blue. Negotiations with the German government had gone on for more than a year. Already at the party convention of February 1951, the Lamerhav faction had urged that the fight against the agreement be intensified.[56] Then, the demand had elicited no response from the leader.

Begin was a political person, and the explanation for his behavior lies in the political realm. He fought to preserve his leadership. His resignation at the time is also amendable to explanation in the light of the political reality he faced following his party's election defeat. The opposition threatened his leadership and he did not see how he could maintain his standing as party leader.[57] When the reparations issue came up and he decided to act, he immediately secured the backing of the radical opposition that was organized in the Lamerhav group and constituted the major threat to his leadership. Lamerhav rallied to the new cause with a will. Indeed, Shmuel Tamir, one of the faction's leaders, took an even more radical stance than Begin, calling for "underground operations" against the government.[58] When Begin called a halt to extra-parliamentary activity, this group was sorely disappointed. Yet to their surprise it was Begin who once more took control of Herut, while they, who had taken part in Begin's militant but futile activity against the Reparations Agreement, found themselves neutralized by the leader. Toward the end of 1952 Shmuel Tamir and Shmuel Marlin, both leading lights in the Lamerhav group, resigned from the Herut Council because the party had "in practice abandoned the campaign to crush the criminal and corrupt way of life and regime."[59] Begin was the one who found the way to the hearts of the party's rank and file. They, who had followed Begin in the campaign against the reparations and had responded to the fiery orator who defended Jewish national pride, were not bothered by the disparity between his high-flying rhetoric and his dearth of achievements in the fight against the reparations. Through this symbolic discourse Begin was able to make contact with Herut's rank and file.

Henceforth, he would not need groups of intermediaries in the party to act as his bridge to them—the very role coveted by the intelligentsia. Thus, the intelligentsia remained without a function and became super-fluous.

In the years that followed, Begin made no effort to encourage the return of the intelligentsia to the movement. When, for example, after the Six Day War of 1967, Ya'akov Amrami, a former Irgun commander, who had left Herut in the early 1950s, expressed a desire to resume his activity in the party, Begin's response was evasive. Amrami indicated that he awaited a proposal that would enable him to engage in "vigorous activity," but Begin replied laconically that "you will give me and all your friends deep satisfaction if you renew your activity." Amrami stayed out.[60]

In this way, Begin freed himself of the need to account for his actions before the party forums. Meetings of Herut institutions became show-cases for speeches by Begin. Instead of discussions, an exchange of views, and decision making, accompanied by an attempt to strike a compromise between different views and interests, the major event at every such gathering was Begin's keynote speech, ardently received by the party faithful. Through this process a party organization was formed that was unique in the Israel political arena.

5

The Supremacy of Politics

A National-Democratic Party

The third Herut party convention, held in 1954, was the first in the new political style. Two sessions were held, in February and April. The convention's importance lay in its affirmation of the party's new disposition. The intelligentsia did not attend, and as a result, an observer noted, "a great silence befell Herut."[1] It was hardly a quiet convention, but the noise emanated largely from the leader's zealous supporters. Begin was in absolute control.

Begin proposed a draft constitution that would obligate the party to hold a convention every two or three years, which would elect the chairman. In this it resembled the Betar constitution. The difference was that the Herut document declared the party's allegiance to the democratic regime and asserted that all party activity would be carried out within the parliamentary-democratic framework. Herut would achieve power, Begin stated, via the ballot box alone and not by any other means.

This decision of principle was the logical followup to the decision to establish Herut as a mass party composed of branches and administered by a body elected via an internal vote. However, now that the proposal was being submitted for ratification by the convention, many Betar veterans voiced their objection to the principle that participation in democratic elections was the sole legitimate means to attain power in the State of Israel.

The dissenters explained their position in a special pamphlet devoted to a discussion of the issues on the convention agenda, which was published by the Central Committee on the eve of the gathering, and in the general debate at the convention itself. One discussant said: "My inner conviction is that whether all of us here are a majority or a minority—is immaterial." He added: if the majority of the nation agrees to forgo the state, "Then what? Will we bow our heads before His Highness Democracy?"[2] The overwhelming majority of the people were a "mass," a veteran Betari held, drawing on terminology and reasoning

85

that had characterized the radical right during his youth, and the mass was inherently conservative and anti-revolutionary. For the revolution to succeed, then, "there is no need, necessarily, for a mass majority," but for a supreme effort of individuals. Therefore, "any change in the situation of a people derives not from the will of the people but from the will and the struggle of individuals."[3]

Other speakers urged that all options be left open, as was the case in their Betar past. They had to be ready both to bring out people to the street, and be a movement of the ballot box.[4] Even some of Begin's most trusted and loyal deputies, such as Haim Landau, were reluctant to rule out the possibility of a coup. Today, Landau agreed, there is only one way to achieve power, and that is through the ballot, but in three years the situation might be different.[5] Betar and Irgun veterans were loath to accept the idea that only via the democratic route could power be attained.

But Begin was adamant. In his reply to the debate he explained why the ballot was the road to power in Israel. What are the alternatives, he asked. One way is to bring out the masses to the street, give them arms, place them on the barricades, and act. But in this century every government will have at its disposal means of suppression that the insurgents do not have. "In this way: bloodshed, yes; power, no." A second option was a military coup. This was not practical, Begin said, but even if it "were practical, I would suggest that it be rejected. The danger in a military coup is a danger for generations. A nation that embarks on this road of military coups will find itself wallowing in its blood, not for a single generation but for generations. Today I will stage a coup, tomorrow someone else will stage a coup against the first coup, and so on and so forth." A third way was to go underground. But "what will an underground do? Take a few pistols and try to push them against the ministers' hearts and say to them: We are in charge?" Not even against the British were personal attacks used, Begin reminded the convention. His conclusion: none of the three options was feasible. On the other hand, he also spurned the NWF proposal that Herut join a Mapai-led coalition. They will just throw us crumbs, he said. "Mapai distributes portfolios to its partners without power." So this possibility, too, was ruled out, and in any event it was not politically practicable, he concluded. Therefore the sole remaining possibility was a parliamentary opposition party striving to replace the ruling party in elections.[6]

Begin's defense of democracy in 1954 was a departure from the approach he had voiced at the convention three years earlier. At that time, he had viewed democracy as a supreme and absolute value entailing the assurance of individual freedoms, the defense of individual and minority rights, and, to guarantee these freedoms, a separation of powers and the supremacy of the law. Now he accepted the rules of Israeli democracy—what I have called "formal" or "procedural" rather than liberal democracy—in reference to the election process and to competition for voters' support among groups desiring an input in political decisions. Begin accepted the same concept of democracy that impelled Mapai and which was dominant in the Israeli society.[7]

Yet the party structure he erected in Herut differed from that of the other Israeli parties in several key respects: Begin did not establish a bureaucratic apparatus, he did away with intermediary groups, and he became an absolute leader in the party. Herut's new constitution was adopted without dissent at the convention, the debates notwithstanding. Many of the delegates were ardent followers of Begin, who referred to him only in superlatives of love and reverence. One such delegate, for example, declared during the general debate that the leader's "tremendous and brilliant" speech was a "renewed *Shulhan Arukh* [a sanctified code of Jewish law]" and that "a definitive answer was given to all problems." Another asserted that Begin's address had recalled "the orators of Greece and Rome."[8] Indeed, Begin utilized his rhetorical skills to maintain power in his movement. He was able to address his followers without recourse to the mediation of the intelligentsia and without the assistance of a bureaucratic organization.

Henceforth, Herut professed allegiance to the idea of procedural democracy, and formal democracy also prevailed within the party. Begin, however, was able to maintain absolute rule. He was the sole source of authority in the organization and formulated party policy by himself.

But there was one fly in the ointment of the new structure. The National Workers Federation was an organizaiton with vested interests and an apparatus of salaried workers. A condition for Begin's control of the organization, without the help of an apparatus and without having to accede to the interests of specific groups, was the weakening, perhaps even the liquidation, of the NWF. Begin took up the task at what was to be the last closed Herut convention, subsequent Herut conventions were opened to press coverage.

Begin and the National Workers Federation

The NWF was a trade union founded and headed by Betaris who supported the idea of corporatism—which rejected socialism and the class war—and aspired to mutual understanding and harmonious relations between the classes, a unity grounded in the national interest. They themselves represented the workers and expected that the state, which embodied the overall national interest, would mediate between the interests they represented and the interests of the employers. In the prestate period, they had been active in the Irgun under Begin's leadership. Now their primary concern was to promote a trade union. Yet, although they viewed themselves as the representatives of the working class, they opposed a separate economic sector, controlled by the Socialist parties, of the kind that existed in the Histadrut Labor Federation, and instead sought to forge relations of understanding between workers and employers with the state as arbiter. The logic of their position also led them to oppose Begin in his refusal to join a government coalition led by Mapai.

Their displeasure with Begin the leader grew when it emerged that Begin identified with the interests of the employers. (See also the following section in this chapter.) The NWF believed that Herut should represent the interests of the workers, if only because they constituted the bulk of the party's electoral support. Begin disagreed. He was against giving preference to the workers, but above all he relegated economic issues to a secondary place below politics, that is, foreign policy. Following the departure of the intelligentsia, Begin's relations with the NWF deteriorated; a power struggle began for influence in the party.

In this struggle, the NWF leadership had one major weakness. The majority of the organization's members and activists were former Irgun members who were loyal to the leader. As I explained in the 1949 elections, most of them cast their vote not for the Revisionist list, on which the NWF's general-secretary appeared in the second position, but for their leader Menachem Begin. Shostak later admitted that if the Revisionist list had returned even one representative to the Knesset, they would not have joined Herut. But to counter the strength of the Histadrut, their small union needed the support of a political force.[9]

Begin saw the NWF, which was led by a group of independent minded activists, as a threat to his rule. In short order the differences between the two sides became an overt struggle that peaked in the party convention of 1954. Begin and the NWF leaders were in agreement on the issue of democracy, but the dispute erupted because of the labor union's desire to maintain its autonomy within Herut and have a voice in framing party policy.

Begin had stepped up the struggle against the NWF's autonomy in 1953, immediately after the heads of the Lamerhav group ceased their party activity. He was now free to do battle against the other independent group. A conflict broke out in 1953 when Begin opposed the appointment of an NWF activist as secretary of the organization's National Health Insurance Fund (NHIF—*Kupat Holim Leumit*) in Petah Tikva. The appointment was effected without Begin's approval, and the Herut Central Committee passed a resolution calling for its annulment. Shostak refused to attend the Central Committee meeting on the subject and then resigned from the body altogether. The NHIF secretary in Petah Tikva retained his position; a showdown between Begin and the NWF leadership was now unavoidable.[10]

The NWF leaders came to the party convention prepared. To prevent their takeover of the convention, the Central Committee determined that delegates must be elected on a personal basis and that factional organization in the branches was prohibited. Nevertheless, the NWF estimated their support at 40 percent of the convention delegates.[11] Their success illustrates the organizational weakness of the Begin group, which did not have the necessary bureaucratic machinery to supervise the elections. The NWF, in constrast, had an apparatus staffed by salaried workers who could devote themselves to ensuring that their people were elected in the branches.

At the convention, Begin led the attack on the NWF, demanding that it accept his authority in organizational and ideological matters. Specifically, he insisted that their profit-making enterprises be dissolved. Here he invoked the principle of a separation between politics and economics. Politicians must not control economic enterprises as was done in the Histadrut. "If we are faced with the alternative . . . of either engaging in commerce or disbanding the NWF, I say we should disband the NWF."[12]

The NWF leaders argued in their defense that in the existing conditions and in view of the Histadrut's influence, a labor union concerned for its members' welfare was duty bound to maintain economic enterprises. But in response to Begin's demand they shifted to the offensive and submitted to the convention a comprehensive social-political program as an alternative to the Herut leadership's policy. Specifically, they sought the convention's backing for a social-economic policy that would show preference for the needs of wage earners. At the same time, they objected to the idea of Herut refusing under any conditions to join a government coalition. "The slogan of 'us or them' puts off the people. They don't accept that only we are the pure and the just, while the others are evil," Shostak told the convention. Moreover, a tactical political consideration also militated in favor of entering the coalition: in Israel, this was the way to build up strength and achieve power. "In Israel," Shostak said, "the road to governing is through the government." He also called for a clearly formulated stand in support of the democratic system.

The nation was not certain whether Herut would resort to rebellion to attain power. On this point Shostak differed not with Begin but with many other delegates. But Shostak also rejected Begin's extreme foreign policy notions, such as seizing a favorable opportunity in order to conquer the entire area of historic Eretz-Israel (a subject we will come back to). "The people fear that as a consequence of a patriotic predilection, everything will be jeopardized," Shostak argued.[13] In the last analysis, the moderate wing in Herut—those who had preferred to remain silent in the previous convention during the debate between Begin and the radical wing—had now put forward a comprehensive political and social program.

Begin himself did not present an orderly doctrine. In the debate, he concentrated on one principle only—the separation of economics and politics—although he admitted that the central problem was the question of authority. It was over this issue that he wanted to confront the NWF. The NWF had become a "duchy," Begin complained, a situation that undercut his authority as movement leader. As could be expected in a "leader party," Begin posited the question of authority as both a personal problem and an issue of principle. When the debate grew heated, however, he preferred to emphasize the blow to his personal authority, to the authority of Menachem Begin the leader. "The NWF and the NHIF have become a gargantuan being sucking my very marrow," was Begin's pathos-laden appeal. He was the leader of the movement, and therefore he must have the final say about the NHIF. When Shostak reminded him that he was the elected general secretary of the NWF and that he had the right to represent his organization at the convention, Begin proposed that a referendum be conducted among the NWF membership to determine who spoke for the organization, Begin or Shostak. Let us poll even the NWF's executive in order to prove who speaks in its name, Begin said.[14] Here Begin exposed the Achille's heel of Shostak and his colleagues. The NWF rank and file saw Begin as their leader, and, as the minutes indicate, even many executive members accepted Begin's supreme authority.

Not surprisingly, the NWF leadership tried to have the question of Begin's authority removed from the debate. No one questions his authority, they maintained. The debate over authority is only with his aides, one of their spokesmen explained. Begin himself, this speaker continued, is the supreme commander, and as such he should not intervene in petty organizational matters. But this is exactly what Begin wanted to do. Stopping the speaker at this point, he asked, "If you appoint me commander of the NHIF, will you carry out my orders?" Nonplussed, the

speaker replied, "We will." Begin then said: "The movement that established the NWF can decide to obligate its members, and then we will call
a convention and decide on its dissolution."[15]

The upshot was that the convention obligated the NWF to dissolve
its profit-making enterprises within a reasonable time. This naturally weak-
ened the organization, but the welfare institutions and the NHIF, which
were its principal source of strength, were unaffected. The NWF had some
10,000 members at this time, but its health services numbered 50,000
subscribers.[16] The NWF remained the one organized force in Herut.

More serious for the NWF was Begin's decision to reduce its strength
in the new Central Committee elected by the convention. In retaliation,
one of the organization's leaders declared that its members would refuse
to serve on the convention's various committees. Once more Begin
intervened, stating that no one had the right to speak on behalf of the
NWF's executive. Therefore the announcement was null and void. "In
this convention I will speak in the name of the NWF executive," Begin
asserted to boisterous applause by the delegates. As long as he was
chairman of the movement, Begin said, he spoke on behalf of all the
organizations affiliated with Herut—the NWF, Betar, and so forth.[17]

The shifting of the debate to the personal level played into Begin's
hands at the convention. When the delegates felt that the sharp language
of one of the NWF speakers was disparaging the leader, they prevented
him from continuing. Only after Begin intervened was order restored
and the speaker allowed to conclude his remarks.[18] In this manner, Begin
was able to image himself as a democrat while maintaining absolute
control of the convention. This became his mode of operation in subsequent conventions as well. That the democratic gestures were empty was
illustrated by the fact that those who disagreed with him—even persons
not organizationally affiliated with the NWF—were kept off the list of
Central Committee members that Begin drew up and submitted for the
convention's approval.[19]

Begin blocked all attempts at independent organization in the movement. But because he lacked his own bureaucratic machinery, members
occasionally succeeded in organizing and getting elected as convention
delegates. Still, that was as far as they got: Begin prevented them from
influencing decisions or from being elected to the movement's executive
bodies.

Despite everything, the NWF remained the only strong organized
group in Herut. But although Begin was unable to bring about the
organization's dissolution, he saw to it that its leaders were deprived of

influence on party policy, and for years they did not dare threaten Begin's standing as leader.

The NWF leaders not only headed an organization within Herut; they also saw themselves as representing the interests of the workers and the wage earners who constituted the overwhelming majority of Herut members and voters. Begin and his associates argued that Herut represented not specific sectors but the overall national interest. Begin's belief in the supremacy of politics led him to concentrate almost exclusively on foreign and security policy and to shunt aside social and economic problems. Yet as a Knesset faction, Herut's leaders could not avoid expressing their views and voting on such issues. One might have expected that, even without the prodding of the NWF, they would evince sensitivity toward the needs and interests of their members and electoral supporters. But an examination of the party's economic policy, as it was reflected in their voting in the Knesset and in their electoral platforms, reveals a completely different picture.

Herut's Economic Policy

Herut's policy on economic matters was articulated lucidly for the first time in the resolutions passed by the second convention: "Private enterprise," the convention declared, "is the cheapest, most beneficial and most progressive method of organizing the national economy; on condition that the law and the public prevent the formation of monopolies in the wake of free competition; and that the working rights and economic independence of the small-income earner are guaranteed."

Other resolutions called for natural resources to be placed under public ownership, but for public capital to be invested only in essential enterprises that did not attract private financing. Herut also supported investments in social-welfare institutions and in a national health insurance scheme. In particular the need was stressed for state health services in the light of the Histadrut's control of the country's major health service.[20]

The demand for the nationalization of the health services dovetailed with the general principle accepted in Herut, according to which a total separation was required between economic and political institutions— or, in Herut's terms, between the ruler and the provider. The party lashed out fiercely against the Histadrut's control of economic enterprises and the preferential terms these enjoyed as a result. The most scathing attacks were reserved for the kibbutzim, held up as the very symbol of Mapai's control over the economy and society. The kibbutzim were accused of exploiting their connections with the Histadrut and the political parties to reap economic benefits.[21]

Begin frequently had words of praise for the free market and private enterprise. In a speech he delivered at the third Herut convention, which he devoted primarily to foreign and security issues, he included a demand for the abolition of foreign currency controls. If this were done, he stated, Israel could become the Jewish Switzerland.[22]

Herut backed the business community on topics such as wage restraint and even in its call to eliminate linkage of salaries to the consumer price index (CPI). The principle of linking wages to prices, according to a cost-of-living index, which was originally introduced by the British government during World War II, gained the support of the Histadrut but was roundly condemned by most business owners. Since Herut's Knesset faction had to take a stand on these subjects in the many House debates on wages, Herut's Central Committee also found itself frequently called upon to consider the issues. The NWF representatives tried in vain to convince the Herut leadership to support wage increases. However, the majority not only opposed wage increments but, as mentioned, in the mid-1950s even supported abolition of wage linkage to the cost-of-living index. Shostak found this posture both unfair and detrimental to the party's political interests. After all, he argued, 90 percent of the party's membership consisted of wage earners, so how could Herut oppose wage increases? To which Begin retorted that the tens of thousands of workers who cast their ballots for Herut had voted for a political movement and not a trade union. Finally, the Central Committee approved a compromise resolution drafted by Begin that stated that only higher production by the workers "will enable and not only justify an increase [in wages]." Instead of linkage to the cost-of-living, Begin supported a minimum wage law, though here, too, he entered a reservation that salary disparities between skilled and unskilled workers should be enlarged.[23]

In another protracted discussion, extending over several sessions, the majority, after approving the Knesset faction's stand against wage increases, expressed its opposition to Shostak's publishing an article in the party paper in support of wage rises. Ultimately they relented, but only on condition that the paper's editors add a note stating that Shostak's opinions did not reflect the party's position.[24] At this time, Herut made efforts to forge close ties with the business community. In the Knesset the party cooperated with the General Zionists on economic issues, in the hope that "this would make a strong impression" on commercial and industrial circles.[25]

In mid-1957, the NWF executive was invited to a joint session with the Herut Central Committee to discuss a proposal for unification with the General Zionists. The same forum also considered a proposal to establish a separate faction in the Histadrut Labor Federation. The discussion became heated when the NWF representatives stated that to join the Histadrut would conflict with the party's fundamental principles. They also opposed the idea of unification with a middle-class party, which they perceived as "anti-worker." In response, Begin reminded them that theirs was not a workers' party but a national-liberal party. Yohanan Bader added in support that "if the assumption is that in order to win over workers we have to compete with radical political rhetoric . . . this is not the view of the movement, which is not made up only of the working public."[26]

How, then, did Begin frame Herut's economic policy? Herut activists often adduced proposals for an economic and social policy showing preference for population groups that accounted for the majority of the party's members and voters. A like stance was taken by many members of the intelligentsia in the early 1950s. Begin, however, seems to have ignored this pragmatic reasoning. His persistent reply was that Herut, as a national movement, should not represent or show preference for specific interests or groups. Most likely, this position reflected a prevalent trait of the petit bourgeois class to which Begin and many of his associates belonged, namely, a yearning to be part of the established bourgeoisie through identifying with its world view.

A bizarre situation had developed in Herut. In the absence of party machinery that could monitor the feelings of the elctoral masses and the party members, the leadership could not accede to their desires and interests even had it wished to. They simply did not know, and a leader like Begin had no way of knowing, what those desires were. Begin, at all events, took no interest whatsoever in the desires and interests of his supporters, as his understanding of the leader's role contained no provision for this response. As a leader, he was not driven by a wish to pay heed to his supporters' desires, and certainly not by concern for their material well-being. Begin had the national interest at heart, and was convinced that he understood that interest better than others. Hence, his role as leader was to guide his supporters along the straight and narrow road he had staked out.

How, it may be asked, with a policy of this kind, did Herut succeed in gaining the support of tens of thousands of Israelis? How, moreover, was it able to win a consistent 13 percent of the vote and more or less maintain a stable standing, until its electoral breakthrough in the 1973 elections immediately after the Yom Kippur War? The answer is, as the next chapter will make clear, that Herut's members and backers did not seek the party's help in promoting their economic interests. They looked to politics for answers to completely different needs, and these were provided by Menachem Begin and Herut.

6

A Leader Party

Herut's Organizational Structure

The elimination of the intelligentsia and the enfeeblement of the NWF were crucial stages in the process of Herut's transformation into a party headed by a leader. Begin became the all-powerful leader in his party and worked unremittingly to prevent the formation of intermediate groups in the organization that might limit his absolute leader's freedom of action and decision. To this end, for example, he blocked the formation of small committees to deal with specific realms, such as existed in other parties. He preferred large bodies without defined functions and powers, which were relatively easy to manipulate. The supreme body in Herut was the convention, which in the 1950s and early 1960s consisted of about 500 delegates. A convention was elected every two or three years, with the delegates generally meeting once for a sitting of several days. The convention dealt with matters of principle and elected the party chairman, and, at his recommendation, the Council and the Central Committee. The Council, which also comprised several hundred persons, convened every three months.

The Central Committee, which met frequently, was in theory the administrative body responsible for the organization's ongoing activity. In 1951 it consisted of twenty-one members, but additional members were soon coopted. A body of this makeup was incapable of running the organization on a continuous basis. But proposals to set up committees on specific issues were thwarted by Begin. As he explained it, the establishment of a political committee and an organizational committee, as had been suggested, was the custom in Communist parties and had been emulated by Israeli left-wing parties. "The difference between us," Begin said, "is that in the political sphere even a "Level A" Betari (ages 12–15) grasps more than the greatest among them"—hence no expert committees need be formed. He was equally vehement in rejecting a proposal that a three-person executive be established to administer the organization on an ongoing basis. Members would look on such a body as a "decision-making authority" and would consider its creation an anti-democratic act. What was wrong with the Central Committee sitting for a few extra hours when it convened in order to discuss all the subjects currently at hand? When pressure from below nevertheless brought about the election of a secretariat (and later an executive committee), Begin refused to sit on it, "so that its powers will not exceed those of the Central Committee." As a result, the secretariat concerned itself only with the most routine administrative matters.[1]

As mentioned, the size of the Central Committee gradually grew in the 1950s and 1960s. A proposal made at the 1958 convention to reduce the size of Central Committee members from forty-seven to twenty-nine members was torpedoed by Begin.[2]

The few administrative positions that existed in Herut were held by Begin's loyal assistants. Begin did, however, ensure that there was a rapid turnover in these posts. By the time of the 1968 convention, six different persons had served as convention chairman, and seven as the movement's general-secretary. Of the fifteen members of the Executive, only three had been part of that body since its inception in the mid-1950s.[3]

Only once did Begin deviate from his custom of appointing one of his loyal and devoted cronies as chairman of the Herut Executive. This was in 1971, when he named to the post Ezer Weizman, a former commander of the Air Force, who had joined Herut two years earlier. In short order, Weizman utilized his position to influence the election of convention delegates who supported his plans to change the composition of the party institutions. Only at the convention itself was Begin able to contain Weizman and remove him from the chairmanship. Begin then served as executive chairman himself for a year, before appointing another of his faithful associates. (This affair is discussed in Chapter 8.)

The Weizman episode exemplifies Begin's inability—in the absence of a party apparatus—to oversee the election of convention delegates in the various branches. Thus, groups were able to organize and elect delegates as they saw fit. Those inclined to do so were helped by the fact that very few branch members were actively involved in party matters and in the elections themselves. In 1954, for example, in the Jerusalem branch, only 137 members voted for convention delegates, even though Herut obtained 15,000 votes in Jerusalem in the Knesset elections held the following year.[4] The same situation prevailed in other parties. The difference was that in those parties it was precisely this situation that enabled the party machine to get its delegates elected, whereas in Herut, groups were free to organize and elect their own convention representatives. Only Begin could prevent this process from jeopardizing the Herut leadership, and this he could do only at the convention itself, where he wielded enormous influence. Indeed, as Yohanan Bader noted, at the convention Begin was omnipotent.[5] One obvious method resorted to by Begin was to block his rivals' entry to the Council and the Central Committee. Begin was the one who submitted to the convention a nominal list of the candidates for these two institutions. True, this was preceded by contacts between power-broking groups and individuals, but the final decision was Begin's.

The members of the Central Committee and the Council, and the convention delegates, constituted Herut's main cadre. This was the group Begin had to dominate to remain the unopposed leader. Begin was a superb organizer. At a young age, as the head of the Betar's Organization Division in Poland, he was in charge of conducting a members' census and distributing membership cards when the Revisionists reorganized after breaking away from the WZO. He excelled at this organizational activity.[6] Now he wanted a weak organization, the better to let him preserve his standing as sole leader. But that very weakness confronted him with a new dilemma. On the one hand, the party needed a large number of activists to help organize election campaigns in a country where the electorate was steadily increasing. At the same time, he believed that it was vital to maintain democratic procedures in the internal elections to party institutions: this legitimized his claim to rule in a democratic state. Yet without a party apparatus, it was difficult to ensure the election of his loyalists to the party's executive bodies. As a result, Begin was compelled to invest incessant efforts to get his associates elected to Herut's governing institutions, and with their help to rule the party uncontestedly.

A key source of Begin's influence in Herut derived from his having served as the supreme commander of the Irgun. Many in Herut were former Irgun members and could never forget that Begin had been their leader. Nor did Begin miss an opportunity to remind them of the fact.[7] During these years he worked hard to recruit both former Irgun and former LEHI activists to Herut. (LEHI—Hebrew acronym for "Fighters for Israel's Freedom"; a pre-state underground military organization formed by breakway Irgun members.) On the Sabbath he held open house and they would flock to him as though on a pilgrimage, according to a close associate. They would arrive, "shake hands, exchange a few words, and stay until others came."[8]

Begin attached great importance to personal relations with his supporters. He expected ex-Irgun people, who held office in Herut, always to approach him directly, bypassing their direct superiors.[9] Once he explained frankly that these personal relations were one of the sources of his influence in the organization. "I will not turn my back on a friend who has stumbled," he declared at the party convention of 1954, the first since Herut's failure in the 1951 elections. "People know this, and therefore they did not leave me when I stumbled and made them stumble too."[10]

To preserve his singular personal standing in Herut, Begin saw to it that party officials had no possible routes for independent advancement. He alone was the source of authority, and only through personal relations with him could party funtionaries ensure their place in the pecking order. Not even during elections would he sanction local initiatives. He and his speeches were the centerpiece of the campaign. When some proposed that Herut activists meet with small groups of voters on a regular basis, as was the practice in other parties, opposition to the idea was voiced in the Central Committee, apparently at Begin's instigation. The underlying motive for this posture, in the view of Mordechai Olmert, an activist who tried to organize such meetings in Haifa, was to block the possible emergence of new forces in the party.[11]

To retain his leadership, Begin needed a system of rewards for his supporters and sanctions against his adversaries. The existing party structure made no provision for rewards and penalties along the lines of promotion or demotion within the party ranks. The only genuinely important post that was his to distribute was Knesset membership, and this was reserved for the most devoted loyalists only. The majority of the MKs came from the group of "colonels." Begin distributed the few remaining slots among a small number of activists, all of whom were removed not long after forfeiting his trust.[12]

Yet all this affected a very small number of people. As for the others, he relied largely on the network of personal relations he forged in the organization. He accorded party functionaries affection, comradeship, and loyalty, and expected their allegiance in return. He was a believer in human relations and in the power of persuasion, he explained in an interview, and not in coercion.[13]

One of Begin's methods of persuasion was described by Eliezer Shostak, who was subjected to them on a number of occasions. Begin has several ploys, Shostak explained: "He invites people one at a time, never will he call in a large group for persuasion . . . but one at a time. Most of the time, he talks. He does not threaten, he speaks well and to the point. Sometimes he uses the method of stating that he himself will draw personal conclusions [i.e., resign], because for him it is a life-or-death matter. His eyes are extraordinarily penetrating. So I am thinking, the distinguished Irgun leader is here before me, he keeps me here for a few hours, and my view is injurious. For him it is a matter of life-or death. It's difficult to describe the atmosphere, but it is a very unpleasant experience."

Shostak went on to relate how he avoided looking into Begin's penetrating eyes, until Begin reproached him: "Why don't you look at me?" The force of Begin's gaze is also reported by another activist. He related that in one such persuasion talk he did look into Begin's eyes, until the leader said angrily: "Why are you staring into my eyes all the time? I've already seen that you have pretty eyes."[14]

These methods rarely failed, but if they did, he resorted to personal sanctions. To show his displeasure at the behavior of veteran members who opposed him on a certain issue, he stopped addressing them by their first name. He called them "Mr." and in more extreme cases prohibited them from addressing him by his first name.[15]

Sanctions of this kind, involving the severance of friendship, were experienced by Yitzhak Berman and Yehuda Ben-Meir during the period of their service—as a minister and a deputy minster, respectively—in the Begin government. When they voiced views that displeased Begin in cabinet meetings, he would grow demonstratively impatient as they spoke. His expression changed, clearly reflecting his opinion of their views. Long after the meeting, he would still manifest his irritation by employing a frosty manner toward them, barely saying hello. In this way, the two told a journalist, Begin brought about a situation in which views opposed to his own ceased to be voiced.[16]

During this bitter quarrel with the internal Herut opposition in 1966–67 (a subject we will return to in the next chapter), he took these sanctions of severing friendship even further. In one of the fierce debates with the opposition in the Central Committees, Begin observed the reaction of committee members to the speeches of opposition spokesmen. The upshot was that a number of former Irgun comrades received the following note: "At the Central Committee meeting last night, I saw you applauding after Tamir's letter was read out [Shmuel Tamir was one of the leaders of the opposition to Begin] . . . of which every line rings with abysmal hate for your friend. Therefore, I hereby inform you that, unfortunately, I can no longer regard you as a friend. Do not turn to me, either in writing or orally."[17]

The consequence of this behavior was that most of the party functionaries preferred to praise and extol Begin in meetings, rather than hold a substantive discussion involving an exchange of views and an attempt at mutual persuasion. In one Central Committee session, which was debating a possible merger with the General Zionists, Shostak said: "In matters regarding the movement and its future, it is not the members of the Central Committee who decide, it is Begin's opinion. There are times when at first I disagreed with what he said, but later I understood that he was right. . . . I may think that this is wrong, but if he, with his intuition, considers that he is saving the nation—he is the one to decide."[18]

Shostak, who was an experienced politician, seems to have grasped the advantages that could accrue to his organization if another autonomous body joined the party. But because his colleagues in the NWF did not share his pragmatic political outlook, the appreciation he voiced for the intuition of the leader who sought unity was for him a convenient peg on which to hang his own support for unity. But it is important to note the self-effacing manner in which he chose to present his position, based on his deep familiarity with the rules of the party game.

What lay behind this attitude of Herut activists toward their leader, Menachem Begin? In the sociological literature, we find, following Max Weber, that a political leader is sometimes held in the eyes of his supporters to possess unusual personal qualities that qualify him for leadership. These qualities, which are called "charisma," legitimize his authority to lead and cause others to believe in and obey him. However, other scholars today question this explanation. In a previous study, dealing with Mapai and its leader, David Ben-Gurion, I added my voice to the skeptics. I showed that when Ben-Gurion tried to convince the party to accept his stand by projecting his personal vision and his leader's personality, if his position conflicted with the stand of the party apparatus, he did not obtain the support he sought.[19]

Mapai, though, was a machine party, and Ben-Gurion controlled it by controlling the machine. Begin ruled in a party without an apparatus. Was it thanks to his charismatic personality that he held power? Naturally, it is difficult to prove or to refute the hypothesis that his followers' irrational faith in the leader's unique personality was the secret of his strength and influence. In the following pages, I argue that the source of Begin's strength of leadership in Herut derived not from his supporters' belief in his unusual personal qualities, but in his ability to symbolize the myths they accepted. Begin evoked these myths in his many speeches, and he himself came to symbolize them in the eyes of his followers.

Begin the Orator

Begin devoted the greater part of his activity as Herut leader to delivering speeches. At conventions, in meetings of the Council or the Central Committee, Begin's speeches were the central event. He also spoke frequently at mass rallies, particularly during election campaigns, when he would deliver several speeches in a single day. Similarly, his many articles in the party paper, *Herut*, were usually rehashes of speeches he had already delivered.

Begin himself also considered that his speeches formed the core of his political activity. In contrast, he attached little importance to the written word. When, for example, he toiled to convince the party to join the Histadrut as a separate faction, he noted, as a major reason for this step, that he would be able to address mass meetings in Histadrut election campaigns on behalf of Herut. Since writing had a limited dissemination, participation in the Hisadrut elections, Begin explained, would give him the opportunity to make his views known to the masses.[20] In his speech to the party convention in support of Herut's joining the Histadrut, he spoke of his "dream" of the day when he would hold a Histadrut election rally at Mograbi Square (at that time the principal site of his speeches in Tel Aviv), "and there we will explain our program in the sphere of labor relations." Begin left his audience in no doubt that he would be the keynote speaker in that rally. Perhaps "there are party members who do not know our program on labor issues," he said, "but I am pretty well acquainted with it."[21]

Begin constantly sought the support of party activists for his positions. He adduced logical grounds in support of his stands, and, as Shostak related, in these instances "he spoke well and to the point." (See p. 100) But his oratory in public assemblies, in city plazas, and before large groups of supporters, was a different kettle of fish.

Many observers reported Begin's rhetorical skills and his ability to stir large crowds. There is no doubt that he took considerable pains in preparing his speeches. He loved to speak and he enjoyed the applause immensely. However, a veteran journalist who in 1954 compared Begin's speeches with those of Jabotinsky, expressed disappointment in Begin as a speaker. Jabotinsky could construct a speech possessing a logical internal structure geared to the time allotted, whereas when Begin heard the cheers of the crowd, his carefullly prepared speech "fell apart."[22] This appraisal is based on the assumption that Begin's speeches should be judged according to his didactical ability to present ideas to an audience and explain them in a manner calculated to enable the crowd to follow each line of reasoning and be convinced by the arguments adduced. This was the technique employed by most of the politicians in the Zionist parties, and Jabotinsky had been one of the finest speakers among them. It seems to me that another journalist, Shabtai Teveth, was on the mark when he analyzed Begin's speeches not in terms of their internal power to convince, but as performances by an actor who apparently rehearsed in front of a mirror to prepare every gesture. As an actor, Teveth wrote, Begin was not perfect because he did not forget for an instant that he was performing in front of an audience. Unlike a good actor, who loses himself in his role while he is performing it, Teveth said, "one gets the impression that Menachem Begin is sitting in the audience and is ardently admiring and enjoying Menachem Begin who is on the platform."[23]

Begin's speeches on these occasions hardly ever contain a logical analysis of situations from which conclusions are drawn: their content is completely different. The theme running through all of them is the national honor of the Jewish people, which has a magnificent past and is destined for a glorious future in its historic land, the site of its most glorious achievements. The national honor is threatened by external and internal enemies, but Begin and his party stand in the breach as its guardians. According to Begin's view, the external enemies are not only foreign states and statesmen who do not accord honor to the Jewish people but also, in particular, those who do not recognize Israel's exclusive right to its homeland in its historical borders. The paramount internal enemy is, of course, socialist Mapai, whose sin is its belief in ideas stemming from alien sources. Worst of all is Mapai's readiness to make concesssions on the issue of Jewish national honor, of which the most flagrant example was its signing of the reparations agreement with Germany. This event, it will be recalled, was what triggered the struggle waged by Begin and Herut to defend the national honor against its denigrators.

Begin's speech at the opening of the third Herut convention, in 1954, touched on all the central issues that he would harp on in the years to come. Defense of the national honor against those who threaten it was a major element in this speech. In the section devoted to foreign policy, it was in the light of this criterion that he determined his attitude toward the United States, which at that time was endeavoring to find a compromise to put a halt to the ongoing Israeli-Syrian border clashes. The U.S. dispatched a special emissary to the region who put forward compromise proposals that Begin naturally did not accept. Following a lengthy analysis of the details of the proposals, Begin reached the conclusion that they must be rejected. He explained his position in the following words:

> We must give a reply to Mr. Byroade [the American emissary]. We will tell him in plain language, without arrogance but with faith—faith in the Rock of Israel and its Deliverer, and faith also in friendship based on freedom and independence: There is no friendship except mutual friendship between us and the United States of America. . . . Do not think that the Jewish people lives thanks to the Americans. The Jewish people ascended the stage of history before the birth of the American people . . .

The principal internal enemy of the Jewish people was Mapai. Mapai was a corrupt party that exploited the country's citizens for its own purposes of power. Begin devoted part of his attack on Mapai at the 1954 convention to a diatribe against the kibbutz movement, symbol of the Mapai establishment. The kibbutz movement enjoyed public support even though it lived in wealth and luxury that hardly befitted people who passed themselves off as workers for the nation. The houses and dining rooms they built for themselves were fit only for five-star hotels.[24]

But Mapai's most serious transgression lay in its foreign policy, which debased Jewish national honor, as was glaringly apparent in the German reparations affair. Relations with Germany remained an important element in Begin's speeches. The decision of the Mapai-led government to establish diplomatic relations with the Federal Republic was a burning issue in the 1959 election campaign. This was but one example, Begin asserted, of how Ben-Gurion was "humiliating" the Jewish people in the eyes of the world.[25]

National honor was a key value of all radical-right movements in Europe between the two world wars, and was at the center of their information and propaganda efforts. Thus, although the Nazis were propelled to power in Germany by the economic crisis, even during the Great Depression the focal point of their propaganda remained the submission of the other parties to the Treaty of Versailles and the national humiliation entailed in that shameful act. This was the main theme of Hitler's speeches during this period. (See chapter 1, p. 17) Similarly, national honor was a cardinal issue for the ruling group in Poland—which, as will be recalled, formed the Betaris' Reference group—and in large measure dictated the country's foreign policy in these years.[26]

Begin himself was convinced that his speeches were based on logical arguments and that his support was due to "my ability to formulate and analyze." This was the character of his talks with and lectures to his associates. But an examination of the speeches he delivered at public rallies and in city plazas turns up a very differnt level of argumentation.[27] They present a world view built of myths.

Begin's Myths

Myths are intended to present ideas and not emprical facts. They may be grounded in reality, at least in part, but there is no need or purpose to subject them to empirical tests. Symbols, which are emotionally charged, are the language of myths. They represent the myths and are the proof of their existence. In our case, it was Begin the leader who symbolized the myths of Herut, and his leadership furnished the proof of their existence.

One myth concerned the purpose of Israel's existence; namely, to revive the magnificent history of the Jewish people; this would be done by establishing the renewed state in the geographical area occupied by the Jewish state in its golden age. A second myth dealt with the means to achieve this end; namely, a military struggle, of which the initial phase had been waged by the Irgun and had caused the expulsion of the British. But the military struggle was not yet complete, since only part of the historic Jewish homeland had been liberated. Therefore, the fight must be pursued to achieve the liberation of Greater Israel by force of arms. As to who was capable of executing the mission—this was the subject of the third myth. According to this myth, the task could be performed by Menachem Begin, who, as commander of the Irgun, had already set the project in motion. Begin was also suitable because he was the heir of Ze'ev Jabotinsky, who had envisioned the idea and marked out the ways to its realization. Identification with the idea of Greater Israel and with Ze'ev Jabotinsky was tantamount to identification with Menachem Begin, Jabotinsky's disciple and successor, who had begun the task and was ready and able to conclude it successfully.

These three myths are based on an interpretation of historical events and concrete situations that is not necessarily consonant with reality. To argue that the boundaries of Mandate Palestine (with or without Jordan) were the borders of the historic Land of Israel was devoid of factual historical basis. But Herut, like Betar and like the Revisionist party, which also embraced this principle, never bothered to examine the subject. I found no one among them who refuted this notion, although this camp contained scholars and researchers who knew it lacked historical foundation. Correlation between myth and reality was unnecessary.

The same can be said about the second myth, which grounded the need for a military struggle to liberate Eretz-Israel by adducing the argument that part of the land had already been liberated in this manner, and a Jewish state established in it. Most scholarly studies of the process, by which the State of Israel was established, concluded that developments in the postwar world and the Zionist diplomatic activity, that took advantage of this political constellation, exercised a decisive influence on the state's establishment; and that the military activity of the Yishuv as a whole, and of the Irgun in particular, played only a marginal role in Britain's decision to leave Palestine.[28] But to this day, the wealth of research documenting these historical facts have not shaken the faith of Betar and Irgun veterans that their role was crucial, nor that of the disappointed Betar intelligentsia, who eventually found themselves outside the Herut movement.[29]

The third myth held that it was Ze'ev Jabotinsky, the distinguished and visionary leader, who was the trailblazer for the Irgun; and that Menachem Begin, the Irgun commander, was the most loyal and devoted of his followers and the fulfiller of his vision. The reality, as we know, was different. Begin headed the rebels against Jabotinsky on the issue of the military struggle in Eretz-Israel. This did not prevent Begin from evoking this myth incessantly. Moreover, he could do so with fervor, as few dared question openly the veracity of his claims.

Jabotinsky's portrait was displayed at every movement gathering and hung in every office of the movement's headquarters in Tel Aviv, called *Metzudat Ze'ev* (Fortress of Ze'ev). His name was mentioned in nearly every speech Begin delivered, and the praises heaped on Jabotinsky invariably fired up the crowd. Thus, for example, when Begin addressed the opening session of the party convention in 1958, in front of a gigantic portrait of the leader, and called for the execution of Jabotinsky's last will and testament, in which he requested that the government of Israel reinter him in Israel in a state ceremony, so thrilled was the audience that they rose and sang the Betar anthem—which was written by Jabotinsky.[30]

At the party convention in 1963, a veteran movement member, Dr. Arye Altman, dared to question the myth. The subject on the agenda was Begin's proposal that Herut join the Histadrut. When Dr. Altman argued that Herut's joining the Histadrut would be tantamount to admitting that Jabotinsky had erred when he set up a labor union to compete with the Histadrut, Begin was outraged. In a lengthy interjection from the dais, he explained that Jabotinsky had often considered a return to the Histadrut.

Begin opened his reply to the debate by declaring that there was no truth to Altman's claims. "Anyone who wants to prove the opposite to me," Begin protested, "will have to prove that he has read more of the writings, articles, and essays of the head of Betar than I have, and that in the period from 1929 to 1939 he heard Ze'ev Jabotinsky speak, not only in conventions, councils, committees, and closed meetings, but in private conversations, too, more than I did." Although many in the audience were well aware that there was not an iota of truth in this description of the supposed intimate relations between Begin and Jabotinsky, no one got up and said so. A myth is not assailed, certainly not in public. This is one of the secrets of its potency. To preclude any such attempt, Begin stressed in this same speech that to question the myth was to injure him personally. "In every act of fulfilling the doctrine of the head of Betar," he insisted, "there is a drop of my blood. And if I put forward a proposal, let it not be said that it contradicts the doctrine of the head of Betar. Debate it, support it, reject it. . . . But to claim that I put forward a proposal that conflicts with the doctrine of the head of Betar? You have gone too far."[31]

Begin was passionate in the defense of this myth because of its implicit principle that the leader is loftier than the people. This tenet of the European radical right could not be explicitly adduced in public in the years following the democracies' victory over Adolf Hitler and Benito Mussolini. The reverential attitude toward the dead leader, and Begin's claim of succession, legitimized Begin's leadership without his appearing overtly as an absolute leader. Positing himself as the faithful implementer of Jabotinsky's vision and policy, Begin thus also demanded discipline and reverence. At the same time, he could present himself merely as a successor. Taking into account the public climate, he denied that he was even a leader. "Not only do I not believe in charisma," he declared on one occasion, "I am not a leader at all. I came to Jabotinsky's movement in my youth, and I am one of his pupils."[32]

The myth of the heir is exceptionally interesting. Begin's revolt against Jabotinsky's leadership was no secret. The quarrel between them had erupted openly at a Betar convention in Warsaw and was fully reported in the *Book of Betar*, the movement's official history. But any mention of these events proved bewildering to the party faithful, as they involved a conflict between two principles in which they believed: on the one hand, the leader principle, which obligated them to heed the ideas of Jabotinsky, but on the other hand, the principle that the Irgun must conquer the land by force of arms, which the leader disavowed.

Many of my interlocutors among Herut veterans reminded me of this debate with an embarrassed smile, while accepting Begin's stand. In public, however, they preferred not to talk about it. Begin exploited this predilection by reiterating on numberless occasions that he was Jabotinsky's heir. But his pronouncements concealed another implicit message for his loyalists, namely, that while Jabotinsky was a distinguished leader, he, Begin, who had been right in their historic debate, was therefore the greater of the two. The message was not lost on veteran Betaris. As Shostak explained it, Begin constantly wanted to prove that he had been more successful than Jabotinsky, and that "his power of judgment was superior to everyone's."[33]

To understand the import of this mythical world that Begin symbolized for former Betaris from Poland, we have to return to their historical wellsprings: the European radical right and the modes of operation of the ruling group in Poland—the Betaris' reference group—during the formative period of Begin and his colleagues.

The cardinal ambition of the ruling group in Poland in the 1930s, it will be recalled, was to bring about a return to the boundaries of Greater Poland as they have existed before the partition of 1772. The Polish leaders were convinced that only an enlarged Poland, possessed of a strong military capacity to defend itself, could successfully preserve its independence in the shadow of its two powerful neighbors, Germany and the Soviet Union. The proof was that independence had been gained as a result of Pilsudski's military campaign and guerilla operations as leader of the Polish Military Organization. This account is disputed by historians. They ascribe the establishment of independent Poland to the Allied victory in World War I and Lenin's decision to forgo control over the country. Many of the historians are further convinced that even within the context of appraising the Polish effort as such, greater importance should be attached to the diplomatic activity pursued during the war years by Roman Dmowski in London, where he headed a Polish liberation movement, than to Pilsudski's military activity in Poland itself.[34] The myth that gained credence among many Poles was that their country's independence was due to their military struggle, and that military force would also serve in realizing the right to restore the historic boundaries. This remained the aspiration of nationalist circles in Poland in the interwar period.

Between Pilsudski's death, in May 1935, and the outbreak of World War II, the strong man in Poland was Edvard Rydz Smigly. Smigly depicted himself as Pilsudski's successor. His speeches, too, were laced with references to the former leader, Pilsudski, whose close assistant he claimed to have been. He even formed a new political organization, the Camp of National Unity, which was committed to carrying out Pilsudski's doctrine.

The veracity of Smigly's claim to be Pilsudski's heir is susceptible to doubts. Nevertheless, Smigly sought to utilize the claim to legitimize his rule, which was every bit as authoritarian as Pilsudski's had been. The difference was that Pilsudski had ruled through sheer force of personality. He was also revered by the masses for his contribution to the establishment of independent Poland and for his patriotism. Smigly realized that he, too, must develop his image. Lacking Pilsudski's dazzling personality, he presented himself as having been chosen by the leader to execute a central task, namely, to defend the country's borders and its security.[35]

Begin faced a similar problem in Herut. A comparison between him and Jabotinsky, the brilliant intellectual, was less than flattering to the Irgun commander. He, too, solved the problem by presenting himself as the person capable of fulfilling the mission Jabotinsky had strived to achieve—to restore Israel's historic borders. According to the myth, these were the original borders of the British Mandate and included the West Bank, the Gaza Strip, and the Kingdom of Jordan. Jabotinsky and the Revisionist Party never reconciled themselves to the severence of Trans-Jordan from the territory of the future Jewish state. Nor did Begin and the Herut movement.

The centrality of the borders question was also inspired by the Polish national movement and the European radical right. Nationalism in its extreme version, as it was reflected in the parties of the radical right, played on the fact that there was no general agreement about the borders. The doubts were compounded by the presence of a number of ethnic groups in the same territories. The issue of borders thus became a bone of contention between the various countries.[36] This was the situation in the majority of the East European states that were established after World War I, but Poland was an extreme case. There the problem was rendered excessively acute due to the Poles' cultural ties to their magnificent national past when they were a great European power, and by the fact that about 30 percent of the population was composed of other ethnic groups, many of whose nations were situated just across the border, such as the Germans and the Ukrainians.

Pilsudski and his colleagues preceived the border issue also as a security question. Poland's powerful neighbors, Germany and Russia, constituted a permanent threat. Therefore, only by Poland's becoming the largest and strongest power in eastern Europe could its independence be guaranteed. But, true to their radical-right orientation, they also believed that geographical size would assure the nation's spiritual glory. The Poles stressed primarily the historical dimension and their desire to turn back the wheels of Polish history in order to recapture their former greatness.[37] German nationalists, in contrast, were more concerned about a geographical space that would enable the spirit of the nation to be expressed. Excessive proximity to their neighbors was liable to suppress the German national spirit. This outlook was embraced in the 1930s by the Nazis to justify their expansion plans.[38] The yearning to rule the entire area of the former Mandatory Palestine, which included many of the historic sites of ancient Israel, was shared by other political groups in Israel. But none clung so tenaciously to the myth as did Begin and his associates from Betar-Poland.

Without a knowledge of this cultural-ideological and political background, it is difficult to comprehend the centrality of the aspiration for Greater Israel that informed Herut's world view. Begin's identification with this claim transformed him into the symbol of the demand. In the first years, when the Revisionist and Betar intelligentsia were still active in Herut, ideological tenets were voiced that echoed ideas widespread among the radical right in an earlier period. I. Margolin, for example, writing in *Herut* in early 1949, asserted that the growth of a national culture required space. A nation could not evolve unless it remained by itself in a specific expanse. Such evolution was impossible within the boundaries delineated by the armistice agreements. These were "grotesque" borders, fit only for a state "in a Levantine operetta." Another writer argued that in such borders a community could be maintained, but not a state. A small state like this was no more than a ghetto surrounded by Arabs.[39]

The consensus among former Betaris was that a big state was an aspiration uniting the whole camp. It was "our most cherished principle," "the cement that binds us." as party activists said.[40] Even a moderate like Dr. Shimshon Yuniczman, who eased out of the group of Begin's close associates because he "deviated somewhat from the line," took a hard line posture on this issue. "If we do not eliminate the borders, the borders will eliminate us," he remarked.[41] Ya'akov Amrami, too, who had left Herut in the first years of its existence, and wrote to a member of the *Ha'aretz* editorial board to request that the views espoused by former Irgun personnel not be identified with those of Menachem Begin, added that there was one subject on which the ex-Irgun people shared Begin's outlook: the integrity of the homeland.[42] The opposition leadership in the NWF took a similar line. On this question they had no quarrel with Menachem Begin.[43] The members of the generation unit of Betar and Irgun veterans remained loyal to the myth as it coalesced in their formative period, and of which Menachem Begin, commander of the Irgun, had become the symbol.

The grounds cited in favor of Greater Israel that were products of radical-right ideology were not stressed in Herut. To have done otherwise would have conflicted with the process of repressing the ideological world of the European radical right. Instead, they preferred to emphasize the historical myth that was also central in Poland. This myth legitimized Begin's leadership authority for having begun the task of liberating Eretz-Israel as commander of the Irgun. Herut's fidelity to the idea was absolute, and bolstered Begin's claim to be the movement's uncontested leader.

The myth that the State of Israel was established by virtue of the Irgun's military struggle and existed thanks to its powerful army, was also identical to a myth that prevailed among Polish nationalist circles. This was the myth that Poland's independence was due to the struggle waged by Pilsudski and the Polish Military Organization he headed. Underlying both myths was a myth shared by the entire radical right, holding that military force was the basis of international relations and the sole guarantee of the preservation of every nation's independence and standing in the international arena. Former Betaris and Irgun activists identified with this myth, believing that they alone had grasped correctly the fundamental principle involved, whose validity was demonstrated by their victorious expulsion of the British.

Liberation of the Historic Land of Israel by Force of Arms: Plan of Action or Myth?

The conqest of the whole Land of Israel in its Mandate boundaries by military means was Herut's declared goal in its first years of existence. The very first session of the Herut Council, in October 1948, resolved that the liberation of the whole Land of Israel was a paramount objective. However, since the Irgun, as a military force, no longer existed, new ways were required to achieve the goal.[44] What this meant, it soon became apparent, was that the IDF was to conquer the remaining parts of Eretz-Israel. This stance was adopted as official Herut policy. In his election campaign speeches in 1951, Begin railed that the government had not taken advantage of the assassination of Jordan's King Abdullah in order to invade his kingdom. Begin was convinced that an incursion had been feasible. "By the very fact of committing our force without casualties, [we would have] found ourselves beyond Jerusalem's wall, on the Jordan, and all the nations would have affirmed this *fait accompli* as they did in the past."[45]

In 1954, following a coup in Egypt, Herut maintained that Israel should have seized the opportunity to take control of the Gaza Strip, then under Egyptian rule.[46] Herut's official policy called for exploiting a propitious moment to conquer these territories without excessive blood-shed. The party's third convention, for example, resolved that "the entire historic territory of Eretz-Israel [must be liberated] by means of a calcu-lated strategy of operational thrusts at opportune times"—a general war was not called for.[47] Begin was convinced not only that the great powers would refrain from intervening, but that military operations of this kind would enhance the IDFs prestige and that Israel's standing in Washing-ton would improve once its true strength was revealed.[48]

In Herut there was widespread and enthusiastic support for the military conquest of Eretz-Israel. One party activist explained that Israel must pursue a policy of "Jewish irredentism," meaning in the political jargon, exploiting every means for the military conquest of neighboring territory.[49] This mission was entrusted to the IDF, which in Herut's preception was the most important institution in the nascent society. On some occasions, the word "sacred" was invoked to describe the IDF. The party's election platforms invariably contained a section extolling the IDF and a call "to deepen the people's affection for the Army."[50] The need for immigration was also explained in terms of its crucial importance for the armed forces. "Every month that passes without the immigration of a thousand Jews", Begin stated, "also means [fewer] citizens for the Army—and that is bad."[51]

Calls for a military offensive to conquer the rest of Eretz-Israel grew increasingly vociferous with the intensification, in the mid-1950s, of raids by terrorist squads across the border. The situation grew dangerous and the IDF seemed unable to find a way to prevent the raids, which became ever more frequent. Begin was convinced that the only answer was a frontal military assault. "If we fight, we will be saved," Arye Naor, who served as Cabinet secretary in the first Begin government, quotes him as saying in those days.[52]

Participants in internal discussions in Herut institutions evinced growing concern over the security situation. Many of them objected to making security issues a matter for public debate. The situation should be discussed in back rooms with other parties and the desirable modes of operation taken up with the government, they argued. Some were apprehensive that talk of war would prove distasteful to the voters and that bellicose declarations would therefore have the sole effect of strengthening Mapai.

Many Herut activists feared that their image as the "war party" would have a negative effect on their constituency.[53] On the eve of the 1955 elections, Begin's aides were worried about the adverse effect generated by his aggressive speeches in the need to conquer the areas of Eretz-Israel held by Jordan. Their feeling was that Begin was frightening the electorate. At the meeting of the Herut Central Committee, a loyal Begin aide, Arye Ben-Eliezer, tried to explain that in his estimation the nation did not want a war. His remark touched off the following dialogue:

> BEGIN: You must tell me what I am to say in [my speech at] Mograbi [Square] in six days time.
> BEN-ELIEZER: You are entitled to say anything you wish.
> BEGIN: I have had my fill of the applause of my friends, and now I want to get votes. If there is a problem about things that should not be said— tell me what I am allowed to say.[54]

Begin's rejoinder drew no response from Ben-Eliezer or anyone else. Even if we interpret his comments not as a reprimand but as a request for advice—a request for which I found no parallel in other internal discussions—he did not elicit a response from persons who undoubtedly had their own ideas about the content of his speeches. Knowing their leader, they did not dare proffer him counsel. No change is detectable in Begin's aggressive warlike style during the election campaign in the wake of this meeting. Begin also sometimes grew impatient at the cautious approach displayed by his associates. Prior to the 1954 party convention, he even suggested, sarcastically, that the two viewpoints compete in two separate lists for the convention. He would head what he called the war list, while someone else would lead what he termed the naive list.[55]

Begin's style of speech became perceptibly more extreme in this period. At a national assembly in Betar, for example, he spoke of the possibility that they would be called on to carry out operations "whose execution, due to national considerations, will not necessarily be based on an official order." In the same speech, he reminded his audience that without recognition of the Jewish people's right to the whole homeland, "we have no mission."[56] This behavior testifies to his belief in his own inner convictions and his certainty that if he could impart them to the people, the nation would follow him. Since he was also convinced that the most effective method to combat the terrorist raids from across the border was by a war of conquest, he argued in 1956 that, despite what his aides believed, the nation was ready for war and that if the government balked, it could be overthrown by the force of the masses.[57]

Very quickly he discovered his mistake. On October 25, 1956, Israel went to war. Israeli forces invaded Egypt, conquering the Gaza Strip and the Sinai Peninsula within a few days. The attack was planned in collusion with England and France, which sent forces to seize the Suez Canal following the Israeli incursion. The subsequent course of events was totally unexpected by the leaders of the three countries. Both the Soviet Union and the United States demanded that they withdraw from all the territories they had occupied—and all three complied. David Ben-Gurion, who had initially regarded the military victory as a turning point in Israel's standing in the region, agreed to Israel's withdrawal from all the areas occupied by the IDF.

No one was more astounded at these developments than Begin and the Herut leadership—first by the Israeli incursion and then by the decision to withdraw. But when the government's decision to pull back handed them an opportunity to put popular support for their policy to the test, it emerged that they were unable to mobilize the masses to oppose the withdrawal. Public opinion seems to have accepted the government's reasoning that the current reality—the Soviet encroachment into the region as Egypt's patron, and the firm stand of the Americans—left Israel no choice but to withdraw. In the first election held after the Sinai Campaign, in 1959, Mapai scored an impressive electoral victory. The calm that prevailed along the borders after the war enabled the national leadership to depict the war's outcome as a victory. In the 1959 campaign, Herut no longer put forward an operative plan for the conquest of Eretz-Israel. The change of posture came after the organized popular opposition to the withdrawal, which Begin had hoped to arouse, failed to materialize. A perusal of the discussions held by the Herut Central Committee suggests that the party activists read the public mood accurately and therefore did not go out of their way to organize demonstrations against the withdrawal, for they were apprehensive that the rallies would be poorly attended.[58] Begin's appraisal of the demonstrations sounded a new note. He professed himself satisfied that the demonstrations had passed without unruly behavior and without clashes with the police. "This will enhance the nation's prestige in the eyes of the world," he explained to his assistants, "and it will enhance the prestige of our movement in the eyes of the nation."[59]

I found no reassessment of party policy in either Central Committee deliberations or in the party newspaper following the IDF's withdrawal. Most probably, no such discussions were held, and the revision was probably Begin's personal decision; repeating the pattern followed after the demonstrations against the German reparations agreement, Begin again decided not to radicalize his struggle against the establishment. Neither formal resolutions passed by party institutions, nor the party's election platforms, now demanded the conquest of Eretz-Israel by force of arms at an opportune moment. Once more we find that Begin's fidelity to the myths did not cause him to jeopardize his party's standing. On the other hand, he was obliged to display loyalty to the myths that legitimized his authority as party leader. The solution he found was to evince verbal loyalty to the myth of Greater Israel but without adopting it as an operative program. Thus, Greater Israel remained a central declared objective of Herut, but in the form of a declaration of principle; in the practical realm, a deliberate fog prevailed.

Henceforth, Begin and other Herut spokesmen emphasized the Jewish people's historic right to all of Eretz-Israel, and depicted themselves as the sole faithful guardians of this right. When it came to realizing the rights, however, their pronouncements were ambivalent. They raised no categorical demand for a military operation, making do, instead, with a call for tough measures in dealing with terrorists and with militant declarations regarding Israeli security policy and relations with the Arab states. Herut welcomed the Israeli reprisal raids across the border in retaliation to terrorist attacks, but always urged a stronger military response than the operation carried out. The "excessive cautiousness" displayed by the IDF in these raids was assailed.[60] Some party activists continued to urge a war of conquest and their articles were published in *Herut*.[61] But other publicists were always found who assured readers that at stake was no more than a right in principle to all of Eretz-Israel, "even if it is not known when we will be able to transform this principle into reality."[62] It is not always apparent whether official Herut statements enunciated a principle or called for a military incursion to liberate territories. The following, for example, is from a 1964 editorial in Herut on the occasion of the anniversary of the fall of the Old City of Jerusalem in the 1948 war:

> This day fills us with the duty to reiterate to ourselves, and to the whole world, that we do not forgo those parts of the homeland that were plundered from us in those tragic circumstances. For even if the enemy now controls Jerusalem

and Bethlehem, Hebron and Nablus, and other places in our land, we shall not recognize even his minimal right to them. Our right to all parts of the homeland is unassailable, and we will not rest or sit quietly until they are restored to us and become an integral part of the State of Israel.[63]

In his speeches Begin did not elucidate the means he would employ to realize the idea of Greater Israel, but he never ceased talking about the liberation of Eretz-Israel. As we will have occasion to see, whenever internal party opposition threatened his rule in Herut, he became even more assertive in his commitment to the idea of the whole Land of Israel. But the idea of the liberation was also transformed from policy to a myth detached from practical politics of which Begin became the symbol. This myth was a cardinal source for the legitimization of his authority. As a result, he could not cast it off even had he wished to (and no proof exists that he ever did) without jeopardizing his leadership status. In the course of time, particularly after Begin began to identify increasingly with religious tradition (a subject which is discussed in the following chapter), this myth took on religious overtones, but in the background the idea persisted that a nation's greatness was assured by the existence of a large and expansive state whose borders were contiguous with those from its days of splendor. As the myths became Begin's mainstay, he devoted himself to enhancing his oratorical and stage skills, while casting about for slogans and formulations to assure him support on the emotional plane. Thus, for example, prior to the 1955 election campaign, he termed Mapai's policy *havlagah* (restraint) which, he said, was a highly pejorative term in the 1930s. (See our discussion, pp. 57–8) He proposed the use of the epithet "pogrom" for violent operations carried out by Arabs across the border against a Jewish population. These were terms the public knew and recognized, Begin told the Central Committee.[64] However, he was apparently unsatisfied with the reverberations generated by these slogans. In the 1965 election campaign, he began using the slogan "love of Israel," hammering it home in his many speeches. This soon became a central catchword. It did not commit him to a practical program of any kind.[65] At the same time, it is clear that there was nothing accidental about the choice of this and similar slogans. The sociologist S. N. Eisenstadt points out that in the exilic period, the phrase "love of Israel" connoted the Jews' self-imposed separation from their neighbors in reaction to the discrimination practiced against them by the peoples among whom they lived. In some cases, Eisenstadt notes, the term expressed extreme xenophobia.[66]

There is no doubt that Begin's formulations reflected inner feelings and psychological needs, as well as his early education. The applause of his listeners encouraged him to persist in invoking these phrases in the coming years. But a construct of Begin's inner world, and of this level of communication between him and his audience, its importance notwithstanding, is outside the scope of the present work.

The symbolic politics and the preaching of the Greater Israel idea without concern for the means to attain it, were not understood outside the Herut camp. Journalists and observers of the Israeli political scene reached the conclusion that in foreign policy, "the differences between Herut and Mapai have been reduced to a minimum." Herut propaganda was garbed in purely emotional dress, it was said, and all that differentiated it from Mapai was its militant tone and the call for tougher military actions against terrorists. On the other hand, these observers added, in economic policy, no difference existed between Herut and the General Zionists. Herut's only remaining distinctive feature, then, was the emotional rejection of Mapai rule.[67]

What these observers failed to perceive was that Herut functioned at the level of symbols and myths and not in the pragmatic world, which was the setting for the other parties who were partners or potential partners in government coalitions. The emotional rejection of Mapai rule was part of Herut's world, with the myths and symbols helping to create a complete world view. Drawing on them, Begin retained the loyalty of his party.

Status Politics

Myths and symbols play a major role in politics. Drawing on them, political elites, parties, and groups mobilize the support and allegiance of their members and supporters. But in democratic societies, most parties, being bureaucratic organizations, are moved to attain their major organization goal—the winning of elections—in a calculated and pragmatic fashion. They consequently differentiate between enlisting support through myths, and promoting material interests of groups in order to obtain their support as a quid pro quo. Thus, the politicians in such parties must distinguish between the two types of political activity. Their political skill resides in the ability to comprehend the two types of activity and to distinguish between them.

This was not the situation in Herut, which was a leader party and lacked a bureaucracy. Its leaders did not mobilize the support of groups by helping to promote their material interests, but saw themselves as representing the overall national interest. To obtain support, they did not rely on the use of a party machine, but primarily on forging a direct tie between the leader and his supporters through speeches at rallies whose purpose was to convince them, by evoking the myths—which constituted Herut's program—to back them.

Until now, the explanation adduced for this exceptional phenomenon in the Israeli party system was a historic-cultural one. The Herut leaders imbibed this political style in the socialization process they underwent in Betar-Poland. Their reference groups were the national groups that ruled in Poland and the movements of the radical right in Europe. From them they also received the contents of the myths that became part of the culture of their generation unit.

By drawing on anthropological studies, which maintain that myths exist in a society because they give expression to the claims of groups for their place in the social structure, I want to propose an additional explanation for the bond that was formed between Herut members and the party's myths. The myths gave expression to the yearning of Herut members for status in the Israeli society. That is why they identified with them, and through them, with the leader who symbolized them, even though he led them from one electoral failure to another in the course of nearly thirty years and did nothing to enhance their status.

Prior to their immigration from eastern Europe, the Betaris, or their parents, like most of the immigrants to the Yishuv, had belonged to the petit bourgeois class, a class that suffers chronically from economic and social insecurity and constantly aspires to upgrade its status. In Palestine, many of them, like many immigrants, became manual laborers. This represented a decline in their status. As I explained in a previous book, after years of pioneering activity, the members of the pioneer-labor parties were also struck by a desire to better their socioeconomic status. They were able to fulfill their wish thanks to the rapid development of the bureaucracy and its absorption of many settlers who thus left the labor force and were elevated to managerial and other positions. Following the establishment of the state, when the Jewish population was almost tripled within a few years, the government and Histadrut bureaucracies expanded rapidly and took in many of the pre-1948 immigrants.

These developments passed over former Betar and Irgun members almost completely. They found the public bureaucracy—that of the government and the Histadrut—closed to them. Moreover, these early years of the state provided few opportunities for advancement in the private market either. The upshot was that many of them were forced to remain part of the proletariat. Their resentment at being relegated to this status was aggravated when they saw their peers from other Zionist parties climbing the economic and social ladder while they marked time. In addition, their inability to enter the public bureaucracy, after they had risked their lives in the struggle for the creation of the state, deprived them of a sense of participation in the nation-building process.

The yearning of Herut activists for status was reported as early as 1951 by the journalist Arye Ziv in his coverage of that year's election campaign. Ziv found it surprising that even though the majority of Herut voters were from the lower social strata, the party supported the interests of the propertied class. Ziv attributed this puzzling behavior, which seemed to conflict with Herut's political interest, to the aspiration for status of Begin and his cohorts. Their origins "in the stratum of the middle class with its petit bourgeois cast," Ziv wrote, and their consequent longing for status, led them to identify with a higher social stratum. Ziv relates that at this time Begin frequently stressed that Herut people were not "good-for-nothings" but numbered also lawyers, doctors, and the like. Herut's economic policy also reflected this yearning for status.[68]

The preoccupation of Herut members with status explains Begin's unconcern with his supporters' economic needs (described in the previous chapter). The primary concern was less with material interests than with the decline in status. The longing for status also accounts for the disregard Herut evinced toward the "oriental" communities—that is, Jews from Arab lands—with their low status, and the absence of any effort to integrate them into the party. The few discussions held on the subject by the Central Committee revealed the same patronizing approach to the orientals that existed in other parties. Like them, Huret decided to coopt a small number of them into its institutions, but even this was done, in the mid-1950s, with some misgivings. Some party veterans said that even though the candidates proposed were "good lads," there was no need to hurry and bring them into the party institutions prematurely. The party's general-secretary noted that no urgency was involved because these people from the ma'abarot (temporary tent camps set up for new immigrants in the early 1950s) had no interest in the question of representation. But those who favored the move pointed out that the step was being taken not to ask for their counsel but to accord these persons a certain standing when they appeared before their colleagues.[69] The oriental communities provided votes, but since they possessed none of the prestige aspired to by Herut circles, no effort was made to absorb them in the party. It was not until the mid-1960s that this cautious and patronizing approach began to disappear, and then for reasons connected with internal developments in Herut, as the next chapter will show.

Begin had no solution for overcoming the status blockage that affected the former Betaris and Irgun activists. Instead, he offered them as a substitute the world of myths they had known since their formative period in Poland. It is obvious that they were not fully conscious of the nature of the problem that was bothering them. They themselves did not comprehend how powerful was their desire to enhance their status both in their own eyes and in the eyes of others. But this is what Begin did for them by evoking the myths. The message he transmitted to his followers was that their prestige was determined according to myths different from those that were dominant in the society that had shunted them to the fringes. It was they, not the Haganah, who had driven out the British, and it was thanks to them, and not to Mapai, that the state had been established. Only they were capable of leading the nation to the liberation of all the historic Land of Israel, an act of crucial significance for the country's future.

This emphasis on myths through which they claimed for themselves a central standing in the society, transformed politics for them into what we term "status politics." As I explained in the Introduction, groups that are unwilling to accept their low status in the system and shift their struggle to the political sphere, transform politics into a dispute over the distribution of prestige.[70]

Similarly, the political style that Begin adopted in Herut resembled that of status politics as it is known from other societies. It was a politics that fled from reality into a world of pretense and stressed emotional rather than rational action. This was effected by politicians who utilized their rhetorical skills to conjure up for their supporters a reality that differed from the actual social and political situation. As Kalman Katznelson explained it, Begin and his cohorts could not be defined as statesmen "because they do not have in mind any political goal per se. . . . Their proper title is performers and conjurers." They are "stage people, actors, directors, makeup artists, and so forth, who make a supreme effort and demonstrate very earnest seriousness in trying to vest the artificial thing they create with concreteness and substance, in order to get the audience to conclude that the thing is not artificial but realistic and genuine beyond any doubt."[71]

This was a political style different from the bureaucratic politics practiced by Mapai and the other parties. Unlike them, Herut did not concern itself with establishing party organizations and a party apparatus in order to supply the various needs of its members and voters, and thereby gain their loyalty and bind them to the party. The needs of the Herut community were different, and Menachem Begin was able to satisfy them.

Herut's status politics placed the party outside the Israeli political system, which was engaged in distributing resources and benefits to the various groups. Herut's myths isolated the party from the system. They divided the society into good and bad, just and wicked, loyalists and traitors. This world view had no room for compromise, a central principle of democratic politics. True, Herut's entrenchment behind the myths and symbols fortified the members' allegiance to the party and its leader, but at the same time it generated equally intense opposition to the party and its leader in others, and heightened the antagonism between the two camps. This phenomenon was discernible in elections as well. The elections held between 1955 and 1973 saw shifts of voter support from one party to another, but few crossed the lines between Herut and the other parties. In 1959, Mapai's share of the vote increased by 6 percent, while in 1961 it lost 4 percent due to a bitter leadership struggle. Other parties were hurt by Mapai's successes and benefited from its failures. As for Herut, however, it obtained 12.6 percent of the popular vote in 1955, 13.5 percent in 1959, and 13.8 percent in 1961. The vicissitudes that affected the political system left Herut untouched. (Voter behavior is discussed in chapter 8.)

The party's isolation and its inability to increase its strength did not reduce the ardent support of the rank and file for their leader and for the myths he stood for. But many party activists expressed their disappointment in the election results. They wanted to succeed, and every failure discomfited them. Many blamed the leader.

To uphold his authority, Begin convened the Central Committee after every election defeat and demanded a vote of confidence. Naturally, he won unreserved support on these occasions. But the unease lingered in Herut activists, including many NWF members, who constituted a standing threat to Begin's leadership.[72] Under the impact of this threat, Begin decided to undertake an effort to improve the party's electoral prospects, which entailed structural revision in the party organization. This step, which very nearly cost him the leadership, is the subject of the next chapter.

7

Breakout and Insularity

Striving for an Electoral Breakthrough

In the late 1950s and early 1960s, following the elections of 1959 and 1961, Herut found itself in a rut, unable to increase its electoral strength. As a result, it continued to be an opposition party without influence in the political system, to the chagrin of those party activists whose loyalty to the myths and whose admiration for Begin the leader and orator who symbolized the myths, was insufficient compensation for their party's weakness.

Political analysts in this period thought that Herut, in its existing format, had exhausted its reservoir of voters. It had the backing of certain middle-class groups, notably Irgun members and supporters, and new immigrants, particularly from the Oriental communities, who felt that they were getting a raw deal in the new society. To strengthen its hold in the public and to attract new groups, the journalist "Poless" wrote in *Ha'aretz*, Herut had "to move from being a raucous opposition to a substantive opposition." But were it to take this step, it would be no different from the General Zionists, a right-wing opposition party.[1] The effort to stake out a unique niche in the political system was a mission the intelligentsia had tried to cope with in Herut's early days, before they were routed by Begin. Now the task fell to the leader who was the absolute ruler in Herut.

Mordechai Olmert believes that Begin drew up a program to increase Herut's electoral support as early as 1956. To attract religious voters, he backed their views on the religion-state issue. He also sought a merger with the General Zionists to secure middle-class backing, while moving to set up a faction in the Histadrut to enlist the support of new-immigrant workers who disdained the Socialist world view. The program's flaw, according to NWF's Olmert, was that it was devoid of a new ideological or programmatic message. Without such a message, he thought, it would be impossible to gain the support of new groups.[2]

In Olmert's view, this and other weaknesses derived from Begin's intellectual incapacity for thought at the ideological level. It is my estimation, in addition, that Begin could not permit himself ideological innovativeness. As already explained, Begin depicted himself as a leader who expressed the national interest and not the interest of specific groups. This national interest was anchored in agreed myths between him and his supporters. Since this was the core of the legitimization of his standing as leader, he did not dare discard the myths. But many activists in Herut, who devoted themselves to party politics, desired influence and personal advancement in the political system. Their pressure, together with his desire to lead the Jewish people, spurred Begin's efforts to increase his party's electoral strength.

Olmerts's three components should not, in my estimation, be understood as a deliberate and comprehensive strategy. They were tactical moves.[3] Only one of them originated as an initiative of Begin's, unaccompanied by the pressure or persuasion of his aides. In 1958, he suddenly began to declare, on frequent occasions, that for the Jewish people, nationality and religion were two sides of the same coin and were inseparable. The immediate cause of this formulation was an exacerbation of the debate between the religious and secular sectors. The Interior Minister, Israel Bar-Yehuda, had recently reached a decision according to which anyone declaring himself to be a Jew could be registered in his identity card as such without the examination or approval of any religious authority, and thus become an Israeli citizen in accordance with the Law of Return. (This law accords citizenship to all Jews who so desire.) The religious parties took great exception to this decision, which was also denounced by the Chief Rabbis. (There are two Chief Rabbis in Israel, one Ashkenazi and one Sephardi.) They maintained that only the religious authority is vested with the right to decide who is a Jew. In the wake of the public furor, Begin demanded, at the party convention, that the directive be rescinded. Amongst Jews, he declared, no differentiation should be made between religion and nationality. "A Jew is a Jew from the viewpoint of nationality and religion alike." This principle had assured "the wellbeing of the nation from ancient times unto the last generation."[4]

Begin also cast himself as the defender of the honor and authority of the chief rabbis, who headed the campaign for the sole right of the religious authority to determine who is a Jew.[5] The sixth party convention resolved that "the Herut movement protests the deprecation of the Chief Rabbi, and demands that the Chief Rabbi who has been or will be elected hold the lofty post for life." In 1964, when a public storm erupted over the refusal of the Chief Rabbinate to recognize the Jewishness of Israelites who immigrated from India, Herut, too, objected to this ruling. However, in its draft motion on the subject presented in the Knesset, it saw fit to add: "The Knesset calls on the whole public to show honor and respect for sages and teachers as has been the custom among our people according to our sanctified tradition from ancient days."[6]

The great publicity that Herut's Information Division gave to Begin's speeches and numerous pronouncements on this issue, was undoubtedly designed to attract religious voters. But neither did this posture deviate from the position taken by Betar-Poland. Jabotinsky, too, it will be recalled, believed, like others on the radical right, in the power of religious tradition to support a national outlook that aspired to glorify the nation's historical tradition. Their hope was that religion would imbue the national orientation with the moral dimension it lacked. The fusion of the two, Jabotinsky was certain, would attract youth. He, too, urged respect for rabbis and Torah sages. At the same time, he was a secular person and apparently did not expect loyalty to religious ritual. But already then, Betaris took Jabotinsky's message literally, making no differentiation between the abstract idea and the ritual, and insisting that their members observe religious precepts. (See pp. 40–41)

In reinstating this Betari tradition, Begin inevitably outraged the remnants of the Betar and Revisionist intelligentsia. Even Yohanan Bader admitted that on this point he found it difficult to accept Begin's posture. But Bader also explained that for Begin himself, no deviation was involved. Unlike the cosmopolitan Jabotinsky, Bader noted, Begin was a provincial from a remote town who accepted religious ritual and religious mysticism at their face value.[7] Equally simplistic was Begin's reasoning, which he reiterated endlessly: the Jews must preserve their fidelity to religious tradition because this was what had maintained them as a separate nation throughout their exile.

True, there had been a period of several years, following Begin's arrival in the country and when he served as Irgun commander, when he had abandoned this orientation, apparently under the impact of his encounter with the native-born secular nationalists who joined the Irgun. At that time he agreed to use the word "Hebrew" instead of "Jewish" to differentiate between nationalism in the resurgent homeland and Jewish tradition in the Diaspora. Most of the Irgun members who had espoused these views were no longer in Herut. Uzi Ornan, himself a former member of LEHI, had become the head of the League for the Prevention of Religious Coercion, for which he was savaged in *Herut*. This development angered Ya'akov Amrami, a senior Irgun commander, who ceased his activity in Herut in the early 1950s along with the rest of the intelligentsia.[8] After Begin published an article in *Ma'ariv* reiterating his assertion that in Judaism religion and nationality were inseparable, Amrami wrote him a lengthy letter on the subject. He reminded Begin of his days in the underground, when he had accepted the principle of a separation between religion and nationality. "How you have changed, Begin," Amrami lamented. But even while writing the letter—it was in 1972—Amrami realized that there was no prospect of the leader's changing his mind, so he did not bother to send it. As he noted on the document, to do so would be without "point or purpose."[9]

The contradiction between the identification of religion and nationality, and the liberalist principles, which obligated a separation of religion and state, did not concern Begin. Nor does he seem to have been aware of the idea's conflict with the Zionist principle that the Jewish people is a nation and not a religious sect. But these questions were very much on the minds of the remaining members of the intelligentsia in Herut.

In the first years, their voice was still heard in the party paper, where they made known their views on this issue. In 1964, *Herut* ran a debate between supporters and denigrators of Begin's stand. But a note was appended to the articles stating that the opinions expressed in them were solely those of the authors.[10] *Herut* was closed down shortly afterward, thus eliminating the last movement forum in which the vestiges of the intelligentsia could make known their views, albeit in a controlled manner.

Unlike the principle identifying religion and nationality, the ideas of Herut's merging with the General Zionists and of joining the Histadrut as a separate faction, were first broached not by Begin but by party officials who were looking for ways to boost Herut's electoral strength. The proposal for union with the General Zionists was already floated in the early 1950s. Begin had dismissed the idea until after the 1955 elections on the ground that the disparity in the size of the parties' Knesset factions—at that time the General Zionists had twenty MKs, to Herut's eight—would result in Herut's being swallowed up as a mere faction within the bigger party. A further obstacle, he said, was the General Zionists' opposition to the principle of Greater Israel.[11] However, following the 1955 election, when Herut returned fifteen to the General Zionists' thirteen MKs, he agreed to approach the General Zionists with a merger proposal.[12]

In the deliberations conducted by the Central Committee, the merger advocates took a scornful, at times overtly hostile attitude, toward the General Zionists. "I despise them," Yuniczman said, "but this is the way to power." "I am not enthusiastic about them," Yosef Szofman added, "but what interests me is those who will vote for them." Many were perturbed by the General Zionists' indifference to the idea of Greater Israel. Haim Landau, who opposed the merger, explained that if "we are perceived as having decided to obscure the ideological principle that is important to us, then woe unto us."[13]

Why, then, did they work tirelessly to bring about this union from 1955 until the establishment of the electoral bloc ten years later? Mordechai Olmert and his NWF colleagues could not understand why Begin and his aides were seeking closer ties with the middle-class General Zionists when their main constituency was the working class. Eventually, he concluded that the striving for status was what tipped the scales. Through this kind of organizational merger, Herut leaders wanted to enter "the salons of society."[14] When talks with the General Zionists (by now part of the Liberal Party) went into high gear in 1964, articles began to appear in *Herut* deploring the bad manners of Israelis and urging more refined etiquette.[15] Naturally, it is difficult to prove a connection between the two developments, but this concern of veteran Betaris with good manners did crop up precisely on the eve of the formation of the Herut-Liberal Bloc, or Gahal in the Hebrew acronym. As will be recalled, the subject of bourgeois manners had already concerned Betaris back in their youthful movement days.

But Begin was above all a politician who strove to be a sole leader. His decision to seek a merger was related to his assessment that he would not find it difficult to prevail over the united party. From the outset of the discussions, he was clearly cognizant of the advantage possessed by the leader party he headed over the cadre party of the General Zionists. "By uniting with them," he told the Central Committee, "you are uniting with the masses, and our speakers will conquer the masses who will be the framework of the united party."[16] Hence Begin did not relax his efforts to achieve unity, which held out the promise of both power and status for Herut.

In the first round of the unification talks between the two parties, held in 1955–56, the main stumbling block was the General Zionists' refusal to assent to the principle of the integrity of the homeland. Their opposition, Begin believed, was not grounded in principle. They were guided by political considerations. "If the principle remains, the public will have the impression that they entered the Herut movement."[17] Their consideration in this regard was understandable, as was Begin's refusal to forgo a myth that constituted the legitimization for his authority and assured the continued unity of the Herut camp around his leadership in the unified party.

When the talks between the two parties resumed, in 1958, the General Zionist leadership agreed to a concession on the issue of principle that had been the bone of contention two years earlier. As already mentioned, following the Sinai Campaign, Herut had ceased demanding a military operation to conquer Eretz-Israel and now couched this demand in the form of a declaration of principle only. A mere declaration was not fraught with significance for the pragmatic-minded General Zionists. Their feeling in this regard was reinforced when Herut agreed to a vaguely worded formulation of the principle. The text, as agreed by both delegations, was: "The right of the Jewish people to Eretz-Israel in its historical wholeness—is an inalienable right." For its part, Herut assented to basic liberal principles such as: "Man was not created for the state, but the reverse: the state was created for man." In the proclamation of principles, Herut also agreed that the economy would be based on the principle of free enterprise and that state services would be guaranteed to all inhabitants. They disparaged the idea of the class war and demanded the continued supremacy of the national interest that was common to all strata of the nation.

This time it was disagreements over organizational issues that produced a deadlock in the negotiations. The General Zionists sought not only numerical equality in the united party, but insisted on preserving the separate organizational frameworks to the point where the party would have two chairmen—one from each party—two general secretaries, and so forth.[18] Begin could not possibly accede to this request, as he had no bureaucratic organization at his disposal. In this situation, even an organizational structure as loose as that of the General Zionists' cadre party posed a danger, which was compounded by the fact that the only true organization within Herut belonged to Begin's rivals in the NWF. Negotiations with the General Zionists were resumed in 1963, with Begin putting forward a new idea. He now proposed, instead of union, an electoral alignment between the two parties which, in time, would engender organizational unification. In the meantime, he assented to the continued existence of two separate organizations and agreed that the principle of Greater Israel—which was a "sacrosanct principle"—would be binding on Herut members only.[19]

Yet even now the General Zionists, who in 1961 had joined with the Progressive Party to establish the Liberal Party, found it difficult to accept the idea of forging an alignment with Herut. The Progressive Party branch was dead set against the idea, and ultimately did not join the new bloc, setting up the Independent Liberal Party instead. The General Zionist leaders in the Liberal Party drew encouragement from Herut's decision to form a faction in the Histadrut. This was taken to be a sign of a tendency toward moderation within Herut, and gave rise to the hope that together they could form a national-liberal party. Such a party held out the prospect of becoming an alternative to Mapai, with the Liberals enlisting the support of middle-class populations such as those of Rehavia in Jerusalem or in North Tel Aviv, and Herut gleaning the support of disadvantaged populations such as Tel Aviv's Hatikva neighborhood and the Upper Galilee development town of Kiryat Shemona.[20] The Herut-Liberal Bloc—Gahal—was established somewhat in advance of the 1965 elections.

Establishing a Faction in the Histadrut

The idea of joining the Histadrut also originated among Begin's assistants. As early as 1955, Avraham Drori, the party's general-secretary, noted that Herut had obtained the support of many Histadrut members who were not Socialists and who could, therefore, be organized in Herut if the party were to set up a faction in the Histadrut.[21] But internal developments also played a part in this decision. While Begin's victory over the NWF at the third convention, in 1954, had sapped the labor federation's strength, the NWF nevertheless remained the only organized force in the movement. At its disposal were salaried employees, and in many branches its apparatus was congruent with the movement's.[22] Herut even had recourse to the NWF's financial support: in 1960, for example, the movement's paper was saved from closure thanks to the NWF's readiness to underwrite part of its budget.[23] (It is not certain that Begin favored this move—at all events, he shut down the paper a few years later.) The NWF's organizational and financial clout was a source of ongoing displeasure to Begin. The formation of a Histadrut faction by his assistants was a means to neutralize the NWF's influence. Some NWF leaders estimated that Begin had sought to establish such a faction as early as the 1956 convention, and they were convinced, moreover, that his paramount objective in doing so was to liquidate their organization.[24] The NWF activists may have been right in thinking that the electoral consideration was secondary for Begin, but he found it convenient to posit it as the primary motive because entry into the Histadrut entailed a grave ideological deviation that would certainly trigger serious opposition, and not only from the NWF hierarchy.[25]

In the first stage, Begin and his associates tried to convince NWF members to support Herut's entry into the Histadrut and thereby to split the strength of the leading group in the federation. These efforts enjoyed a modicum of success. But when a leading NWF figure expressed his support for joining the Histadrut in public, he was forced to resign from the NWF Executive.[26]

The tension between Begin and his group, and the group of NWF leaders, had not abated since the 1954 convention. NWF members spoke of "blind hatred" between the two groups.[27] Begin, for his part, said bitterly that the NWF had blamed him for the electoral failures of 1959 and 1961. True, they had not demanded his resignation, "but my blood was spilled."[28]

In the 1961 convention, NWF delegates managed to take over the Standing Committee. They tried to bolster their strength in the new Central Committee proposed by the convention, and also demanded rotation among the party's Knesset Members. It was proposed that a third of the MKs be replaced in every term of office, a move which, if accepted, would have decimated the Knesset ranks of Begin's cronies. Begin reacted by proposing rotation in the post of movement chairman as well—in other words, by threatening to resign. This was sufficient to torpedo the NWF proposal.[29] At the NWF executive meeting held after the convention, Shostak said that "at the end of the convention an organized bloc was initiated against us, led by the movement chairman."[30] A head-on collision between the two groups was now inevitable. An NWF personality explained: "The movement understood that it would not be able to liquidate us directly, and therefore it made the proposal for the [Histadrut] faction its top priorty."[31]

The preparations for setting up a Histadrut faction led by Begin's assistants were undertaken even before the subject was placed on the Central Committee agenda. Some veteran members, such as Arye Ben-Eliezer, renewed their membership in the Histadrut, while others, such as Arye Altman, mobilized to fight the idea. Protracted, tension-filled discussions took place in the Central Committee in 1962. At their conclusion, Begin moved that Herut members of the Histadrut set up a faction within the Federation of Labor. The motion was defeated by a vote of 37-26.[32]

The vote was a resounding failure for Begin, who had ensured, at the 1961 convention, that his supporters among the veterans retained their places on the Central Committee. Many of them now voted against his proposal. The idea of entering the Histadrut flew in the face of the anti-Socialist tradition they had brought from Poland; but it is also possible that the proposal rankled because it did not conform with their aspirations for status. They, who were a proletariat under duress, had no desire to join the workers' Socialist labor union.[33]

Begin refused to accept this defeat, the more so as it was perceived as an NWF victory. Having failed in the Central Committee, he shifted the arena to the party convention of 1963. The struggle commenced even earlier, with the election of the convention delegates. The NWF turned out to be strong in the city branches, but were unable to make inroads among the new-immigrant population in the development towns. (So-called development towns were built in Israel after its establishment to absorb the mass immigration primarily of Oriental Jews who immigrated from Arab countries in North Africa and the Middle East.) The Begin group took advantage of this weakness and renewed the old alliance from Irgun days, "an alliance that the Betar elite forged with the oriental communities."[34] It was an opportune moment for Herut to organize these groups. Mapai was in the midst of an internal leadership struggle that had the effect of enervating the party apparatus. For the Herut leadership, this was an organizational success whose ramifications for the party's structure will be discussed below.

The debate at the convention over entering the Histadrut was fierce, marked by turmoil and vitriolic exchanges between the two camps. Begin's indefatigable endeavors produced only a small majority for his proposal, 291 in favor, 275 against. For a crucial decision such as this on an issue of fundamental principle, Begin needed a bigger majority. He therefore appealed to the convention to demonstrate the movement's unity by a greater show of support for the proposal. The revote produced a majority of 347–257. As the number of opponents was only marginally less, I infer that many of the new supporters of the plan had abstained in the original vote.[35]

But the struggle between the two camps was not yet over. It would be resumed following the 1965 Knesset elections, which resulted in a crushing defeat for the new Herut-Liberal Gahal bloc.

The 1965 Elections and the Ensuing Crisis

Gahal's defeat was particularly galling because the political conditions in the 1965 elections seemed quite propitious for the opposition parties that had now banded together. Mapai had split on the eve of the elections following a leadership fight that brought about the resignation of the party's elderly leader, David Ben-Gurion, who formed a new party, Rafi, and savaged Mapai without mercy. Nonetheless, Mapai was able to retain its dominant standing and form a coalition relatively easily without either Gahal or Rafi. Gahal, whose two component parties had separately won a total of thirty-four Knesset seats in 1961, obtained only twenty-six seats in 1965. Worse, the internal division of Knesset seats had landed Herut with three fewer seats than it won by itself in 1961.

Disappointment was widespread in the party, notable among figures such as the well-known lawyer Shmuel Tamir, a leader of the Lamerhav faction, who had resumed his party activity following Herut's entry into the Histadrut and the formation of Gahal. Many of Herut's younger generation were embittered, as were activists in Herut's newly formed Blue-and-White faction in the Histadrut. NWF leaders were outraged, and pinned the blame for the failure on Begin personally. Following the election, Begin once more convened the Central Committee to request a vote of confidence. In the debate he said he was taking this step because of the accusations leveled at him by the NWF. Already in the 1959 poll they had blamed him for the failure, though without demanding his resignation. This time he would not be silent, Begin asserted.[36] This outburst ended any possibility of compromise.

In fact, relations had reached the boiling point even before the elections. True, after the convention some NWF leaders, such as Eliezer Shostak, still entertained the hope that Begin desired a united movement and would therefore seek a compromise.[37] But relations deteriorated rapidly. The NWF was shortchanged in the party institutions and in the list of Knesset candidates. The Petah Tikva branch, one of the most radical in the NWF group, reacted by running separately in the municipal elections.[38] After the general elections, it was obvious that an internal fight was unavoidable. Begin, an NWF activist said, would never reconcile himself to the organization's existence "because it is headed by a group which harbors independent opinions and is not dependent on him. They are still thinking in terms of the Betar hierarchy and do not tolerate dissenting views."[39]

For the NWF leadership, the electoral debacle was a convenient jump-off point for an offensive. They were able to mobilize a broad coalition among disappointed Herut activists against Begin's leadership. An examination of the social status of the internal opposition is most illuminating. Many were members of the liberal professions or businessmen. They included lawyers such as Shmuel Tamir, professors such as Eri Jabotinsky, and university trained youngsters such as Ehud Olmert and Akiva Nof. Possessing prestige and status in the general society, they also sought political power and influence. The same phenomenon would repeat itself in the case of the opposition that formed against Begin in late 1972. At that time, the activists would be Ezer Weizman, a former chief of operations and commander of the Air Force, and the businessmen Yosef Kremerman and Ya'akov Meridor. They were less bound to the mythical world symbolized by Begin than Herut members whose social mobility was blocked.

The heads of the opposition group were united in their belief that Begin's extremism, such as his uncompromising demand for Greater Israel, had put off many voters. To judge by his election speeches, the fact that he now headed a bloc in which one of the partners pursued a moderate foreign policy line, drove him to express views that were exceptionally radical. The purpose was to maintain his standing as the symbol of Greater Israel. In one speech, for example, he declared that the alternative was peace without a state or a state without peace—there was no third option.[40] Around this time, the President of Tunis, Habib Bourguiba, had issued his famous statement advocating negotiations between the Arabs and Israel. This was an unprecedented declaration in the Arab world of that period, notwithstanding that Bourguiba proposed peace in the 1947 boundaries agreed upon by the United Nations. The war in 1948–49 between Israel and its neighbors created a larger state than agreed in 1947. It was to this declaration that Begin was responding. Akiva Nof, then of Herut's young guard, joined the opposition after the elections (he was subsequently an MK for the breakaway Free Center), urging a more positive response to Bourguiba's declaration. The principle of negotiations adduced by Bourguiba must be accepted, "and mutual concessions are the very soul of negotiations."[41]

The NWF-led dissidents decided to organize the opposition to Begin around a debate over the party's future course. The leadership issue was naturally a by-product of any policy change. In the debate, many of the arguments that had been adduced at the third convention were voiced again. To their demand for the adoption of a more flexible posture in order to expand the ranks of the Knesset opposition, they added their long-standing readiness to participate in a coalition even with Mapai, as this was the road to power. They sought to lead their party on a different, more pragmatic route.

Their policy began to take shape at the NWF executive meeting held after the election. It was clear, as Shostak made a point of explaining, that the struggle must be directed against Begin's leadership. This was unavoidable, even if, for tactical reasons, they attacked not Begin himself but the political line he espoused. Shostak explained the position in the following words at this meeting:

The basis of Greek tragedy is that a person chooses his own fate, and the same can be said about Begin. He himself chose his fate. Ever since he emerged from the underground, he has been possessed of the feeling that he will wield power in the country. This belief he conveyed to his close friends. Begin himself determined the tragedy of the movement. He alone wanted to prove that he was more successful than Jabotinsky, that his power of judgment is superior to everyone's, and that there is no place for discussion, for debate, or for mistakes. For seventeen years we have been following him and doing his will, and he is leading us to a desert without an end. For years upon years we gave him credit and did what he asked . . .

The attitude toward Begin and his way was mystical, Shostak added. Many decisions that members did not understand and did not agree with were accepted in the hope that perhaps he knew best. Now the time had come to propose a different way.[42]

After Shostak and his associates explained their program to the Central Committee, Begin refused to allow an ideological debate. He told Shostak bluntly: "Before you can embark on your road, Shostak, I will have to be eliminated."[43]

To outside observers, Shostak's program appeared both logical and unavoidable. Those who did not comprehend the symbolic politics of Herut expected that this would be the coming stage on the road of the party that had already formed a bloc with the Liberals and had established a faction in the Histadrut. Herut's adversaries, who were accustomed to thinking about politics in terms of practical criteria, anticipated a reshuffle in Gahal in the wake of the election failure. They were particularly fearful of Gahal-Rafi cooperation. Thus, Aharon Yadlin, a leading Mapai figure, explained that Gahal's failure "is the result of the voters' recoil from the assumption of power by the person Begin and everything he stands for." Yadlin was therefore certain "that Gahal will draw conclusions from its defeat. And if this bloc does not fall apart once more, then sooner or later it will carry out a sweeping revision of its attitude toward its leaders and toward its public image." The upshot would be Gahal's cooperation with Rafi, Yadlin predicted, with no little concern.[44]

The immediate threat to Mapai, as Yadlin, too, understood, was indeed a possible linkup between Gahal and Rafi. Immediately after the elections, private talks on this question got underway between leading figures in Rafi, the Liberals, and Herut. In February 1966, the Liberal

Party's Central Committee deliberated cooperation with Rafi and other groups, and a formal resolution was passed supporting the establishment of a broad electoral alliance.[45] Within days, Begin convened the Herut Central Committee and reiterated his unshakable loyalty to the Greater Israel idea. Without assent to this principle, there would be no merger with the Liberals, he told the Central Committee.[46] Immediately after the Central Committee session, Begin's assistants echoed his demand and thus poured fuel on the debate. Bader wrote an article entitled "Adventurism" in which he advocated a military adventure in order to achieve the goal. Everything that had taken place in the country until 1948, and which had brought about Israel's establishment, Bader reminded his readers, had been an adventure. Therefore, he hoped that the youth would not flinch from adventurism when it was called for, "and will do its duty to the nation and the homeland."[47] Peretz Bernstein, the president of the Liberal Party, wrote a rejoinder to Bader's piece, which he called "Irredentism." Bernstein made no secret of his surprise that the debate on this issue had erupted now, of all times: "Surprisingly and for a surprising reason, the question of Eretz-Israel, of which the greater part is not incorporated in the state of Israel, has now arisen to engage public opinion."[48] The journalists who covered the political scene were less surprised at the timing of the debate. To them it was obvious that the floating of the Greater Israel slogan was meant to halt the process of rapprochement between circles in the Liberals, Rafi, and Herut. Begin had no desire to expand the alliance, "Poless" wrote, as this would adversely affect his standing, which was uncontested in Herut and quite stable in Gahal.[49] If a new coalition were to be formed which included, besides Ben-Gurion, the elderly leader, well-known public figures such as Moshe Dayan, Shimon Peres, and others, Begin, even if he managed to retain his leadership—in itself a doubtful proposition—could certainly not remain the authoritative leader that he was in Gahal.

Thus, parallel to the preparations for the Herut convention, the debate over Begin's continued leadership in Gahal grew ever more heated. Explicit testimony of the situation was provided by a leading member of the Liberal Party, Simha Ehrlich, in an article he published in *Ha'aretz* while the internal elections for the Herut convention were at their height. According to Ehrlich, one of the reasons for Gahal's poor showing in the elections was that Begin had refrained from making a categorical peace declaration, despite importuning that he do so. Begin's adamance regarding Greater Israel had heightened his radical image and scared off many voters. Before it could become an alternative to Mapai as the ruling party, Herut must cease to be a sect of fanatics and Gahal must expand its ranks, Ehrlich argued. This was possible only if Herut abandoned its declarations on the principle of Greater Israel, and placed at its head "a personality possessing a broadly acceptable public image."[50]

The opposition that organized within Herut around the NWF showed more caution than Ehrlich, who operated on the outside. To assail Begin's leadership, it was necessary to call into question Herut's sacrosanct myths, not an easy matter for the opposition figures, many of them veteran Betaris such as Shmuel Tamir, Eri Jabotinsky—Ze'ev Jabotinsky's son—and others. But there was no getting around it. Jabotinsky, in articles he published on the eve of the convention, said he considered it harmful to raise the issue of the integrity of the homeland, because doing so prevented the unification of the forces opposing Mapai. While he did not dare deny the sacredness of the principle, he did insist that the area of Israel sufficed for its economic development, took a stand against a deliberate war, and argued that "the problem of territorial expansion and the rectification of the borders, with all its economic and strategic importance alike, does not resemble in its urgency and serious-ness the problem of the need for an independent state, which we faced" before 1948. He had no doubt, Jabotinsky added, that the Herut hierar-chy was raising the question of the whole Land of Israel purposely in order to prevent the unification of the opposition forces.[51]

It suddenly appeared that the formation of the Gahal bloc, along with the entry to the Histadrut, which had been tactical moves of Begin's intended to bolster Herut's electoral attractiveness, had created a mo-mentum that Begin did not expect. Many activists were now ready to effect compromises in the Herut platform in order to attain power. Begin grasped that his leadership was at stake and began demanding the allegiance of the party faithful in the name of the myths he symbolized. He presented himself as the loyal fighter for Greater Israel and even revived the idea of liberating Eretz-Israel by force of arms. By evoking the myths, he hoped to rally the Herut ranks around him. To preserve his authoritarian leadership, he not only opposed expanding the elec-toral bloc but was even ready to dismantle Gahal and restore Herut to its state of political isolation in the period before the formation of Gahal.

The opposition, headed by Shostak and Tamir, which included many of the Herut young guard and even functionaries from the Blue-and-White faction in the Histadrut, organized itself well for the convention. Begin and his cohorts, in contrast, pinned their hopes on their evocation of the myth of Greater Israel and the need to liberate the homeland, along with their leader's ability to control the convention proceedings. In his opening address, Begin reiterated his views on the whole Land of Israel and reasserted his refusal to hold contacts with Germany.[52] It was only when they were defeated in votes on two technical procedural issues that the Begin group realized how strong and cohesive the opposition was.[53] Their own organizational weakness was now revealed in all its gravity. Not only had they been unable to prevent the election of opposition activists as convention delegates, but they were also even unable to estimate accurately the opposition's strength until the two votes.

The opposition, for its part, set itself limited goals, such as the election of Shmuel Tamir as chairman of the executive, and the attainment of a majority in the Central Committee to be elected by the convention. In this manner they hoped to take control of the organization while sidestepping the need to attack Begin frontally. To this end, they proposed to Begin that he support Tamir's election, and in return they would back Begin's reelection as movement chairman. They evidently expected that Begin, seeing they had a majority at the convention, would be willing to reach an agreement with them.[54]

It is startling, on the face of it, that these opposition figures, who had known Begin for so many years, actually believed that he would enter into this kind of agreement. But they probably feared that in a head-on clash on the convention floor, he would be able to overcome their efforts to mobilize a majority. Begin's response was characteristic of his leadership style. Suddenly, without warning, and without consulting with his associates, he announced his resignation as chairman of the Herut movement. A "conspiracy" had been staged behind his back, he explained, and in view of this disloyalty of colleagues in whom he had believed and with whom he had traveled such a long road since the days of Betar and the Irgun, he was unwilling to go on as leader. Naturally, in a democratic movement it was legitimate to want to appoint a member to a position in the movement even against his—Begin's—will, he said, but as the founder and leader of the movement, he expected that those so inclined would speak with him first and not act behind his back. Begin's true opinion of party democracy is revealed in this statement. How was opposition to the leader feasible in a party in which the opposition were duty bound to consult with the leader about how to proceed? By depicting the opposition group as conspirators, who had offended him personally, Begin hoped to deter many of the delegates from supporting them. His resignation was meant to stir them into action.

Expectably, the resignation touched off a storm of emotions at the convention. The journalist Amos Elon described the atmosphere as charged with emotion to the point where it threatened to slide into violence. "Our dear father, we are headed for the grave," "You are our father," "Do not cast us off," "Do not abandon us"—these were some of the reactions recorded by the reporters.[55] The furor on the convention floor reached new heights when Ehud Olmert, of the young guard, dared to attack Begin's leadership and to propose a reassessment of the concept of the integrity of the homeland. Olmert's speech, and the inevitable reaction of the delegates, enabled Begin to reappear as the defender of democracy. He demanded vehemently that Olmert be allowed to conclude his remarks.[56]

But only after Begin's resignation did the convention truly take an astonishing turn. When Yohanan Bader decided to take advantage of the turmoil to stop the discussions until the convention persuaded Begin to retract his resignation, his motion was defeated. By a vote of 235 against 179, it was decided to proceed with the order of business.[57] Begin's people, and evidently Begin himself, were stunned.

Not even at this hour of crisis did Begin see fit to convene his aides and consult with them on his coming moves. He continued to act alone. On the evening after his resignation, he delivered a three-and-a-half-hour speech that lasted into the small hours of the night. He catalogued everything he had done for the movement since the days of the Irgun, and with great emotion told how deeply injured he had been by the opposition's conspiracy against him. He flayed Shmuel Tamir personally for his disloyalty. He repeated his uncompromising faith in the idea of Greater Israel. But he made no proposal to extricate the convention from its deadlock.

Toward the end of the convention, two members of the Begin group took the initiative—Yohanan Bader and Ya'akov Meridor, who were considered in Herut to be the only members of Begin's coterie to evince even a modicum of independence. Their relative independence, as compared with Begin's other aides, is, I believe, also related to their place and status in the general society. Bader was a well-known lawyer even before settling in Palestine, while Meridor was a successful businessman. As for Begin's other associates, they had attained their standing in Herut as a result of their loyalty to Begin. Were it not for their standing in Herut, they, like many of their colleagues, would have been low down in the socioeconomic scale. Bader suggested that the convention elect a Central Committee and an executive on the basis of parity between the two camps. Bader himself would serve as chairman of the Central Committee, and Meridor as chairman of the executive. Since Knesset Members—most of whom were Begin loyalists—were automatically members of the Central Committee, the net result of Bader's proposal would be to give

Begin the barest majority on the new Central Committee. Bader's motion drew 252 votes in support and 249 against. Observers thought that even this tiny majority was obtained thanks to Begin's emotional speech the previous evening, which had induced a number of opposition members to support the leader after all.[58]

It was impossible for the movement to function in this situation of a permanent showdown between two opposing camps. Begin, moreover, refused to lead his own troops. A Bader-Meridor initiative to maintain the movement's institutions until Begin agreed to retract his resignation, did not get the leader's blessing. For the same reason others of the Begin group, such as Haim Landau and Arye Ben-Eliezer, refused to attend meetings of the new executive.

The situation that was created paralyzed the movement, and Bader was convinced that only Begin's return to open activity could save Herut. Without Begin, Bader feared, Herut would not be able to preserve its standing in Gahal and in the Gahal Knesset faction indefinitely. In a letter to Arye Ben-Eliezer, Bader asserted that pressure must be put on Begin to resume his activity in the movement publicly.[59] But Begin refused. At the same time, and again in a solo action, he stepped up his attacks on the opposition. In an article in the daily *Hayom* (the Gahal paper) entitled "My Resignation and My Griefs," he repeated his accusations against the opposition and Shmuel Tamir, who had fomented a conspiracy against him. He said he refused to return to his post because the opposition wanted a "referee in the ring" who would bring about compromises between the camps, instead of a leader who laid down movement policy. To this he would not agree.[60] Clearly, Begin would consent to lead the movement again only if the opposition were routed. But the opposition remained united and the impasse dragged on.

It was Yohanan Bader who broke the deadlock for Begin. In September, Bader learned that a letter to the editor in *Ha'aretz* attacking Begin had been published under a pseudonym. Its true author was a fairly minor opposition figure named Amsterdam. The letter itself, which said that it would be disastrous for the country if Begin attained power, did not go beyond what other opposition activists were saying about Begin's leadership.[61] However, Bader presented it as an illicit act instigated by none other than Shmuel Tamir. He demanded that both Amsterdam and Tamir, as well as another opposition figure, be brought to trial in the movement's court.

The dispute now became even more fierce, and the Begin group took advantage of its miniscule lead in the movement institutions to combat the opposition. Meridor dissolved the executive and appointed a new executive from which Tamir was suspended until the Herut court had its say, as Meridor explained. In reaction, other opposition members refused to attend executive meetings, while the Begin associates, who had refused earlier to take part in these meetings, began turning up for them. The tension grew, and with it the efforts of various middlemen to find a way out through a compromise. All such proposals were rejected by Begin. He sought not a compromise but the elimination of the opposition.

Throughout this period, Begin waged a struggle of his own against the opposition. He took part in Central Committee meetings when the arguments and mutual vilifications flew thick and fast between the sides. He held talks with figures from the opposition camp in an effort to persuade them to switch sides.[62] In one Central Committee meeting, when a member of the opposition camp accused Ben-Eliezer of not speaking the truth, Begin got up and stalked angrily out of the hall. Only after the speaker apologized did Begin agree to return. He then delivered a speech lasting one-hour-and-a-half, attacking the opposition and re-peating his accusations. He declared that he would not accept a compro-mise and he rejected all the proposals to have the convention meet and elect him chairman. However, he also expressed his confidence several times that he would be chairman once again and that under his leader-ship the movement would once more prosper. Clearly, this would be possible only after the opposition was routed.[63]

The meeting just described took place in mid-November 1966, but the deadlock lasted until the end of February 1967, when the movement's court concluded its deliberations and ruled on the fate of the opposition activists. Amsterdam was expelled from the party for life, Tamir for one year. The opposition could not take this blow to their leader with equanimity. To remain in Herut without Tamir would be tantamount to an admission of weakness and would result in the certain defection of many of their followers. Their only viable option was to leave the party. Those who took this step formed an independent party called the Free Center. No sooner had the opposition camp left, when the Central Committee convened and elected Begin as movement chairman. Only two members abstained. One of them was Begin himself, who resumed office immediately after the vote.

On the day of Begin's reelection as Herut chairman, Simha Ehrlich published a second article in Ha'aretz. He reiterated his original charge that Begin's leadership had contributed to Gahal's failure in the general elections and that Begin's removal as leader would have enabled coop-eration between Gahal and Rafi. There were signs, Ehrlich pointed out, "that Mr. Begin's resignation did indeed lead Gahal and Rafi to draw closer," and the process had good prospects for a successful outcome. But Begin's return to power had stifled this process and had thus ended the prospect of creating an alternative to the existing government.

Ehrlich again charged that Begin's stands on the integrity of the homeland had disenchanted many potential Gahal voters. But the fundamental problem, Ehrlich said, was not ideological: it was the structure of the Herut movement and Begin's absolute leadership in that party. If Herut were to become an open movement in which there was room for the free interchange of ideas and views, the political cooperation could continue and along with it the striving to create an alternative to the Labor Alignment. But "now Mr. Begin is returning to the Herut movement, a movement that has been purged, and once more peace and quiet will prevail and Mr. Begin will rule without reservation and without contestation as always." Finally, Ehrlich asserted: "By its actions and its blunders, Herut has effectively dismantled Gahal; the formal aspect of the dissolution is not decisive at this moment, but it will come, because the only goal Gahal set itself—the creation of an alternative—will now never be attained."[64]

We have no answer to the question of what course Israeli politics would have taken had the opposition taken over in Herut. There is no way of knowing whether it would have been possible to expand the Herut-Liberal alignment, or what its chances might have been of achieving power. But in view of the split in Mapai, followed by the collapse of the party apparatus and the economic crisis that afflicted Israel in this period, a reasonable possibility existed of forming an opposition that could have overcome the ruling party.

Another question is whether, had it not been for the Six Day War, Gahal would have fallen apart in the wake of Begin's victory, leaving Herut a marginal and isolated party in the Israeli political system for the indefinite future. Since I did not make a study of the Liberal Party, I will not enlarge on this subject, and I will make do, instead, with a thumbnail sketch of developments in the party in this period.

The decision of the Liberal Party leadership to establish an alignment with Herut derived from their desire to have a hand in ruling the country. In 1961, they merged with the Progressive Party, which had been a Mapai coalition partner since the establishment of the state. Mapai, however, refused to bring the united party into the government, perhaps because it preferred the partnership of smaller parties with which it could more easily maintain its dominance in the governing institutions. In their desperation, the Liberal politicians turned to Herut, in the hope that an electoral bloc of this kind could constitute an alternative to Mapai.[65] They drew encouragement from circles in the middle class who viewed with concern the establishment of the Socialist alignment between Mapai and Ahdut Ha'avodah, a party espousing a more orthodox Socialist viewpoint than the social-democratic Mapai.[66]

One group that helped push the Liberals into a bloc with Herut was the editorial board of *Ha'aretz*. They believed that the country had been ruled too long by one party and that a change of government was essential for the health of the democratic regime. Since there was no difference between Mapai and Herut on foreign affairs and security issues, the victory of such a coalition would generate a much needed change in Mapai-style economic policy, which had suppressed free enterprise.[67]

Both the Liberal Party and *Ha'aretz* were pleased at Herut's decision to establish a faction in the Histadrut. An alliance between the middle-class supporters of the Liberals and the lower-class backers of Herut, they were certain, would catapult them into power.[68] As we know, this prognosis proved mistaken. In the 1965 elections, many middle-class voters opted for the Socialist bloc. They preferred the status quo with which they were familiar, over a change that they feared might be excessively radical under Herut. In addition, they probably shared the gut reaction of most of the veteran Yishuv against the myths of Herut and against Begin, who symbolized them. S. Z. Abramov, a leading figure in the Liberal Party, noted that when incipient signs appeared of a challenge to the status quo, the middle class was gripped by an atmosphere that he termed "counter-revolutionary." The middle class preferred the continuation of Mapai rule. Herut maintained its electoral strength in 1965, but the defection of large numbers of former Liberal Party supporters produced the election setback.[69] As a consequence, the Liberals effectively became the weaker of the two parties in the Gahal bloc. Hence, also their dismay when Begin emerged as the uncontested leader of Herut, dashing any hopes of removing him from Gahal. Probably the Liberals would have eventually dissolved Gahal, since it did not achieve its goal of becoming an alternative to the rule of Mapai. But two and one-half months after Begin's resumption of the leadership in Herut, the crisis began that culminated in the Six Day War, and a new political situation was created.

However, before the emergence of the new political reality—which will engage us in the next chapter—Herut under Begin's leadership appeared incapable of extricating itself from the political wasteland. The world of myths, which Begin symbolized, isolated the party in the Israeli political system. This was grasped by the one intellectual who remained in Begin's camp, Yohanan Bader. Unlike Begin's other assistants, Bader evinced no personal reverence for the leader. In his autobiography, he wrote that "Begin's rationalism yielded to his deep, almost mystical faith." Bader was nevertheless not deterred from supporting Begin because his own belief in Greater Israel was total. For him, this was "neither a slogan nor a messianic vision, but realistic foreign policy."[70] His statement to a reporter during the party crisis that he preferred "to live in the desert with Begin rather than sit in the government with Tamir," was more a declaration of loyalty to the path that Begin symbolized for him than it was to the person himself.[71]

Bader's allegiance to the myths, and not the man, was absolute. It is difficult not to surmise that this was the reason Begin did not appoint him a Cabinet minister after Herut joined the coalition.

It was Bader whose analysis of the 1965 elections and the flight of the middle class led him to conclude that Herut's only prospect of coming to power lay not in alliances with other groups but in a national crisis. "Although our heart rejects, negates and disdains an answer that identifies an opportunity with a national crisis," Bader wrote, "cold logic confirms this analysis."[72] To attain power without compromises and without concessions, and with Herut's myths intact, was unfeasible, Bader assessed, without a national crisis. Loyal to the myths, he reconciled himself to this situation. All that remained was for him to hope that a crisis was in the offing.

Herut Changes and Marks Time

Before turning to deal with the effects of the Six Day War crisis on Herut's standing in Israeli politics, I want to discuss the implications of the events described in this chapter on developments within the party. Events as fraught with significance as the establishment of a faction in the Histadrut, the creation of the bloc with the Liberals, and the internal crisis that generated a split, were bound to leave their mark in Herut. The question is whether and to what extent they caused a modification of the leader party structure as I described it in earlier chapters.

It was Israel Eldad, one of the group of Betar intellectuals, who did not join Herut, who pointed out, immediately after Herut entered the Histadrut, that this was a watershed in the party's history. No longer would Herut rise above sectorial interests and no longer would it be a party that considered the national front more vital than the economic front. By taking this decision, Herut lost its singularity and became a party like any other party that represented interests.[73] True, on the surface it is difficult to discern a change of this kind in Herut policy in the years after it joined the Histadrut as a separate faction. Its major preoccupation continued to be foreign affairs and security questions, and it seemed to stand pat on social and economic issues. But a closer examination reveals that in the areas of wages and labor relations, Herut did undergo a policy revision. In the 1950s, it will be recalled, Herut espoused free enterprise and tended to support the interests of the propertied class precisely on matters of wages and labor relations, although even then these issues were not its primary concern, and we discovered this posture only by examining the stands taken by the Knesset faction. Likewise, policy changes on economic issues beginning in the mid-1960s will become apparent only if we monitor closely the positions Herut took in the Knesset. It is particularly important to take note of the declarations of those Begin associates who now led the Blue-and-White faction in the Histadrut. The two key spokesmen in this regard were Arye Ben-Eliezer, the leading figure in the faction, and Yohanan Bader, in charge of economic and social matters in the party, who assisted Ben-Eliezer.

In the 1950s, Herut had opposed wage increases and had supported the abolition of cost-of-living increments. Now it supported wage increases and opposed the abolition of the cost-of-living payments.[74] An instructive example of the changes that occurred in Herut's positions on economic issues is provided by the proposal to nationalize Histadrut enterprises. This subject was raised in Herut institutions in the 1950s, and again in the mid-1960s. In the discussions on the election platform for the 1955 elections, Shostak's proposal to transfer some Histadrut enterprises to state ownership was opposed. Finally, it was decided that the platform would not specify where they would be transferred to. In contrast, in the 1965 Histadrut elections, with Herut taking part for the first time, Ben-Eliezer's proposal to transfer Histadrut enterprises in part to the state and in part to the workers themselves, was adopted.[75] On another occasion, Bader called for worker partnership in Histadrut enterprises, asserting that "this should be the difference between a private plant and a plant that pretends to be [part of] the workers' sector and to differ from a capitalist plant."[76] This did not deviate significantly from previous ideas, but it nevertheless reflected a new spirit. Bader, however, flew in the face of Herut convention when he expressed opposition to compulsory arbitration. To justify this change in his stand, he adduced the doubtful argument that compulsory arbitration should be resisted because all the arbiters would be members of Mapai. This position angered another veteran member, Eliahu Lenkin, who protested the change in the pages of *Herut*. However, the paper gave Bader its editorial support.[77]

Bader, though, did not adopt an excessively radical posture on these questions. On the contrary, in a "Blue-and-White" supplement in *Herut*, he found it necessary to restrain the workers. Thus, for example, he explained why there should be no tax hikes for the wealthy. "The worker has no interest in the taxes of others being raised," he wrote. "He will not be happy if others are harmed, he wants his own lot made easier."[78]

It is interesting to compare this new orientation of Begin's cronies on labor relations with the stand of the NWF. The latter, faithful to corporatist ideology, sought to introduce harmonious relations between workers and employers. They generally supported demands for wage hikes but vehemently opposed strikes. Thus, they had no qualms about denouncing a strike by academics on the eve of the 1965 elections, contending that they were setting "a bad educational example" for other workers, particularly as they were not fighting for mere subsistence.[79]

On another occasion, an NWF leader wrote about his disappointment with the Port of Ashdod management, which had not stuck to its stand of paying wages in accordance with norms based on workers' productivity. "Why did the port management surrender to the workers' committee, and why did it accept the deliberate infirmity of the manufacturing councils—so that norms would not be measured and they would work as much as they pleased and how and when they pleased," the disappointed corporatist leader demanded to know.[80] The Blue-and-White faction in the Histadrut did not share this outlook, and always supported the workers in labor disputes.

Unlike his aides, Begin tried to avoid any specific preoccupation with economic and labor relations issues. He preferred to talk in general terms about concern for the disadvantaged and the need to permit them a decent existence. This approach had remained consistent since the 1950s. However, the establishment of the Histadrut faction obliged him to make more frequent reference to these subjects in his speeches. Thus, in 1966 we find him supporting the same cost-of-living increments he wanted to abolish ten years earlier.[81] Begin expressed this stand at the Herut Council that preceded the eighth convention in 1966, when the opposition tried to seize control of the party. It is difficult to escape the impression that the purpose of this support for cost-of-living payments was to secure the backing of the development town delegates to the forthcoming convention. Still, his act demonstrated sensitivity toward the changes that had occurred in the social profile of the Central Com-

mittee in the wake of Herut's joining the Histadrut. This was an innova-
tion. But the leader's response was reserved. In his meetings with the
Blue-and-White faction, Begin did not hesitate to reassert his old conservative views on wages and labor relations. In one of the first conventions
of the Histadrut faction, in March 1965, he argued that without such
wage disparities, everyone would grow lazy and there would be no
point in making an effort.[82]

Herut's stands on social and economic issues, and the changes they
underwent, merit a separate examination. But from the mid-1960s, we
seem to witness a certain response by the leader to the economic interests
of the party's new members. This was not the case in the past, when Betar
and Irgun veterans formed the majority of the membership. For the most
part, Begin's response was reflected in his devoting more time in his
speeches to social and economic questions, although his central theme
continued to be foreign affairs and security.

Begin's addresses to conventions of the Blue-and-White faction
suggest that he decided that he must incorporate social issues into
speeches to Herut members of the Histadrut, however uncongenial he
found this. After devoting the majority of one address to foreign affairs,
he admitted that "it is my duty this evening to speak about a number of
social problems as well," and went on to discuss economic questions.[83]
He also honed his rhetoric, and evinced increasing virulence in his
attacks. An illustration is the following passage from his speech to the
Herut Council in June 1972:

Last Thursday I was at Lahavot Habashan, a kibbutz of the
Hashomer Hatza'ir movement. It was a very pleasant encounter with this kibbutz. I replied to questions. I asked
whether it is good, whether it is logical, whether it is fitting
that a Socialist should be a millionaire. One of the kibbutz
members called out: What's wrong, I want to be a millionaire
too. Very nice. So we already have a kibbutznik who wants
to be a millionaire. And from Mapam [United Workers Party,
a party to the left of Mapai, of which the Hashomer Hatza'ir
movement was a part] at that. So I said: We have nothing
against you, but what sort of combination is this? Then I had
to tell him. You want to be a millionaire? That's fine for your
wife. But maybe you'll wait a little? A Socialist like you? A
radical like you. We have today 47,000 families, a quarter of
a million souls, who live in housing of between four and

seven people per room. This is a social horror . . . 47,000
families like this. Maybe you will agree to solve that problem
first and then to start being a millionaire, a radical Socialist
like you?[84]

But his speeches in this vein contained no practical proposals for
dealing with the problems of poverty. It was the same regarding discrimination against the Orientals, another subject to which he began devoting
more time in his speeches. As far back as the mid-1950s, when it emerged
that the bulk of Herut's electoral support came from the lower strata of
Oriental origin, the party leadership began considering how to draw
them closer to the party. To one activist who admitted that he did not
know how to handle the question of the Orientals, Begin replied that no
promises should be made to the new immigrants. Instead, they should
be asked: "Are you an equal citizen in the country? We see you as a
human being and citizen with equal rights. The others want you to
remain a new immigrant."[85] Begin now adopted this style when addressing workers, who were largely from the Oriental groups. In one of the
first meetings of the Blue-and-White faction, for example, he told his
audience: "We want you to be a proud citizen. We want you to feel good
in the Jewish state, truly good. We will do all we can to represent you, to
convey your message, so that they will not abuse you, so that they will
not be able to shunt you back and forth, because there are such, how did
they call them?—Directors, who think they can do whatever they please
because they have the power . . ."[86]

In this manner, he maintained maximum freedom of action as a
leader without any commitment to interest groups in the party. Moreover, even though from very nearly the outset the majority of Herut
voters were from the lower-strata Oriental communities, no effort was
undertaken to enlist them in party activity. Only at the lowest level of
political activity, primarily during election campaigns, did Orientals
play an important role, from the first years of the state, in the various
parties.[87]

The entry of Oriental Jews into Herut institutions was stepped up
following the establishment of the party's Histadrut faction. But only
after the split, when the opposition, headed by the NWF, left the party,
was the way cleared for the entry of large numbers of new activists from
the Oriental groups. David Levy, for example, a Deputy Prime Minister
at the time of this writing, moved into the Herut hierarchy only after
Avraham Tiar, an Irgun veteran who had until then been considered "the

representative of the North African communities," chose to join the breakaway Free Center group.[88]

To upgrade the standing of the new members, the party bodies were enlarged. The Central Committee was expanded from sixty-seven members in 1963 to 120 members in 1968, and to 170 two years later. By 1972 it already comprised 278 members. A few years later, the Council was abolished and its members swallowed up in the Central Committee, which by the end of the decade had almost 1,000 members. The number of convention delegates also increased apace, from 500 in the early years to almost 2,000 in the 1970s. Concurrently, the powers of the Central Committee were extended. In 1975, the appointment committees, which were composed of Central Committee members named by the leadership, were abolished, and the Central Committee itself was empowered to elect directly the party's candidates for public and government office. In 1977, it was decided that the candidates would be elected by secret ballot, with the exception of the head of the list, who would be elected in an open vote.[89]

I was unable to find the minutes of the discussions that preceded these decisions, and it is not clear whether formal discussions were actually held in the party institutions. Most probably, the decision on these organizational changes was made by Begin himself, like many other decisions concerning party organization. Nor do I possess information as to whether this was the result of pressure from below and a desire to imbue these members with a sense of partnership, or whether Begin realized that his control would be more effective in larger forums that would all but preclude the formation of an opposition majority at the convention or in the Central Committee. Invariably, opposition to Begin originated with the veterans. This was the case in 1966–67, as we saw. The opposition was led by an NWF group of Betar and Irgun veterans—former Irgun senior commanders such as Shmuel Tamir, Amichai Paglin, and Eri Jabotinsky, and youngsters who were the offspring of veterans, such as Ehud Olmert and others. Ezer Weizman, who tried to seize control of Herut in 1972, as the next chapter will show, also drew heavily on the help of veterans such as Yosef Kremerman, Ptachiya Shamir, and others.

In a leader party, which lacked a mediating intermediate level, new members who were co-opted to party institutions gained a sense of belonging and partnership that was unavailable in machine-ruled parties. Evidently, they also did not partake of the frustration of the veterans who found themselves cut off from the party's decision-making process. As members of the new-immigrant generation, they derived immense satisfaction from their very ability to express themselves at conventions and in Central Committee meetings, something that was unfeasible in the veteran machine parties. A resident of the development town of Beit She'an, who was elected a delegate to the Herut convention after eight years as a member of Mapai, explained his feelings:

> Until I saw for myself the complete freedom of expression at the convention, I did not know what democracy meant. The truth is that I believed that the Herut movement also had the same system that I had seen on numerous occasions, according to which only those who were first in the kingdom could say what they felt. Even though I was a member of Mapai for eight years, I never once had the privilege of expressing my own ideas from its platform. On the other hand, in the Herut movement, I have already had the privilege of being on one of its platforms and expressing myself freely.[90]

Begin's speeches to Herut institutions increasingly resembled his speeches to mass rallies in town squares. They were not didactic addresses, directed at the rational faculty. They were more like performances aimed at the emotions, in which Begin the actor presented himself as the symbolizer of myths.

Social and economic issues were not paramount in Begin's speeches even after the mid-1960s. His constant theme remained the need for national pride, the claim that a nation with such a magnificent past could anticipate an equally magnificent future in the historic Land of Israel, and Begin's ability, as the commander of the Irgun and the successor to the great leader Ze'ev Jabotinsky, to lead the struggle for Greater Israel. These myths, which focused on foreign affairs and security, and not on socioeconomic questions, were what legitimized his leadership. Hence, it was vital that he preserve their centrality in Herut. Political developments played into his hands. In the wake of the Six Day War, which broke out a few months after he succeeded in eliminating the opposition from Herut, foreign affairs and security issues became the central questions in the political discourse between the parties. Beyond this, the new members who joined Herut, and the voters from the Oriental communities, who catapulted the party to power, were themselves victims of status problems not unlike those suffered by Betar veterans in the early years of the state. They, too, found Herut's status politics attractive, as we shall see in the next chapter.

8

The Road to Power

A New Political Discourse

On May 17, 1977, ten years after the events discussed in the previous chapter, as a result of which Herut remained outside the dominant party system prevailing in Israel, Herut won the election and Menachem Begin, its leader, became Prime Minister of Israel. Herut gained power while preserving allegiance to its mythic world view and to its leader who symbolized that world. With its victory, the dominance of the Labor party came to an end, along with the entire dominant party structure.

This surprising turn of events was not due to anything that happened in Herut, but stemmed from developments in the dominant party and from a series of events involving Israel's relations with its neighbors.

A dominant party, it will be recalled, is one that during a prolonged period obtains greater electoral support than any other party. This electoral phenomenon is bound up with developments on the cultural-ideological plane of the society in which the party functions: its principles, ideology, working methods, and style are accepted by the majority of the population, including those who refuse to vote for it. (See the discussion p. 1) The acceptance of the spiritual dominance of the Labor party by the other parties created what I termed a dominant party system. Herut, which did not acknowledge Labor's dominance, found itself outside this system that prevailed in Israel.

Mapai's spiritual dominance was also anchored in myths and symbols. These myths placed the party and its leaders at the center of the history of Zionism and the State of Israel. The myths held that it had been the leaders of Mapai, who by organizing pioneering settlements, establishing the Histadrut Labor Federation, and creating the Haganah, had built the new society, which it then led to political independence. The party was thus identified with the process of the state's establishment, and its leaders were perceived as the founding fathers of the new society. Myths, according to our definition, it should be recalled, represent ideas, not empirical facts. They may be grounded in reality, at least in part, but

151

there is no need to subject them to empirical tests. Drawing on these myths and symbols, Mapai recruited the support of the other parties in the dominant party system, and the support of the electorate. Being a bureaucratic machine party, as were the other Israeli parties except Herut, Mapai enlisted the support and loyalty of the various population groups both by the manipulation of the myths, and by responding to the material needs of these groups. Indeed, party policy was determined in large measure by the need to provide these material interests of the party faithful. Even though they supported the establishment of the kibbutz and the moshav—two forms of agricultural collective—and called on their members to settle in them in the name of the Zionist-Socialist myth, they set up trade unions, welfare institutions, and economic enterprises in the cities to which the majority of new immigrants flocked; and even though they inscribed on their banner the myth of economic equality, they increased the wage differentials between laborers on the one hand, and the clerks and members of the liberal professions, whose support they needed, on the other hand.[1]

As a ruling party, Mapai articulated a policy in both foreign-and-security and social-and-economic questions, the latter revolving around problems of immigrant absorption, welfare programs, supervision of the public and private sectors of the economy, and so forth. In Herut, it will be recalled, the party program consisted of myths dealing with foreign and security issues. Social and economic questions were not of primary concern to the leadership, and to the degree that they did have views on these subjects, they resembled those espoused by the General Zionists. They accepted the orientation of that bourgeois party that supported a free economy regime and disdained the bureaucratic interventionism that Socialist Mapai had foisted on the economy.

Until the Six Day War, Mapai conducted the political discourse on economic and social issues, as on foreign and security matters, primarily with the other parties of the left. At the core of the foreign policy debate with these parties was the question of relations with the Soviet Union and the United States. In contrast, in its discourse with Herut, Mapai vehemently rejected the latter's myths, scorned its claims that the State of Israel had been established thanks to the Irgun's military struggle against the British, and spurned its demand to realize the Jewish people's right to a state in the Mandate boundaries by means of military force. The Mapai leaders depicted Herut policy as irresponsible and certain to entangle Israel in a military adventure that might jeopardize its very existence. They opposed any further conquests, particularly after the Sinai Campaign of 1956, and they believed that their policy was judicious and responsible and guaranteed Israel's well-being and security.

At the same time, the Mapai hierarchy accepted that the country's military security was of central importance. This was the reason, the Mapai leader, David Ben-Gurion, explained, that he had always retained the Defense portfolio along with the premiership.[2] But in contrast to Herut, Mapai insisted that Israel's security was not contingent exclusively on military strength. World public opinion was equally important. The days were past, Ben-Gurion asserted in election campaign speeches, when historical problems could be resolved by military force. The reaction of the great powers, as well as of other countries, must be taken into account. "There is an Asian-African world that now consists of independent nations," he said in a 1959 election speech, "and they cannot abide military actions. Their opinion is important in the eyes of the nations of the world, and it is just as important to us."[3] Ben-Gurion stressed that security depended not only on the military but also on world sympathy. He was especially critical of Herut's demand to expand Israel's territory. The goal of the state was to establish peace with its neighbors, and "anyone who says that peace can be achieved with the Arabs on the basis of the historical borders knows that this is a deception."[4] Ben-Gurion hammered home the theme that the state's staying power was not measured in military strength but "in the total moral, professional and economic resilience of the nation."[5]

The pragmatic and realistic element in Israel's foreign policy was emphasized particularly by the second rank of the Mapai leadership, the intermediate group in the party. They cautioned against an emotional and impulsive approach like that of the Herut leader. They also demanded that their own party leadership pursue a policy informed by intelligent and calculated political judgments. A judicious and rational policy was called for even in reaction to the acts of the murder squads, who infiltrated across the border, they insisted. "Against the possible usefulness that security activity will bring Israel in the realm of Israeli-Arab relations, toward the improvement of routine security," Meir Bareli, party functionary, wrote on the eve of the 1955 elections, "we must calculate the damage that this causes in another sphere—in Israel's relations with the great powers." In contrast to the praise heaped on the IDF by Begin after the 1953 reprisal operation against the Jordanian village of Kibiyeh, in which local women and children were killed, Bareli explained that "hardly anyone disputes the severe harm that the Kibiyeh action caused to Israel's good name, its international prestige, and its relations with nations and states."[6] In the 1965 election campaign, another party activist pointed out that a change was occurring in superpower relations and that an era of dialogue between them was beginning that might bring in its wake the emergence of more rational trends in the Middle East. The Alignment (of Mapai and Ahdut Ha'avodah, formed in 1965) was capable of exploiting these developments, he noted, whereas "Gahal is not prepared, unfortunately, either emotionally or intellectually" for this development in international politics.[7] In the eyes of Mapai leaders and functionaries, the goal of foreign and security policy, which was to ensure Israel's safety and strive for peace, was composed of many elements, of which military considerations were merely a single factor, and not the central one at that.

At the same time, the Mapai leadership was aware of the country's longing for security and the desire "to teach a lesson" to the armed Arab squads that infiltrated across the border and attacked Jewish settlements. One school of thought has it that the IDF's reprisal policy—its cross-border raids against targets of these squads—stemmed less from purely military considerations than from a response to this desire for revenge. Military operations were indeed executed, but without entangling Israel in a war with the Arab states, which the majority of the nation did not want. As Dan Horowitz and Shlomo Ahronson explain, these reprisal raids were "an instrument in the internal struggle over Israeli foreign policy," that is, in the interparty political discourse.[8] This hypothesis gained credence from the fact that many of the most spectacular reprisals were carried out close to general elections.[9] It was a policy that Levy Eshkol, Ben-Gurion's successor as leader of Mapai and as Prime Minister, described as "a strong hand combined with judicious political behavior," and which assured Mapai—so its leaders believed—broad support for its foreign and security policy.[10]

The crucial test of the public's support for the policy of the hard hand and judicious political behavior was the government's decision following the Sinai Campaign, to withdraw from the Sinai Peninsula and the Gaza Strip to the armistice lines of 1949. Herut, which had backed the military incursion but opposed the withdrawal, could not drum up public support for its policy, whereas Mapai made gains in the elections that took place following the pullback.

The aftermath of the Six Day War saw a change in the Labor Party's policy on foreign affairs and security issues, which brought in its wake a change in the interparty political discourse on these subjects. It was Labor that annexed East Jerusalem and its environs to Israel and that set in motion the settlement policy in the occupied territories, which had the aim of extending Israel's borders. The new policy held that there was to be no return to the borders that existed on the eve of the Six Day War, not even in exchange for a peace treaty. In a previous book, I ascribed this shift in Labor Party policy to internal party developments.[11]

As I explained there, power struggles in the Mapai hierarchy since 1960 led to the resignation of its leader, Ben-Gurion. He was followed by many from the party's younger generation, who established a rival party, Rafi (Hebrew acronym for Israeli Workers List). Control in Mapai remained in the hands of an aging group of leaders who decided to set up the Alignment with Ahdut Ha'avodah. As we saw, these developments hastened the creation of Gahal. In the wake of Gahal's electoral failure, a crisis erupted in Herut—described in the previous chapter—that concluded with Begin's victory and that put an end to the attempts to expand the electoral bloc headed by Herut.

Although these events reduced the danger that a strong political camp would be formed that might have a serious shot at wresting the country's leadership from Mapai, the latter continued to be hampered by an internal problem that jeopardized its continued rule. The aging of the party's elite—which was closed to new forces—became an increasingly acute dilemma. While this elite was agonizingly trying to extricate itself from the situation in which it found itself, the whole system was jolted by a series of events that commenced in the middle of May 1967, less than three months after Begin's return as chairman of Herut.[12] Egypt suddenly closed the Straits of Tiran and moved a large part of its Army into Sinai. Under the terms of the understanding that had been reached after the Sinai Campaign between Israel and the Western powers, Egypt's actions constituted a threat to Israeli security and obliged the powers to intervene. However, the big powers showed no inclination to do anything of the sort. The aging elite was at a loss in the face of the crisis, while the Arab states drew encouragement from this display of impotence, and Syria and Jordan also massed forces along Israel's borders. In these weeks, the weakness of the elite in the face of the danger was glaringly apparent. The IDF, including the reserves, was deployed along the borders, and the whole country waited for the Israeli government to act—but in vain.

It was Menachem Begin who initiated the series of consultations with party leaders that culminated in the co-option of Rafi and Gahal to the government. Begin himself was appointed a Minister Without Portfolio, but the crucial appointment was that of Moshe Dayan, a Rafi leader, as Minister of Defense. The import of Dayan's appointment was a decision for war. The Six Day War, which broke out a few days later, ended in a dazzling Israeli military victory on all fronts. Israel conquered Sinai and the Gaza Strip from Egypt, the West Bank from Jordan, and the

Golan Heights from Syria. The conquest created a new political reality that necessitated a new policy.

The method of the Mapai elite to recapture the initiative and retain its rule was to merge with Ahdut Ha'avodah and the majority of Rafi. A younger generation, from these two parties, joined Mapai's elite, which hoped in this way to retain control in the country.

But the merger did not result in the emergence of a stable and strong elite at the head of the Labor Party. If an elite is to preserve its rule, it must be amenable to a constant and gradual co-option of new forces. The ongoing entry of new forces enables adaptation to changing situations, while the gradualness of the process allows for the integration of the new forces, and assures the continued cooperation and solidarity of the elite's members who learn to work together. Both processes are vital for the reproduction of an elite.

In our case, the elite was joined, all at once and in the midst of dramatic events, by groups of native-born representatives of what I termed the "post-revolutionary generation;" they were co-opted into the group of foreign-born veterans of the revolutionary generation that created the new state. The senior members of the post-revolutionary generation had devoted their productive years in the Haganah and the IDF to military activity, in which they had been engaged since adolescence. Throughout this entire period, they had been divorced from the practice of national party politics. To overcome this lacuna, a division of labor was decided upon between the two groups in the new party elite. The veterans retained responsibility for domestic and economic issues, while foreign affairs and security, realms in which the older generation had stumbled, were made the responsibility of the native-born generation. The latter's proficiency in security matters helped legitimate their authority and compensated the entire elite for the weakness of the veterans, which was revealed on the eve of the Six Day War.

The co-option of experts, technocrats, to the political elite is a common phenomenon in contemporary developed countries. It is a consequence of accelerated technological developments and the growing role of the state in giving direction to these developments. Technocrats, though, find it difficult to function within the framework of a cohesive, solidified political elite. The ability to override differences and curb the competitiveness of those in the elite, striving to reach the top, is a strong suit of professional politicians, who recognize that only in a group manifesting solidarity can they maintain their rule.[13] A political elite composed of professionals, who reached the top thanks to their professional expertise, studies suggest, is characterized by an absence of solidarity and by disagreements that hamper their ability to govern.[14] The research indicates that the encounter in a ruling group between technocrats and professional politicians engenders a new species of politician-technocrat who combines technical proficiency with the skills of the professional politician. In this manner, an elite is able to overcome internecine strife that could jeopardize its very existence.[15]

In the Israeli Labor Party, the entry of the technocrats into the elite following the Six Day War gave rise to a host of problems in the functioning of the elite. In addition to the flawed political socialization of this native-born generation (as I explained in *An Elite Without Successors*), the majority of the generation that entered the elite of the Labor Party were military technocrats. As C. Wright Mills notes in his book, *The Power Elite*, the nature of the activity, thought processes and behavior demanded of those who operate during many years within a military organization, causes difficulties in their adjustment to non-military structures. Even after taking off their uniform, he argues, they are unable to discard the military world view they acquired in the course of their lengthy service.[16]

A further impediment encountered by the former senior officers, who joined the political elite in the course of their adjustment to civilian modes of thought, was their immediate need—after the flagrant weakness shown by the remnants of the founding generation in the Six Day War crisis—to establish the legitimacy for their authority. As they had been active since adolescence in security matters, they cited this activity to legitimize their authority as political leaders, and defined military goals for themselves in their new position. In the wake of the conquests, they were united in their desire to demarcate borders that would be more readily defensible. As is often the case among experts, they disagreed about the optimal solution. Some insisted that a strip along the Jordan River must be retained, others spoke of holding the ridge line, and so forth. But as politicians, they were obliged to translate military discourse into political discourse. That discourse took shape in the course of the establishment of the Labor Party and during the period of coalition government with the Gahal bloc from the eve of the Six Day War until August 1970. This coalition partnership was based on the shared consensus of the two parties that a common effort was required to ensure Israel's security. Realizing that their desire to assure Israel's security by way of extending its territory and annexing East Jerusalem would be repudiated by the international community, they wished to secure maximum support among the Israeli public to help them withstand world pressure. This, they thought, could best be achieved by preserving a grand coalition. It was for this reason that Labor decided to continue the coalition with Gahal even after the former's impressive election victory in 1969. In those elections, the Labor alliance received 56 of the 120 Knesset seats against Gahal's 26.

For Menachem Begin, the Six Day War was a veritable gift from heaven. Immediately everyone in Herut united around the idea of Greater Israel, a concept that was shared by all Betar, Irgun, and Revisionist Party veterans. Even before the war ended, Yohanan Bader declared that the West Bank and Gaza Strip were part of the soil of the homeland and therefore must not be returned.[17] Immediately after the war, Menachem Begin told a festive joint meeting of the Central Committees of Herut and the Liberals: "Neither in our hearts nor on our lips can we imagine the possibility that a single inch of our land will be restored to alien rule." A resolution identical in wording to Begin's declaration was adopted by both bodies.[18]

"Life is more important than the standard of living," Yohanan Bader said on the eve of the 1973 elections. "Economic resilience, a solution for the country's domestic problems, the ingathering of the exiles, social justice are a *sine qua non* for our existence." But at this stage, Bader insisted, one single goal should be dominant, that of the liberation of the entire Eretz-Israel.[19]

In the new political discourse between the two coalition parties, it was agreed that Israel required new borders. But whereas the Labor Party leaders from the new generation placed military considerations at the center of the discussion, Herut remained loyal to its myths. It claimed the right to Eretz-Israel in its historic borders, which according to the myth were the boundaries of Mandate Palestine.

The joint participation in the government, which, both sides concurred, with the goal of preserving the fruits of the military victory, had the effect of drawing them closer on the political-military issue. In translating the military discourse into political discourse, the Labor Party leaders mixed military considerations with political considerations, and in the process adopted stands espoused by Herut. Thus, for example, Yigal Allon, a leading member of the new generation of Labor Party leaders, stated in election campaign speeches in 1969 that Israel's future borders would be determined on the basis of three principles: security needs, the historic affinity of the people of Israel for the Land of Israel, and the political possibilities.[20] Ben-Gurion, it will be recalled, was guided solely by the third criterion even on the question of borders. But the military technocrats-turned-politicians were preoccupied with the question of boundaries that would ensure military security. The wrangling among them on this issue continued until after the 1973 Yom Kippur War, when Labor Party institutions agreed to adopt the Allon Plan that called for the annexation of about 30 percent of the West Bank to Israel.[21]

To a certain extent, Herut, too, adjusted its stands to the new inter-party discourse. At first they demanded that the country's future borders be the historical boundaries. Demilitarization was suggested for the Sinai Peninsula, which was not part of this territory. However, as the discourse progressed and it emerged that Labor leaders advocated extending the borders to parts of Sinai for military reasons, Herut added its voice to this demand and asserted that the borders of the state must incorporate areas of Sinai.[22]

This new discourse affected the policies of both parties. It even penetrated the thinking of the remnants of the revolutionary generation. They, who did not recover from the trauma of the eve of the Six Day War, when they had led the country, also partook of the new discourse. Even Ya'akov Hazan, the leader of Mapam, an ideological Socialist party, assimilated this new discourse. In election campaign speeches he delivered in 1969, after his party had joined the Labor Party in an electoral alignment, Hazan asserted that the security border in the east must be the Jordan River. Likewise, "we will not leave the Golan Heights," "in Sinai we will not return to the former border," "we will not pull out of the Gaza Strip," and "obviously we will not leave Jerusalem."[23]

Still, Labor did not completely jettison the pragmatic elements that characterized its policy during the years when the revolutionary elite ruled. This difference between Labor and Herut became apparent in the dispute that flared up between the two coalition partners in August 1970, when the U.S. asked Israel to assent in principle to a withdrawal on all fronts, including the West Bank, as part of the terms of a future peace treaty. Arab readiness for peace did not appear to be at hand, Labor Party leaders noted, and this facilitated their agreement in principle. Menachem Begin, however, refused to accept withdrawal of any kind, even of a declaratory character, from the whole Land of Israel. When the Labor Party gave its assent in principle, Begin decided to leave the government.

Begin's refusal to agree to withdrawal, even though void of practical ramifications, stems from the essence of Herut politics, as I described it in the previous chapters. Yoram Lichtenstein, a Herut activist, thought that Begin feared that a ceding in principle of Greater Israel, even if this had no concrete applications, would detract from his influence over his followers. Lichtenstein spoke of the apprehension that "he would lose

something of his charisma in the eyes of his faithful."[24] My own interpretation is that what was involved was an inability to compromise the
myth he symbolized and which constituted the legitimization for his
authority in the eyes of his Herut supporters. Once more, he was not
guided by electoral considerations or a desire for popularity among the
public at large. In public opinion polls, 80 percent of Israelis expressed
their desire for the continuation of the unity government.[25]

Begin's decision to leave the government sparked a series of events
that recalled the crisis in Herut discussed at length in the previous
chapter. Again an internal opposition sprang up urging that the party
adopt a pragmatic approach, which would enable its continued participation in the government, and which tried to take over the party. Some
members of the Liberal Party, disappointed in the pullout from the
government, attempted to bring about Gahal's dissolution.

The Liberal Party leadership put forward a proposal in this spirit to
the Knesset faction following the breakup of the coalition with Labor.
The proposal was debated in the faction, and narrowly rejected; the
leadership decided not to pursue the initiative. Elimelech Rimalt, at this
time the deputy of party leader Yosef Sapir, said that the leadership had
not wished to submit to the party institutions a proposal that was liable
to trigger a serious dispute. Rimalt attributes the opposition to the
dissolution of Gahal in the Liberal Party to the fact that there was broad
acceptance of the Greater Israel idea in the party, but primarily to
electoral considerations. It was clear to everyone that if the party stood
separately in the elections, it would invite defeat.[26]

A more serious attempt to revise Gahal policy was undertaken in
Herut itself. On this occasion the opposition in the party was led by Ezer
Weizman.[27] Weizman, a former commander of the Air Force, was Chief
of Operations when he retired from the IDF and joined Herut after the
1969 elections, having secretly been promised a ministerial post by the
party. He served as Minister of Transport in the unity government.
Immediately after Gahal left the government—a move Weizman opposed—Begin appointed him chairman of the Herut Executive. The
appointment was a surprising move on Begin's part; until then, as will
be recalled, he had named only his close associates to senior administrative positions. Weizman's meteoric rise in Herut was extremely unusual,
and indeed not altogether to Begin's liking. The explanation offered in
Herut to Begin's assent was that he was enthralled by Weizman's high
military rank. "Herut has always admired and continues to admire the
IDF and its commanders," Mordechai Zippori, himself a high ranking
career officer who was to serve as a minister under Begin, noted years

later.[28] In addition, Begin's position and activity as a minister may have caused him to relax his close monitoring of party affairs, and thus enabled a group of activists in the Tel Aviv branch to evince a degree of independence that was unusual in Herut. It was they who initiated Weizman's entry into Herut and his simultaneous appointment as a minister.

Begin's momentary relaxation of oversight deluded Weizman and his supporters into thinking that they could take over the party. This opposition group, which included many from the Herut apparatus, a large number of young people, and the Tel Aviv group that had brought Weizman to Herut, was, like the opposition of 1966, united in its preference for a more pragmatic political orientation. Weizman, too, believed that in politics, influence was acquired by sitting in the government and not outside it.[29] The new group's mode of operation also resembled that of the previous opposition. Weizman exploited his position as chairman of the Executive to bolster his strength through the election of delegates to the convention. There, his people constituted the majority in the Standing Committee and drew up the list of new Central Committee members, dropping a few of Begin's veteran followers along the way. Weizman saw to it that his backers would command a majority in the new Central Committee.

Only at this stage did Begin's assistants grasp the danger and moved to avert it. Begin went into action immediately. As a first step, he summoned the chairman of the Standing Committee, Ptachiya Shamir, an Irgun veteran, and tried to induce him, in one of his famous tête-à-tête talks, to change the composition of the proposed Central Committee. When this failed, he appeared before the committee and in a dramatic speech accused his adversaries of fomenting a conspiracy against him. He further charged that they were concerning themselves with internal issues when they should be engaged first and foremost in the struggle for the integrity of Eretz-Israel. This was also the focus of his address to the convention plenum. It had been essential to leave the government, Begin explained, in order to prevent the partition of Eretz-Israel. Had they stayed in the government, the body, Herut, would have remained, but the soul would have gone out of it.[30]

This time Begin placed himself openly at the head of his associates and called them the "Begin group." To this he added the threat that if his proposal for the makeup of the Central Committee were not accepted, he would not serve as movement chairman. This was enough to remove the wind from the opposition's sails. No organized body such as the NWF faced him this time. His motion for the composition of the Central

Committee was adopted unanimously by the Standing Committee and by the entire convention. Weizman resigned as executive chairman: he, too, had discovered that the party was democratic as long as it did not counter Begin's will. In the event of a clash between the will of the active members and the will of the leader, Weizman told the press, the leader decided and not the democratic process.[31]

After the convention, Begin named himself executive chairman in place of Weizman, and saw to it that the very first meeting of the new Central Committee approved his proposal to remove from the executive all those who had had the effrontery to suggest changes in the makeup of the party institutions without first consulting with him.[32] Since this time, the struggle had been waged behind closed doors and not on the convention floor, Begin declared his victory and his absolute rule in Herut in an article he published in Ma'ariv. The opposition had fallen apart as soon as he went into action, he wrote, but even if the dispute between himself and Weizman—"who doesn't even have platoons behind him"—had reached the convention floor, the opposition would not have obtained more than 10–15 percent of the votes.[33] Begin had achieved a total rout. Once more it was shown that the road to pragmatic politics was blocked by him.

These events in Herut led many observers to write off the party as a viable alternative to Labor's rule. Shmuel Schnitzer, the editor of Ma'ariv, wrote after the convention that an opposition was needed, and opposition to the Labor Party had good prospects of succeeding, but Herut was incapable of threatening Labor's dominance because "a psychological barrier exists which dissuades many people from joining Herut. What can one do if, between the opposition which seeks a party, and the only party that could conceivably form that opposition, lie a thousand memories of old quarrels which the Herut movement joyfully renews every time the danger arises that they will be consigned to oblivion."[34] Schnitzer's thousand memories are, in our language, the myths of Herut that cemented the activists' loyalty to their leader, but put off the rest of the population.

Herut's inability to divest itself of its myths and to revitalize its leadership, brought Schnitzer to the conclusion that Herut had no chance of ever attaining power. "Menachem Begin triumphed," Schnitzer wrote. "His party will remain cohesive, small, faithful. No one can conquer it from within, and it will conquer nothing outside. Everyone in it will be devoted to the traditional leadership and no one will dare be too gifted, too popular, too independent. Everyone will take the place assigned him in the hierarchy, and no one will stand out or arouse admiration or frighten the old guard. It will rule forever, and never will it attain power."[35]

This pessimistic assessment did not deter the groups that decided, on the eve of the 1973 elections, to join a broad electoral bloc headed by Menachem Begin, the leader of Herut. The Likud, as the new body was known (Hebrew for "unity" or "cohesion") was formed through the co-option to Gahal of the group that had left Herut in 1967 and had itself split into two Knesset factions, along with a group of Rafi activists who refused to return to the Labor Party. They were influenced by the fact that in the new political discourse, Herut was no longer stigmatized as a radical party whose policy was said to be injudicious and irresponsible. Both central parties now adduced stands that were considered legitimate in the new political discourse. Moreover, Herut was now the guardian of the status quo that had emerged in the wake of the Six Day War, while Labor was ready to make concessions. But this assessment was evidently not yet shared by the electorate. Public opinion polls conducted after the establishment of the Likud in September 1973, indicated no more than a minor shift toward the new bloc.[36] The new immigrants from the Oriental communities, who had come to Israel after the establishment of the state, did not share the memories of the veteran community that Schnitzer believed prevented them from supporting Menachem Begin the commander of the Irgun. But in view of the continued antagonism toward Herut among the veterans, the more recent immigrants probably needed some additional convincing before they dared cast their ballot for the opposition Herut party. Here the hand of war intervened again.

The elections were scheduled for October 23, 1973, but were postponed until December 31 because on October 6 the Yom Kippur War erupted. This war caught the IDF off guard. The Egyptians and the Syrians surprised the Israeli defensive deployment, and the IDF was forced to retreat. The war exacted a very heavy toll in Israeli casualties, and ended only after the Americans organized an emergency arms airlift to the IDF. In the terms of the new political discourse, in which the two parties argued about which espoused a better policy to ensure Israel's security against its foes, it is not surprising that many voters abandoned Labor, which had pledged security and brought the Yom Kippur War, and voted Likud. As against 39.6 percent of the voting public who cast their ballot for Labor after the war (a decline of about 7 percent), 30.2 percent voted for the Likud (an increase of about 7 percent).[37] A party is dominant as long as it gains a significantly greater number of votes than any other party. In this election, the Labor Party lost its dominance. True, it was still able to form a coalition, but it encountered considerable problems in doing so. The first Labor coalition government of Prime Minister Yitzhak Rabin obtained the support of only sixty-one Knesset Members (out of 120). The dominant party structure had come to an end.

The Parties and Their Constituencies

At the end of the previous section, I attributed the change on the behavior of the voters, who abandoned the Labor Party (the Alignment) in 1973 and voted for Herut (the Likud), to a process whose beginnings lay in the new political discourse that made Herut a legitimate interlocutor, and which continued with the Yom Kippur War. In the language of the new discourse, Labor had difficulty in proposing an interpretation that would absolve it of blame for the military problems encountered by Israel, because this war broke out when the borders were secure in the terms that were accepted by both major partners to the discourse. Therefore it was punished by the voters, who turned to a party that proposed an alternative for Israeli security.

Voter behavior is not the subject of this study. It belongs to a different sphere of analysis, requires the presentation of different research questions, and the examination of different data. The voters' degree of political involvement differs from that of party activists and party leaders. An examination of that involvement requires an analysis of the system of relations between individual persons, their pyschology, their political socialization, and the reciprocal influences between them and the broader economic, social, and political system.

Nonetheless, Herut's success in attaining power cannot be understood without reference to its new voters. To this end, I turned to the literature that deals with voter behavior in Israel. The problem is compounded by the fact that we have no studies of voter behavior prior to the 1969 elections, when Asher Arian conducted the first election study in Israel.[38]

All the studies conducted since 1969 support the thesis that the central factor underlying the Likud's rise was the vote of the Oriental Jews, who abandoned the Alignment in favor of the Likud. The analysts offer a wealth of explanations for this turn of events. Some argue that the Orientals are members of a lower class and therefore voted for a party that was able to cast itself as the defender of their interests, in contrast to the establishment Alignment. Others speak about a feeling of ethnic deprivation among the Orientals, who blamed the ruling party for their low status in the Israeli society. Still others ascribe their behavior to the political culture they brought with them from their countries of origin, which was traditional not secular, paternalistic, and authoritarian not democratic—hence they responded positively to a leader party. The culture and low social status of the Orientals, others maintain, spurred them to hate the Arabs and support a hawkish approach in Israeli's relations with the Arab states. Shamir and Arian, who examined these conjectures, showed that they were unsupported postulates, hence they remain mere speculations. They themselves hold that the vote is bound up with Israel's political history, Mapai's role in immigrant absorption, and subsequently in the enfeeblement of the party apparatus that reduced the new immigrants' dependence on the party. They point, further, to the legitimization accorded Herut when it was co-opted into the government and the rise of nationalism following the Six Day War, as elements that brought the Orientals' vote to the Likud. But they admit that the data in their possession are insufficient to substantiate these ideas too.[39]

What all these studies have in common is the assumption that the influence of political factors, such as political elites and parties, on the political behavior of Israeli voters is negligible. Michal Shamir, summing up the changes in voter behavior after the 1969 elections, which brought about the rise of the Likud, asserts that it was the electorate and not the political elite that initiated the change.[40]

I do not accept this assumption. There is no doubt that a climate of protest among voters against the dominant party admits of pyschological and sociopsychological explanations. Their vote was also influenced by economic and social factors. But the manner in which the protest is given expression in the political arena by the electorate is in great measure influenced by the behavior of the parties and the political elites. I would agree with the conclusion of Rainer Lepsius, the German sociologist who studied the dramatic changes in the electoral balance of power among the parties in the final years of the Weimer Republic, that the role of the parties themselves is a crucial factor in these changes. Parties can be more radical or less radical than their voters, more loyal to the regime or less loyal; but the willingness of the voters to support radical parties is in large measure dependent on the parties' ability to absorb the protest and how successful they are in providing a plausible interpretation of the existing situation. The reverse is equally true: the ability of moderate parties to retain their constituencies is in large measure dependent on how successful the radical parties are in offering a more convincing interpretation of the existing situation. Herein, I believe, also lies the explanation for the developments in Israel in the 1970s.[41]

Naturally, this hypothesis must be examined with the aid of public opinion surveys and election studies, and these, as mentioned, have existed only since 1969. I have tried to fill in the lacunae from the pre-1969 period by drawing on the voting data published by the Central Bureau of Statistics, and surveys that appeared in the press during election campaigns.[42] My findings must be considered provisional until a systematic examination is made of the existing data. This provisional examination reveals that Oriental Jews constituted the majority of Herut voters since the elections of 1955. They accounted for some 55–60 percent of all votes cast for Herut. However, they constituted only 25–30 percent of all voters from the Oriental communities; a far higher proportion of votes was cast by the veteran Orientals, who lived in the country before the establishment of the state, than by those who arrived after 1948. The majority of the Orientals, of both the veterans and the new-immigrant communities, some 55–60 percent, voted for Mapai, and another 10 percent for the National Religious Party, at that time Mapai's loyal ally. This percentage of Oriental voters for Mapai exceeded the proportion among the Ashkenazi community, most of whom cast their ballots for other parties.

This behavior of the Oriental communities remained stable until the elections of 1973. Shifts of voting patterns from one party to another occurred principally among persons of European extraction, although they rarely crossed the line between Mapai and the other veteran parties, and Herut. As a result of this behavior of the two populations, Herut was a party of considerable electoral stability until 1973.

The period since 1969 has seen an abundance of studies and surveys on voter behavior. They show clearly that in the 1973 elections a dramatic change occurred in Israeli voting patterns. This change took place among the Orientals. Whereas in 1969 fewer than 30 percent of the Orientals had voted for Gahal, in 1973 the Likud obtained more than 50 percent of their votes. And the reverse: in 1969, more than 50 percent of Orientals voted for the Labor Party, whereas in 1973 only about 30 percent of them did so.[43] The date of the shift can be pinpointed precisely. Polls conducted in September 1973, following the establishment of the Likud but before the Yom Kippur War, showed only a minor shift in this population from the Alignment to the Likud.[44] It follows that the immediate cause of the shift was the war.

We have not yet answered the question of why it was the Orientals who punished Labor, whereas few among the European population followed suit. Studies in other countries show that new immigrants do not readily vote for radical anti-establishment parties. Immigrants wish to integrate themselves into the new society, not change it.[45] The new,

The Road to Power   167

post-Six Day War political discourse removed from Herut the stigma of radicalism, but another war was needed to induce the immigrants and their children to abandon the dominant party. As for the veteran European settlers, even after the war they were still deterred by the myths of Herut, Schnitzer's "thousand memories of old quarrels."

Only after abandoning Labor and voting for the Likud did the Orientals also embrace the myths of the Likud. The shift of Orientals to the Likud, which was dramatic in 1973, continued in the 1977 elections. But only in the 1981 and 1984 polls did Michal Shamir find a correlation between the stands on foreign affairs and security issues expressed by Likud voters from the Oriental communities, and the stands espoused by the Likud on these subjects.[46] This reflected the institutionalization of the electoral change.

Herut's successful absorption of these masses of new voters without the party's modifying its party leadership structure, its system of myths and symbols, or its political style, is explained, I maintain, by the fact that Herut's status politics proved congenial to its new members and the voters from the Oriental communities. Their mobility in the social system was also blocked, and they, too, were deprived of the feeling of partnership in the new society which they longed for, as had been the lot of former Betar and Irgun activists in the early years of the state. Advancement in the public bureaucracy, the central track of mobility in the Israeli society, was closed to them, too, as I explained in my previous book, *An Elite Without Successors:*

> In the years in which the new immigrants and their children underwent the socialization processess . . . the rate of growth of the bureaucracy, which had been extremely rapid in the first years of the state, slowed down. True, in the 1950s and 1960s we still find a rapid proliferation of the liberal professions. But to enter the liberal professions or advance one's standing in the bureaucracy, a high school ʲmatriculation diploma was no longer enough: university degrees were now required. In this realm, the veteran population held a decided advantage over the recent immigrants. The obtaining of a degree entailed a good deal of preparation and a forgoing of material rewards over a lengthy period. Many of the new-immigrant families were not capable of making this effort. Their economic situation precluded it, and their culture had not readied them for it . . . Fundamentally, the competition to acquire suitable certificates and for professional promotion

in the bureaucracy, is an individual competition. In Israel it became a conflict between social groups. The fact that the majority of the veteran population was of European extraction, while the new groups originated primarily from Asia and Africa, imbued the conflict with an additional dimension. The cultural and social differences of the countries of origin were translated into ethnic differences, with the Europeans defining themselves as Ashkenazis and defining those from Africa and Asia as Sephardis. The veteran established Ashkenazi majority accorded less prestige to the ethnic status of the Sephardis, and the low status, which was an ascribed status, rendered it difficult for the latter to liberate themselves from their inferior status.[47]

The timing of the switch of the Oriental voters from Labor to Herut was dictated by the occurrence of the Yom Kippur War and its consequences. Only after Herut's electoral victory did the new-immigrant Oriental Jews realize that in casting their ballots for Herut they had transferred their struggle for status in the new society to the political sphere. In the process, they adopted the myths of the Likud and transformed them into their own status symbols, thereby institutionalizing their tie to them. Herut's political style, which drew on the myths to build a world of appearances, in which politicians, speaking at public assemblies and utilizing their rhetorical skills to evoke an unrealistic world that gives the masses a feeling of importance and centrality in the society, was also well-suited to the party's new supporters. Thus, Menachem Begin came to power without forgoing his credo, his party's structure, or his absolute rule in the party.

Epilogue
Status Politics

In this study of the Herut Party, I followed its founders, leaders, and activists from the time they began their activity in Betar-Poland until they came to power in Israel, in 1977. The political socialization undergone by the majority of them during their formative period in Poland, influenced the party's structure and world view. Theirs was a leader party, which operated without an apparatus and without a program, unlike other parties, which used such tools to help them win the support of various population groups. Herut enlisted the loyalty of its members and supporters through myths that the founding group brought with them from Poland.

This book does not deal with the developments in Herut after it attained power and became a governing party. Herut as a governing party was not identical to Herut in opposition. Its victory changed the entire political structure in Israel. It brought an end to the dominant party system in Israel and brought into being a multi-party system centered around two ruling parties, each of which is capable of forming a government under its leadership. But the major impact of Herut after it became a ruling party lies in the realm of the workings and style of Israeli politics.

In the early years of the party's existence, many among its intelligentsia were convinced that a precondition for its coming to power in Israel was its accommodation to the existing party structure and its style of politics, namely, its adoption of the modes of operation of a machine party. The road to power in Israel, Kalman Katznelson argued, entailed inculcating in Herut activists "practice and expertise in adminstering large apparati, which the other parties acquired back in the Yishuv period."[1] When Begin set up a leader party without an apparatus, Katznelson was certain that such a party could not rule in the country. Even if it were to score an election victory—a possibility even without a party machine—Herut would not be able to keep a grip on the reins of power. In the absence of an apparatus, the Herut leaders became "performers and speakers who make a successful appearance on the Knesset podium and on the platforms of public rallies . . . [but] who will turn out to be pitiful and unproductive when they move from the arena of speeches to the arena of action." Katznelson predicted that "within hours of Herut's possible attainment of power, chaos will reign in the country, and in short order Herut will have to step down under the pressure of outraged and disappointed masses. The slightest interference by the Histadrut sector will suffice to make a Herut government collapse like a house of cards."[2]

This prediction was not borne out by events. The opposite occurred: the bureaucratic politics of Mapai and the other political parties embraced Herut's style of politics. These developments I attributed to the following developments. One was flaws in the process of reproducing the elite in the Labor Party that enfeebled its party apparatus. Equally important were the changes that occurred in the political discourse after the Six Day War. The myths of Herut dovetailed with the new discourse, and under their impact the entire political discourse revolved around myths and symbols. These developments were what paved the way for Herut's transformation into a ruling party without the need to revise its party structure or modify its myths and its working style. But were it not for the dramatic events that were visited on Israel, notably the Six Day War and the Yom Kippur War, it is doubtful whether we would have witnessed the same dramatic reversal in voter behavior that brought Herut to power.

In Israel, as in other democracies, voters are loyal to their parties. Political sociologists maintain that following a formative period in a democratic regime, in which these voter loyalties are shaped, they will be preserved over time. In the 1960s, scholars believed that once the party system had been shaped, it entered a period of quiescense in which the movement of voters from one party to another was minimal.[3] More recently, researchers have cast doubts on whether voter behavior is truly marked by such immobility, though they do not gainsay that the voters' loyalty to their parties is firm, but rather that shifts in voting patterns are not sharp and rapid but slow and incremental.[4] At the same time, it is recognized that powerful shocks to the political system can bring upheavals and forge new loyalties between groups of voters and political parties. The literature uses the term "realignment" for such redeployments among the electorate.[5] A realignment of this kind occurred in Israel in the 1973 and 1977 elections.

I attributed the cause of this realignment in the electorate to developments within the parties and to the relations between them. The shift of the Oriental voters from Labor to Herut was an unexpected consequence of the parties' behavior. It was they who caused the struggle for social status between the Orientals and the Europeans to move from the social to the political system. Thus, politics became status politics.

The politics of Herut, which emulated the modes of thought and the political behavior of the European radical right and the national groups that ruled Poland in the interwar period, was from the outset status politics. This form of politics was apposite for Betar and Irgun veterans whose social progress and participation in the political system was blocked by the dominant party. They were joined in the 1970s by the Oriental communities whose advancement and social integration were similarly stymied in the Israeli society. When an alliance was forged within the political system between Betar and Irgun veterans and the masses from the Oriental communities, and they adopted the myths of Herut as their status symbols, Herut became a ruling party. In the wake of this development, a similar process occurred among those of European extraction who possessed a higher social status in the Israeli society. They, too, shifted the struggle to maintain their social status to the political arena and intensified their support for the Labor Party.[6] The myths of the Labor Party, and their pioneer-fighter leaders, progenitors of the kibbutz, the Haganah military underground, and the IDF, who symbolized those myths, became the status symbols of this group and an expression of their demand to preserve their status in the social system.

This debate over myths between the two parties in the political system, was an expression of the competition between the two groups for their standing within the social system. In this debate, each group engaged in glorifying its own myths and disparaging those of the rival group. Nor is a debate over myths conducive to negotiation or compromise. Instead of bureaucratic politics conducted via committees in which agreements are discussed and sought through negotiation and compromise, the debate becomes the politics of the piazza. The politicians transform politics into a performance in which they try to fire up the audience through a dramatic presentation of a mythic world that appeals to emotion, not reason. The new political discourse between the parties became what anthropologists call a "symbolic discourse." In discourse of this kind there is no need for an empirical examination of myths and symbols. Moreover, if a discourse of this kind is based on knowledge, Dan Sperber explains, no great intellectual effort is invested in it. And, "The intellectual effort expended is disproportionate and poorly applied."[7] Thus, it was that Herut perceived the idea of historic Eretz-Israel, and thus that Labor perceived the idea of "secure borders."

This emotional symbolic discourse conducted between the politicians and their audience, has foisted itself on the whole Israeli political system. It has penetrated ruling institutions, the Knesset, and other public bodies, and even Cabinet meetings. With the aid of the media, all these bodies have become amenable to discourse conducted directly between the politicians and the public at large. Instead of substantive discussion and a search for practical policy, a performance takes place in which the politicians arouse the public's sympathy by evoking the myths they symbolize. In the process, questions of the practical administration of the state and its institutions are pushed aside, and foreign affairs and security issues, the very core of the politicians' interest, take on a dramatic and mythic dimension. In this same manner, the political system has lost its ability to articulate a realistic policy.

Notes

Introduction

1. Yonathan Shapiro, *The Historical Ahdut Ha'avodah: The Power of Political Organization*, Tel Aviv, Am Oved, 1975; *Democracy in Israel*, Ramat Gan, Massada, 1978; *An Elite Without Successors*, Tel Aviv, Sifriat Poalim, 1984.

2. Maurice Duverger, *Political Parties*, New York, John Wiley & Sons, (1955), pp. 308–9.

3. Yonathan Shapiro, "The End of a Dominant Party System," in A. Arian, ed., *The Election in Israel–1977*, Jerusalem, Jerusalem Academic Press, 1980, pp. 23–38.

4. Shapiro, *Democracy in Israel*, Ramat Gan, Massada, 1978, pp. 102–8.

5. For example: Renzo de Felice, *Interpretations of Fascism*, Harvard Univ. Press, Cambridge Mass., 1977; Walter Laqueur, ed., *Fascism: A Research Guide*, Berkeley, University of California Press, 1976; Richard Hamilton, *Who Voted for the Nazis?* Princeton, N.Y., Princeton Univ. Press, 1982; George Mosse, *The Nationalization of the Masses*, N.Y., Howard Fertig, 1975; George Mosse, *Masses and Man*, N.Y., Howard Fertig, 1980; Stanley G. Paine, *Fascism*, Madison, Wisconsin, Wisconsin Univ. Press, 1980; Noel O'Sullivan, Fascism 1983, London, J.M. Dent & Sons Ltd.

6. Gino Germani, *Authoritarianism, Fascism, and National Populism*, New Brunswick NJ., Transaction Publ., 1978. On Peron's movement, see also: David Rock, ed., *Argentina in the 20th Century*, Univ. of Pittsburgh. Pittsburgh Pa., 1975; Jeanne Kirkpatrick, *Leader and Vanguard in Mass Society: A Study of Peronist Argentina*, Cambridge Mass. M.I.T Press, 1971; Robert J. Alexander, *Juan Domingo Peron: A History*, Boulder Co., Westview Press, 1979.

7. On this subject the works of George Mosse are especially interesting: see note 5.

8. On this subject, see: Raymond Firth, *Symbols, Public and Private*, Ithaca, N.Y. Cornell Univ. Press 1951; Edmund Leach, *Political Systems of Highland Burma*, Atlantic City, N.J., Humanities Press, 1954; Abner Cohen, *Two Dimensional Man* Berkeley Ca., Univ. of California Press, 1974; Dan Sperber, *Rethinking Symbolism*, N.Y. Cambridge Univ. Press, 1975.

9. Joseph R.Gusfield, *Symbolic Crusade* (Champaign Ill., University of

Illinois Press, 1963; Daniel Bell ed., *The Radical Right,* Garden City, NY, Doubleday 1953; Seymour M. Lipset, *Political Man,* Baltimore Md., John Hopkins University Press, 1960.

10. Sperber, *Rethinking Symbolism,* NY. Cambridge Univ. Press, 1975, p. 6.

11. Mosse, *Nazism,* New Brunswick NJ., Transaction Pub., 1978, p. 36.

Chapter One

1. One good political biography of Jabotinsky was written by his friend and close adviser Joseph Schechtmann. Notwithstanding the author's close relations with his hero, this is an important and valuable work: Joseph Schechtmann, *The Jabotinsky Story,* 3 volumes, Tel Aviv Karni 1959. Recently, another book on Jabotinsky has been published (in Hebrew): Raphaela Bilsky Ben-Hur, *Every Individual a King: The Social and Political Thought of Ze'ev Jabotinsky,* Tel Aviv, Dvir, 1988. The author says that "the discussion is solely of Jabotinsky's philosophy through use of the tools of research and the method of political thought." It is not accepted today to set before the reader a person's thought "as a single package" and to "construct it" by means of passages from his writings while completely ignoring his personality, life history, and activity as a political being and a party leader. It is therefore difficult to make use of this book to gain an understanding of Jabotinsky the politician.

2. See Matityahu Mintz, *Ber Borochov—The First Circle, 1900–1966,* Tel Aviv, Tel Aviv University Press, 1976. This intellectual effort played an important part in enlisting the support of Jews from the intelligentsia for Zionism in the period before the Russian Revolution.

3. Z. Jabotinsky, "Obscurantist" *Writings: Nation and Society,* p. 107. Jerusalem, Eri Jabotinsky, 1947–53.

4. Walter Laqueur, *A History of Zionism* N.Y. Schocken Books 1972, p. 381.

5. Z. Jabotinsky, "Letter on Autonomism," in Moshe Bella, ed., *The World of Jabotinsky: His Statements and Principles of His Doctrine,* Tel Aviv, Dfussim, 1972, p. 37. See also Nurit Gertz, "The Few Against the Many," *Jerusalem Quarterly* 30 (1984), 94–104.

6. Z. Jabotinsky, *"Homo Homini Lupus",* in *Writings: Nation and Society,* Jerusalem, Eri Jabotinsky, p. 265.

7. Z. Jabotinsky, *Writings: Autobiography,* p. 39.

8. Noel O'Sullivan, *Fascism,* London, J.M. Dent & Sons Ltd., 1983, p. 70.

9. John Plamenatz, "Two Types of Nationalism," in Eugene Kamenka, ed., *Nationalism: The Nature and Evolution of an Idea,* London, E. Arnold, 1976, pp. 23–36.

10. On these organizations and groups, see Peter F. Sugar, ed., *Native Fascism in the Successor States*, Columbus Ohio, C.E. Merrill, 1971.

11. Richard Hamilton, *Who Voted for Hitler*, Princeton N.Y. Princeton Univ. Press., 1982, 461.

12. See Jabotinsky's articles in *Doar Hayom*, 14 and 22 Sept., 1930.

13. O'Sullivan, *Fascism*, passim.

14. Joachim Fest, *Hitler*, London, Penguin Books 1982, p. 271.

15. K. Katznelson, *Conquerors in Distress*, Tel Aviv, Anach, 1983, p. 107.

16. Jabotinsky, *The Idea of Betar*. Tel Aviv, Betar Headquarters, 1934, p. 17.

17. Jabotinsky, "His Children and Ours" in *Writings: The Way to the State* Jerusalem, Eri Jabotinsky, p. 82.

18. Abba Sikra, "From the Notebook of a Fascist," *Herut*, 18 March 1949.

19. On the explanations of his followers, see Eri Jabotinsky, *My Father Ze'ev Jabotinsky*, Jerusalem Steimatsky, p. 102, and the testimony of Binyamin Eliav, Oral Documentation Center, Institute of Contemporary Jewry, Hebrew University of Jerusalem (hereafter: *Oral Documentation*). On the opportunistic explanation, see Laqueur, A History of Zionism, N.Y., Schocken Books, 1972, p. 365.

20. Stanley G. Payne, *Fascism* Madison Wisc. Univ. of Wisconsin Press, 1980, pp. 15-17. Also Juan Linz, "Some Notes Toward a Comparative Study of Fascism in Sociological Historical Perspectives," in Laqeuer ed., *Fascism: A Research Guide*, Berkeley Ca., University of California Press, 1976, p. 29.

21. Speech at the founding convention of the NZO in Vienna, September 7, 1935 in Moshe Bella, ed., *The World of Jabotinsky*, Tel-Aviv, Dfussim, 1972, p. 167.

22. Hamedina (Warsaw), 17 March, 1939.

23. "Zionist NEP" (1927), *Writings: The Way to the State*, 121-130; "On the Zionist NEP (A Second Time): (1928), ibid., 293-302. In her book Bilsky Ben-Hur reveals links between Jabotinsky's thought and liberal thinkers but makes no reference to other sources that influenced his ideas. As a result, she describes the economic arrangements proposed by Jabotinsky in the article cited as "innovative." Bilsky Ben-Hur, Tel Aviv, Dvir, 1988, p. 258.

24. Renzo de Felice, *Fascism*. Cambridge Mass., Harvard Univ. Press, 1976, p. 70.

25. Jabotinsky, "Class Problems," in *Writings: The Way to the State*, Jerusalem, Eri Jabotinsky Press, pp. 171-180; "Social Redemption," in *Writings: Notes*, Jerusalem, Eri Jabotinsky, pp. 293-302.

26. *Doar Hayom*, 23 October, 1930.

27. NZO convention in Prague, August 1930, according to Joseph Schechtman, II, 186.

28. Jabotinsky, "At the Fireside," in *Writings: The Way to the State*, p. 94.

29. *Doar Hayom*, 9 Nov., 1930.

30. John Breully, *Nationalism and the State*, Chicago Ill., Chicago Univ. Press, 1985, p. 344; Payne, *Fascism*, Madison Wisconsin, Univ. of Wisconsin Press, 1980, p. 14.

31. O'Sullivan, *Fascism*, London, J. M. Dent & Sons Ltd., 1983, p. 157.

32. Jabotinsky, "Revolt of the Elderly," in *Writings: Nation and Society*, Jerusalem, Eri Jabotinsky, p.232.

33. Testimony of Ya'akov Weinschel, *Oral Documentation*.

34. Schechtmann, The Jabotinsky Story, Tel Aviv, Karni, 1959, II, p. 186.

35. *Doar Hayom*, 11 Nov., 1929.

36. Schechtmann, The Jabotinsky Story, Tel Aviv, Karni, 1959, II, p. 205.

37. Katznelson, *Conquerors in Distress*, Tel Aviv, Anach, 1983, p. 111.

38. Schechtmann, The Jabotinsky Story, Tel Aviv, Karni, 1959, II, p. 204.

39. Letter from Jabotinsky to Israel Rozov, November 9, 1933, in Moshe Bella, ed., *The World of Jabotinsky*, 161.

40. Schechtmann, The Jabotinsky Story, Tel Aviv, Karni, 1959, II, p. 233.

41. Joseph Rotschild, *Pilsudsksi's Coup d'Etat* N.Y. Columbia Univ. Press, 1966, pp. 198–208.

42. Herut, 8 June, 1964.

43. Binyamin Eliav, *Oral Documentation*.

44. Arye Altmann, Oral Documentation.

45. Yohanan Bader, Oral Documentation.

46. *Hayarden*, 26 Oct., 1934. Quoted in Moshe Bella, ed., *The World of Jabotinsky*, Tel Aviv, Dfussim, 1972, p. 163.

47. *Hamashkif*, 17 Sept., 1948.

48. Edvard P. Wynot, Jr., *Polish Politics in Transition: The Camp of National*

Unity and the Struggle for Power 1935–39 Athens Georgia, University of Georgia Press, 1974, passim.

Chapter Two

1. Letter from the World Executive in Riga to the command in Eretz-Israel, 16 Jan. 1928, Jabotinsky Archives (Metzudat Ze'vi: Herut Movement Headquarters in Israel), hereafter *JA*, B-9.

2. Letter from the Supreme Command to the Zionist Executive, May 2, 1930, *JA*, B-1.

3. Letter to the Supreme Commander of Betar, 12 Nov. 1928, *JA* B-9.

4. Binyamin Eliav, *Oral Documentation.*

5. Notes from the school for madrichim. *JA* B-9.

6. Norman Davies, *God's Playground*, N.Y. Columbia Univ. Press, 1982, II. p. 404.

7. Norman Davies, *Heart of Europe*, New York, Oxford University Press, 1984.

8. Yehoshua Ofir, *Book of the National Worker*, Tel Aviv, The NWF Executive, 1959, I, p. 89.

9. See the books by Davies cited above, and Voclav Benes and Norman J. Pound, *Poland*, N.Y. Praeger, 1970.

10. Ibid., pp. 165–169.

11. Davies, *Heart of Europe*, N.Y. Oxford University Press, 1984, pp. 147–148.

12. For Mannheim's ideas on the generation issue, see Karl Mannheim, "The Problem of Generations," *Essays in the Sociology of Knowledge*, London, Routledge or Kegan Paul, 1952, pp. 276–332.

13. *Doar Hayom*, 12 Sept. 1930.

14. Message from Betar Commission in Eretz-Israel No. 1 (December 1933), *JA* B-11; see also instruction material, *JA* B-9.

15. Proclamation of Jabotinsky to Betar members prior to the 1935 convention. *Book of Betar*, Jerusalem; The Committee for the Publication of the Book of Betar 1973–76, I, p. 391.

16. Ibid., p. 341.

17. Minutes of the Third World Assembly of Betar, Warsaw, 11-16 Sept. 1938 (pub. in Bucharest by the Betar Executive Committee 1940), *JA* B-1.

18. Plan of Work for Young Betar, September 27, 1934, *JA* B-9.

19. *Hamedina,* 3 Feb. 1936.

20. *Book of Betar,* II, p. 183.

21. Ibid., I, p. 342.

22. *Doar Hayom,* 3 Jan. 1930.

23. *Hamedina,* 6 April 1936.

24. Schechtmann, Jabotinsky, III, p. 194.

25. *Book of Betar,* I, p. 412.

26. Eliav, *Oral Documentation.*

27. Edvard P. Wynot, *Polish Politics in Transition,* Athens Georgia, University of Georgia Press, 1974, p. 83.

28. Although no reliable data exist to support this claim, it was the opinion of many who were active in Betar. See Avigdor Kipnis, "Western Wall Rabbi Beaten," in Yosef Achimeir and Emanuel Shatzky, eds., *Behold the Sikarikin,* Rishon Le'Zion, Nitzanim, 1978, pp. 147-148.

29. Yonathan Shapiro, *An Elite without Successors,* Tel Aviv, Sifriat Poalim, 1984, chapter 3.

30. *Book of Betar,* I. p. 407; *Hamedina,* 6 April, 1936.

31. A brochure devoted to the Summer Camp, September 1934, *JA* B-9.

32. *Die Tat,* 20 Jan. 1939; see also Dr. B. Lubotzky (Eliav), *Hamedina,* 19 May 1939.

33. Jabotinsky, "On Militarism," in *Writings: The Way to the State,* Eri Jabotinsky, p. 42.

34. Ya'akov Rubin, *Herut,* 3 Oct. 1948.

35. *Hamedina,* 12 June 1938.

Chapter Three

1. *Hapoel Hatza'ir* 20 (23), 17 March 1927. See also an interview with the widow of Uri Zvi Greenberg, *Yediot Ahronot,* 4 Oct. 1985.

2. Yonathan Shapiro, *The Historical Ahdut Ha'avodah,* Tel Aviv, Am Oved, 1975, pp. 145-147.

3. *Hapoel Hatza'ir* 42 (19), 27 Aug. 1926.

4. *Kuntress* 11, 11 Aug. 1925.

5. *Kuntress* 12, 24 Aug. 1926.

6. Abba Achimeir, *Revolutionary Zionism*, Tel Aviv, The Committee for the Publications of Achimeir's writings. 1965, p. 184.

7. Ibid, p. 79.

8. Ibid, p. 106–111, 123–128.

9. Kalman Katznelson, "The Lenin Example," in Emanuel Shatzky and Joseph Achimeir, Behold the Sikarikin, Rishon Lezion, Nitzanim, 1978, pp. 130–131.

10. Quoted by Yehuda Shuster: "Building a Theoretical Model of Pre-State Fascist Ideology and Applying the Model in a Concrete Historical Case: Abba Achimeir 1928–33." Seminar paper submitted at Efal Seminar, Efal, Israel.

11. Eliav, *Oral Documentation*.

12. Shabtai Teveth, *The Murder of Arlosoroff*, Jerusalem, Schocken Press 1982, pp. 43–46.

13. This is the explanation given by Raya Berman in Shatzky and Achimeir, Behold the Sikarikin, p. 99. Another explanation is the relative lull in the relations between Jews and Arabs at the time, a situation that lasted until 1936. The Irgun started its operations soon afterwards, see Joseph Heller, *Lehi: Ideology and Politics, 1940–1949*, 1989, I, p. 24.

14. Eliav, *Oral Documentation*.

15. Joseph Schechtmann, *The Jabotinsky Story*, III, pp. 212–218.

16. Letter from Jabotinsky to Achimeir, 12 Nov. 1935, *Writings: Correspondence*, 25–7; and his letter to Uri Zvi Greenberg, 20 Jan. 1936, Writings, p. 167; see also his letter to Heschel Yevin, Writings, pp. 177–178.

17. From Betar Mobilization Regulations, 1935, *JA* B-9.

18. Meeting of Betar recruits, 24 Feb. 1934, *JA* B-5; meeting of the Expanded Council for Mobilization, 12–13 June 1930, *JA* , B-9; circular issued by the Betar High Command of the battalions. 14 Aug. 1933, *JA* B-5.

19. Meeting of Betar recruits, 24 Feb. 1934, *JA* B-5.

20. Bulletin No. 2 (Jan. 1934) of Betar High Command in Eretz-Israel, *JA* B-9.

21. Newsletter of the Mobilized Battalion of Betar, 20 Jan. 1938, *JA* B-9.

22. Second meeting of members of the battalions, 11 March 1933, *JA* B-5.

23. Ofir, *Book of the National Workers*, Tel Aviv, The Executive of N.W.F., I, pp. 151–152.

24. Meeting of recruits in Rosh Pina, March 6–8, 1936, *JA* B-9.

25. Ofir, I, 177.

26. Ibid., p. 244.

27. Ibid., p. 230.

28. Eliav, *Oral Documentation*.

29. Ada Robel-Yevin, *The Purple Loom of Yair Stern's Life*, Tel-Aviv Hadar 1986, p. 61.

30. See Eliezer Livne, *Aharon Aharonson: The Man and His Time*, Jerusalem, Mossad Bialik, 1959.

31. On this topic, see a letter from Ya'akov Amrami to Menachem Begin, April 10, 1972, *JA* Amrami Archives.

32. *Book of Betar* II, pp. 704–706; see also Uriel Halperin, "Platform for the World Assembly," *Hamedina* 13, Aug. 1938.

33. On this subject, see Uri Ben-Eliezer, Militarism, Status and Politics: The Native-Born Generation and the Leadership in the decade Preceding the Establishment of the State. Ph.D. diss. Tel Aviv University, 1988.

34. Yosef Zahavi, "Revolutionary Zionism, the Jewish State and Etzel," in Yosef Achimeir, ed., *The Black Prince: Yosef Katznelson and the National Movement in the 1930s*, Tel Aviv, The Jabotinsky Institute, 1983, pp. 290–313.

35. Eliahu Lenkin, *The Story of the "Altalena" Commander*, Tel Aviv Hadar, 1974, p. 47.

36. Menachem Begin, The *Revolt*, Tel Aviv, Achiassaf, 1978, p. 59.

37. Eliav, *Oral Documentation*.

38. *Book of Betar*, II, p. 618.

39. David Niv, *Campaigns of the National Military Organization*, Tel Aviv, Mossad Klausner I, 1965, p. 288.

40. *Book of Betar*, II, pp. 862-864; Third World Assembly (of Betar), 11–16 Sept. 1938, published in Bucharest, Betar Executive Committee, 1940 *JA* B-1.

41. *Die Tat*, 24 Jan. 1939. See also 9 Dec. 1938; 17 Dec. 1938; 4 Oct. 1938; 11 Nov. 1938; 10 Jan 1939; 17 Jan. 1939.

42. *Die Tat*, 28 April 1939.

43. *Die Tat*, 20 May 1939.

44. Binyamin Eliav, *Oral Documentation*.

45. Yohanan Bader, The Knesset and I, Jerusalem, Idanim, 1978, p. 285.

46. Eliav reports on Jabotinsky's opposition to Irgun's plans, *Oral Documentation*, but Jabotinsky himself sent out a circular on behalf of *Shilton* Betar in a different spirit on March 2, 1939, *JA* B-9.

47. Schectmann, III, p. 238; Ya'akov Ornstein, *In Chains*, Tel Aviv, Private Publication, 1973, p. 131; letter from David Raziel to Ze'ev Jabotinsky, 3 April 1939, *JA* Raziel Archives.

48. Schechtmann, III, p. 262.

49. This is also the assessment of K. Katznelson. *The Decline of the Jabotinski Movement*, Tel Aviv, Anach, 1961, pp. 41–42. On the waning of Jabotinsky's leadership, see also J. Heller, *Lehi*, I, pp. 62–80.

50. Letter from Ze'ev Jabotinsky to David Raziel, March 1, 1940, *JA* Raziel Archives; letter from the *Shilton* officer in London to David Raziel, March 4, 1940, *JA* Raziel Archives.

51. Sasson Sofer. *Begin: An Anatomy of Leadership*, Blackwell, Oxford England, 1988, pp. 69-70.

Chapter Four

1. Hamedina, 21 April 1939.

2. Kalman Katznelson, *Israel After the Sinai Campaign*, Tel Aviv Anach, 1957, p. 130.

3. On the romantic nationalism in Poland and its influence on the country's foreign policy in the period between the two world wars, see Adam Bromke, *Poland's Politics: Idealism vs. Realism*, Cambridge Mass. Harvard Univ. Press, 1967, passim. Regarding the influence of Polish romanticism on Begin, see Sofer, *Begin: An Anatomy of Leadership*, Blackwell, Oxford, England, 1988, p. 66.

4. *Herut*, 3 Oct. 1948.

5. See Uri Brenner, *Altalena: A Political and Military Study*, Tel Aviv, Tabenkin Institute, 1978; and Shlomo Nakdimon, *Altalena*, 1978, Jerusalem, Idanim.

6. Herzl Rosenblum, *Yediot Ahronot*, 11 Jan. 1952.

7. K. Katznelson, *Israel after Sinai*, Tel Aviv, Anach, 1957, p. 131.

8. Israel Eldad, *First Tithe*, Tel Aviv, Hadar, 1975, p. 362.

9. Dr. Margolin's proposal, *JA* H-1.

10. The constitution was approved at the second convention, 1951; *JA*, H-1.

11. Maurice Duverger, *Political Parties*, N.Y. John Wiley & Sons, pp. 62–71.

12. Yonathan Shapiro, *Israeli Democracy*, Ramat Gan, Massada, 1978, pp. 102–103.

13. William E. Wright, *A Comparative Study of Party Organization*, Columbus Ohio, C.E. Merrill, 1971, p. 216.

14. Shapiro, *Democracy in Israel*, pp. 124–129.

15. Yohanan Bader, *The Knesset and I*, Jerusalem, Idanim, 1978, p. 21.

16. *Davar*, 12 Jan. 1949; see also Eri Jabotinsky, *Oral Documentation*.

17. Ofir II, p. 49.

18. K. Katznelson, *Israel After Sinai*, Tel Aviv, Anach, 1957, p. 146.

19. Minutes of Herut Central Committee Meeting, 27 Feb. 1955 *JA* H-1; Shlomo Reuven, *Herut*, 25 July 1951; Ofir II, p. 61.

20. On the definition of the intelligentsia, see Shapiro, *Elite Without Successors*, Tel Aviv, Sifriat Poalim, 1984, p. 17–19.

21. Eliav, *Oral Documentation*.

22. *Ha'aretz*, 30 Aug. 1985.

23. Arye Altman, *Oral Documentation*; Dubie Bergman, The Herut Movement: From Underground to Political Party. Tel Aviv University, 1978, M.A. thesis.

24. *Yediot Ahronot*, 27 Feb. 1951.

25. Katznelson, *Israel After Sinai*, Tel Aviv, Anach, 1957, p. 147.

26. Voclav Benes and Norman J. Pound, *Poland*, N.Y. Praeger, 1970 pp. 207–208.

27. Ibid., pp. 205–206.

28. Yoram Lichtenstein, *The Herut Movement: Structure and Internal Processes*. M.A. thesis, Hebrew University, 1974.

29. *Ma'ariv*, 2 March 1951; Ze'ev von Weisel, *Herut*, 23 June 1950, 25 Aug. 1950; S. Gepstein and Avraham Axelrod, *Herut*, 16 Feb., 1951.

30. Yediot Ahronot, 27 Feb. 1951; Ya'akov Weinschel, *Oral Documentation*.

31. K. Katznelson, *Herut*, 18 Aug. 1950, 10 Nov., 1950; Meir Eisheimer, *Herut*, 22 Nov. 1950, 12 Aug. 1951.

32. Letter from K. Katznelson to Herut Central committee, 24 Feb. 1955, *JA*, H-1.

33. This is attested to by his brother Ya'akov Weinschel, *Oral Documentation*.

34. Shmuel Katz, *Neither Audacity Nor Grace*, Tel Aviv, Dvir, 1981, pp. 12-13.

35. See Ya'akov Amrami Archives, *JA*.

36. See note 34.

37. *Herut*, 1 Feb. 1949; see also Begin's article on the subject, *Herut*, 4 Feb. 1949.

38. *Herut*, 4 Feb. 1949.

39. *Herut*, 17 Oct. 1949.

40. *Herut*, 18 Sept. 1950.

41. *Herut*, 7 Feb. 1950.

42. Menachem Begin, *A Worldview and a National Orientation (Basic Guidelines)* Tel Aviv Betar Headquarters in Eretz-Israel, 1952; also published in *Herut*, 23 March 1951, 30 March 1951, 13 April 1951.

43. *Ma'ariv*, 28 Feb. 1951.

44. S. Marlin, "Who Will Save the State," *Herut*, 8 Sept. 1950; proposals of the Lamerhav faction, *JA* H-1 and see also *Yediot Ahronot*, 27 Feb. 1951, *Ma'ariv*, 2 March 1951.

45. *Ha'aretz*, 30 June 1954.

46. Avraham Axelrod, "Moving Freely in the Same Direction," *Herut*, 16 Feb. 1951; NWF Council, 21 Jan. 1951, *NWF Archives*; Ofir II, pp. 93–94.

47. *Herut*, 30 July 1951, 4 Aug. 1951.

48. *Herut*, 27 Feb. 1951.

49. Ofir II, 111.

50. *Herut*, 8 Jan. 1952; see *Herut* from late December until this date, where these events are described extensively, especially Menachem Begin's letter to the public. *Herut*, 1 Jan. 1952.

51. *Herut*, 26 Jan. 1952.

52. *Herut*, 20 Jan 1952.

53. Katznelson, *Israel After Sinai*, Tel Aviv, Anach, 1957, p. 150.

54. See Herzl Rosenblum, *Yediot Ahronot*, 11 Jan. 1952.

55. Eliahu Ben-Horin, "Muddled Thinking in Jerusalem," *Congress Weekly*, 2 Jan. 1952.

56. See note 44.

57. Arye Altman, *Oral Documentation*.

58. *Herut*, 7 Jan. 1952; see also 28 Dec. 1951.

59. *Ha'aretz*, 26 Dec. 1952.

60. Letter from Amrami to Begin, 2 July 1968, and Begin's reply, 9 July 1968, *JA* Amrami Archives.

Chapter Five

1. *Ha'aretz*, 30 June 1954.

2. Minutes of the Third Convention, 20 April 1954, *JA* H-1.

3. *Platform* for issues at the Third National Convention, Pamphlet 1, *JA* H-1.

4. Minutes of the Third Convention, 20 April 1954, *JA* H-1; see also *Platform* for issues at the Third National Convention, Pamphlets 1 and 2, *JA* H-1.

5. Minutes of the Third Convention, 22 April 1954, *JA* H-1.

6. Ibid.

7. See Y. Shapiro, Israeli Democracy, Ramat Gan, Massada, 1978, ch. I.

8. Minutes of the Third Convention, 20 and 22 April 1954, *JA* H-1.

9. NWF Executive, 6 Sept. 1965, *NWF Archives*.

10. NWF Council, 23 Aug. 1953, *NWF Archives*.

11. NWF Council, 29 April 1954, *NWF Archives*.

12. Minutes of the Third Convention, April 22, 1954, *JA* H-1.

13. Ibid., NWF Council, 11 and 29 April 1954, *NWF Archives*.

14. Minutes of the Third Convention, 22 April 1954, *JA* H-1.

15. Ofir II, 147.

16. NWF Council, April 29, 1954, *NWF Archives*.

17. Minutes of the Third Convention, 21 April 1954, *JA* H-1.

18. *Ha'aretz*, 23 April 1954.

19. *Yediot Ahronot*, 29 April 1954.

20. Resolutions of the second convention, 1951, *JA* H-1.

21. Begin's speech at the Third Convention, *Herut*, 30 April 1954.

22. *Ha'aretz*, 20 April 1954.

23. Herut Central Committee, 20 and 27 Jan. 1956, *JA* H-1; and Ofir II, pp. 172–173.

24. Herut Central Committee, 30 Dec. 1954 and 9 Jan. 1955, *JA* H-1.

25. Herut Central Committee, 3 Feb. 1955, *JA* H-1; see also a letter from Yohanan Bader to Avraham Kahane, July 1950, and an announcement in *Herut* on this subject 31 Oct. 1950.

26. Herut Central Committee, 28 June 1957, *JA* H-1, Herut's leaders were aware of the fact that the majority of their members and voters came from the working class and the poor: see Central Committee report to the first convention, 1949, *JA* H-1, and *Herut*, 14 Aug. 1951.

Chapter Six

1. Herut Central Committee, 16 Feb. 1956; 19 Feb. 1956; 20 Sept. 1955, *J* H-1.

2. *Ma'ariv*, 28 Nov. 1958.

3. Memorandum regarding the Ninth Convention, 1968, *JA* Arye Ben-Eliezer Archives.

4. Herut Central Committee, 26 Aug. 1956, *JA* H-1. See also Yoram Lichtenstein, *The Herut Movement*, M.A. Thesis, Jerusalem, Hebrew University, 1974, p. 30–31.

5. Bader, *The Knesset and I*, Jerusalem, Idanim, 1978, p. 187.

6. Eliav, *Oral Documentation*.

7. See, for example the testimony of Ptachiya Shamir, and the testimony of Begin himself, in Lichtenstein, *The Herut Movement*, 1974.

8. Mordechai Olmert, *My Road on the Public Road*, Tel Aviv, Or-Am, 1981, p. 171.

9. Ibid.

10. Minutes of the Third Convention, 22 April 1954, *JA* H-1.

11. Olmert, My Road on the Public Road, Tel-Aviv, Or-Am, 1981, p. 183; see also Shmuel Tamir, *Davar*, 8 Nov. 1959.

12. Olmert, My Road.

13. *Yediot Ahronot*, 5 March 1971.

14. Lichtenstein, *The Herut Movement*, pp. 169–170.

15. *Ha'aretz*, 9 Sept. 1966; *Yediot Ahronot*, 9 Jan. 1973; see also Lichtenstein, *The Herut Movement*, p. 170.

16. *Yediot Ahronot*, 24 Sept. 1985.

17. *Davar*, 13 Sept. 1966.

18. Herut Central Committee, 4 Dec. 1955; *JA* H-1.

19. See Yonathan Shapiro, *Israeli Democracy*, 1978, p. 128, and Arthur Schweitzer, *The Age of Charisma*, Chicago Ill., Nelson-Hal, 1984.

20. David Yishai, *Between Blue White and Red*, 1980, Tel Aviv, The Blue White Faction, pp. 121–122.

21. Ofir, Book of the National Worker II, 305.

22. *Ha'aretz*, 30 June 1954.

23. *Ha'aretz*, 28 Nov. 1958.

24. *Herut*, 21 April 1954; see also his article, "Around Our Convention," *Herut*, 30 April 1954.

25. *Ha'aretz*, 7 Oct. 1959; and *Ha'aretz* 1 Nov. 1959.

26. On the foreign policy of the Polish leadership, see Adam Bromke, *Poland's Politics: Idealism vs Realism*, Cambridge, Mass., Harvard University Press, 1967.

27. Lichtenstein *The Herut Movement*, p. 154. Amos Funkenstein drew my attention to the distinction between the two types of Begin's speeches.

28. On this subject, see the article by Gabriel Cohen, "British Policy on the Eve of the War of Independence," in *We Were As Dreamers*, Yehuda Wallach, ed., Ramat Gan, Massada, 1988, pp. 13–177.

29. Conversation with Shmuel Tamir on this subject, Jan. 1986.

30. *Ha'aretz*, 28 Nov. 1958.

31. Ofir, II, 293, pp. 301–302.

32. See note 27.

33. Meeting of the executive, 11 Nov. 1965, *NWF Archives*.

34. Benes and Pound, *Poland*, N.Y. Praeger, 1970, p. 173.

35. E. Wynot, *Polish Politics in Transition*, pp. 38, 53, 71.

36. Juan Linz, Arthur Stepan, Eds. *The Breakdown of Democratic Regimes*, Baltimore, Md. John Hopkins Univ. Press, 1978.

37. Benes and Pound, *Poland*, pp. 180, 186.

38. Joseph Bendersky, *Carl Schmidt: Theorist for the Reich*, Princeton N.Y., Princeton Univ. Press, 1983, pp. 251–252.

39. I. Margolin, *Herut* 4 March 1949; Yirmiahu Halperin, *Herut*, 31 March 1950; K. Katznelson, *Herut*, 20 Jan. 1952; Shlomo Meretz, *Herut*, 1 Feb. 1952.

40. Herut Central Committee, 27 July 1956, *JA* H-1.

41. Letter from A. Remba to Yuniczman, 24 Feb. 1950, *JA*, Yuniczman Archive; Platform for Issues of the Third National Convention, 1954, *JA* H-1.

42. Letter from Ya'akov Amrami to "Poless," 18 Feb. 1972, *JA*, Amrami Archive.

43. Mordechai Olmert, Herut Central Committee, 26 Aug. 1956, *JA* H-1.; Ofir, II, 93.

44. Herut Central Committee Report to Herut Council, 19-21 Oct. 1948, *JA* H-1.

45. *Ha'aretz*, 29 July 1951.

46. Herut Central Committee, 25 Feb. 1954, *JA* H-1.

47. Resolutions of the Third Convention, April 1954, *JA* H-1. See also Herut platform for the Third Knesset, 1955, *JA* H-1.

48. Herut Central Committee, 27 Feb. 1955, *JA* H-1.

49. Platform for Issues of the Third National Convention, 1954, *JA* H-1.

50. Herut Platform for the Third Knesset, 1955.

51. Herut Central Committee, 17 March 1955, *JA* H-1.

52. Arye Naor, *Government at War*, Tel Aviv, Lahav, 1986, p. 47.

53. Herut Central Committee, 18 March 1954; see also 3 March 1955; 4 March 1956, *JA* H-1.

54. Herut Central Committee, 6 March 1955.

55. Herut Central Committee, 18 March 1954, *JA* H-1.

56. Begin's speech to the opening session of the Betar National Assembly, *Herut*, 12 April 1955.

57. Herut Central Committee, 4 March 1956, *JA* H-1.

58. Herut Central Committee, 6 Dec. 1956, *JA* H-1.

59. Herut Central Committee, 14 March 1957.

60. See, for example, editorials in *Herut*, 30 May and 3 June 1965.

61. Emanuel Katz, "Is This An Opportune Moment," *Herut* 12 March 1965.

62. Yosef Szofman, "This We Pledge," *Herut*, 29 Oct. 1965.

63. *Herut*, 1 May 1964.

64. Herut Central Committee, 20 Feb. 1955, *JA* H-1.

65. Report by Shlomo Nakdimon on Begin's election campaign, *Herut*, 29 Oct. 1965.

66. S. N. Eisenstadt, *The Transformation of Israeli Society*, Westview Press 1985, p. 45.

67. *Ha'aretz*, Editorial, 17 Nov. 1958; see also *Ha'aretz* 30 Oct. 1959.

68. Arye Ziv, "The Image of the Herut Movement," *Ha'aretz*, 6 July 1951.

69. Herut Central Committee, 5 June 1955, *JA* H-1.

70. See also Joseph Gusfield, *Symbolic Crusade*, Champaign, Ill. Univ. of Illinois Press, 1963, pp. 16–19.

71. Katznelson, Israel After Sinai, pp. 154–5.

72. Ofir, II, 274.

Chapter Seven

1. *Ha'aretz*, 13 Nov. 1959.

2. Olmert, *My Road on the public road*, Tel Aviv, Or-Am, 1981, p. 240.

3. On Begin's inability to think beyond the tactical level, see Yehoshafat Harkabi, *Fateful Decisions*, Tel Aviv, Am Oved, 1986, p. 130.

4. Begin's speech at the fifth Herut Convention, November 24, 1958, Tel Aviv, Herut Information Office, January 1959.

5. See "Jew, Nationality and Religion," Begin Knesset speech, 17 Aug. 1964, Tel Aviv, Herut Information Office, 1965; "Consideration for Sincere Religious Feelings Is Not Weakness," Tel Aviv, Herut Information Office, 1965.

6. Another pamphlet of Herut Information Branch containing Begin's Knesset speech of August 17, 1964; see also resolutions of the Sixth Convention, 2–5 April 1961, *JA* H-1.

7. Bader, *The Knesset and I*, Jerusalem, Idanim, 1978, pp. 184–185.

8. Ya'akov Amrami to the editor of *Hayom*, 17 March 1966, *JA* Amrami Archive.

9. Unsent letter from Ya'akov Amrami to Menachem Begin, 10 April 1972, *J A* Amrami Archive.

10. *Herut*, 3 and 17 Jan. 1964.

11. Minutes of the Third Convention, 22 April 1954, *JA* H-1.

12. Herut Central Committee, 27 July 1955, *JA* H-1.

13. Herut Central Committee, 27 July 1955, *JA* H-1.

14. Olmert, *My Road on the public road*, Tel Aviv, Or-Am, 1981, p. 288.

15. Irena Guthrie, "Israeli Manners in Public and at Home," *Herut*, 15 and 22 May 1964; I. Benari, "Israelis Are Not Polite," *Herut*, 29 May 1964.

16. Herut Central Committee, December 9, 1955, *JA* H-1.

17. Herut Central Committee, 27 July 1956, *JA* H-1.

18. Report to the Fifth Convention, Nov. 1958, *JA* H-1.

19. *Herut*, 15 Feb. 1963; Gahal agreement, *Herut*, 27 April 1965.

20. *Herut*, 3 Feb. 1963; *Haboker*, 19 Feb. 1965.

21. Herut Central Committee, 26 Aug. 1956, *JA* H-1.

22. Ofir, II, 187.

23. Ofir, II, pp. 258–589.

24. Quoted by David Yishai, *Between Blue White and Red*, Tel Aviv, The

Blue-White Faction, 1980, p. 71. Ofir had a different opinion, maintaining that in 1957 Begin and Ben-Eliezer still opposed this step, Ofir, II, 74.

25. Herut Central Committee, 21 May 1959, *JA* H-1; *Herut*, 22 May 1959.

26. Ofir, II, pp. 225–229.

27. NWF Council, 14 July 1957, *NWF Archives*.

28. Herut Central Committee, 14 Nov. 1965, quoted by Ofir, II, 403.

29. Yishai, *Between Blue White and Red*, p. 78.

30. NWF Council, 11 May 1961, *NWF Archives*.

31. NWF Council, 3 Feb. 1963, *NWF Archives*.

32. Ofir, II, p. 314.

33. The term "a proletarian under duress" appeared in an editorial in Herut on the eve of the first Histadrut elections in which Herut participated, Herut, 17 June 1965.

34. *Hamashkif*, 12 Aug. 1948.

35. *Ma'ariv*, 23 Jan. 1963.

36. Herut Central Committee, 14 Nov. 1965, in Ofir, II, pp. 416–418.

37. NWF Executive, 20 Feb. 1963, *NWF Archives*.

38. Ofir, II. pp. 413–415.

39. NWF Executive, 11 Nov. 1965, *NWF Archives*, and Ofir, II, 353.

40. *Herut*, 21 May 1965.

41. *Herut*, 18 April 1965.

42. NWF Executive, 11 Nov. 1965, *NWF Archives*.

43. Ofir, II, p. 417.

44. *Davar*, 26 Nov. 1965.

45. *Ma'ariv*, 18 Feb. 1966.

46. *Ha'aretz*, 10 and 18 March 1966.

47. *Hayom*, 18 March 1966.

48. *Hayom*, 18 March 1966.

49. *Ha'aretz*, 11 March 1966; see also *Yediot Ahronot*, 3 March 1966.

50. *Ha'aretz*, 26 April 1966; see also article by Pinhas Goldstein, *Hayom*, 9 May 1966, and by Yitzhak Modai, *Hayom*, 15 May 1966.

51. *Hayom*, 8 June 1966.

52. *Ha'aretz*, 29 June 1966.

53. *Ha'aretz*, 29 June 1966.

54. I do not have the minutes of the convention, and I collected the fact principally from reports in *Ha'aretz*, *Ma'ariv* and *Yediot Ahronot* published at the time of the convention and immediately afterwards.

55. *Ha'aretz*, 29 June 1966; *Ma'ariv*, 1 July 1966.

56. *Ha'aretz*, 29 June 1966.

57. *Ma'ariv*, 29 June 1966.

58. *Ma'ariv*, 1 July 1966; Ofir, II, p. 440.

59. Letter from Yohanan Bader to Arye Ben-Eliezer, 25 Sept. 1966, JA Ben-Eliezer Archive.

60. Menachem Begin, "My Resignation and My Griefs," *Hayom*, 8 July 1966.

61. *Ha'aretz*, 26 July 1966.

62. Lichtenstein, *Herut Movement*, p. 171.

63. *Yediot Ahronot*, 18 Nov. 1966; *Ma'ariv*, 18 Nov. 1966.

64. *Ha'aretz*, 27 Feb. 1967.

65. Interview with Elimelech Rimalt, 23 Dec. 1985.

66. Dr. Forder speech at the Commercial Club, *Haboker*, 3 Jan. 1965; Yitzhak Ziv-Av, *Haboker*, 26 Feb. 1965; Yosef Tamir, Haboker, 21 Feb. 1965.

67. *Ha'aretz*, Editorial, 23 Jan. 1963; "Poless," *Ha'aretz*, 6 Sept. 1964, 19 Oct. 1965; A. Schweitzer, *Ha'aretz*, 6 Sept. 1964. *Ha'aretz* also invited Menachem Begin to write an article for the paper, an unprecedented act in those days, *Ha'aretz*, 26 Sept. 1965.

68. Articles by S.Z. Abramov, *Herut*, 3 Feb. 1963; *Haboker*, 19 Feb. 1965.

69. S.Z. Abramov, *Ha'aretz*, 14 Nov. 1965.

70. *Hayom*, 24 June 1966; Bader, *The Knesset and I*, pp. 284–285.

71. *Ha'aretz*, 13 Sept. 1966.

72. *Herut*, 12 Nov. 1965.

73. *Haboker*, 1 Feb. 1963.

74. *Herut*, "Blue-and-White" supplement, 15 Jan. 1965; *Herut*, 26 June 1964.

75. Resolution not to determine to whom to transfer Histadrut enterprises Herut Central Committee, 5 May 1956, JA H-1; resolution to transfer them to the state and to the workers, *Herut*, 4 Dec. 1964.

76. *Herut*, "Blue-and-White' supplement, 15 Oct. 1965.

77. Article by Yohanan Bader, *Herut* 29 May 1964; response by Eliahu Lenkin, *Herut*, 5 June 1964; editorial on compulsory arbitration. Herut, 25 May 1964.

78. *Herut*, "Blue-and-White" supplement, 29 Jan. 1965.

79. *Herut*, "National Worker" supplement, 3 Sept. 1965.

80. *Eretz-Israel*, October 1971; see also Eretz-Israel, March 1972.

81. *Yediot Ahronot*, 3 March 1966.

82. *Herut*, 12 March 1965.

83. *Eretz-Israel*, May 1975.

84. *Eretz-Israel*, July 1972.

85. Herut Central Committee, 27 Feb. 1955, *JA* H-1.

86. *Herut*, 30 March 1964.

87. *Ma'ariv*, 13 July 1951.

88. Arye Avneri, *David Levy*, Tel Aviv, Revivim, 1983, pp. 84, 88.

89. This information was gleaned from the reports of the Central Committee that were submitted to Herut conventions.

90. *Herut*, 23 Jan. 1963.

Chapter Eight

1. Yonathan Shapiro, *An Elite without Successors*, Tel Aviv, Sifriat Poalim, 1984, ch. 2.

2. *Davar*, 21 June 1951 and 24 June 1951.

3. *Davar*, 1 Oct. 1959; see also *Davar*, 1 Jan. 1949.

4. *Davar*, 5 Oct. 1959.

5. *Davar*, 16 June 1955; see also S.N. Eisenstadt, 1985, pp. 182–183.

6. *Davar*, 17 June 1955; see also Yigal Allon's remarks in *Davar*, 19 Oct. 1965, and Haim Zadok's in *Davar*, 24 Oct. 1965.

7. *Davar*, 29 Oct. 1965.

8. Shlomo Ahronson and Dan Horowitz, "The Strategy of Controlled Reprisal: The Israeli Case" [Hebrew], *State and Government*, vol. 1, no. 1 (Summer 1971); pp. 77–99.

9. For example, the Air Force's reprisal raid against Syria for the murder of police officers in May 1951, the month before the elections; and the bombing of water-pumping stations in Jordan on September 5, 1955, two months before the elections.

10. *Davar*, 24 Oct. 1965.

11. Shapiro, *An Elite without Successors*, Tel Aviv, Sifriat Poalim, 1984, pp. 145–147.

12. Michael Brecher, *Decisions in Israel's Foreign Policy*, Yale University Press, 1975.

13. Robert Michels, *Political Parties*, N.Y., John Wiley & Sons, 1955.

14. Thomas A. Baylis, *The Technical Intelligentsia and the East German Elite*, Berkeley Ca., University of California Press, 1974, introduction.

15. Robert Putnam, *The Comparative Study of Political Elites*, Engelwood. N.J., Prentice Hall, 1976, pp. 212–215, 242.

16. C. Wright Mills, *The Power Elite*, N.Y. Oxford Univ. Press, 1956, p. 285.

17. *Hayom*, 9 June 1967; see also Editorial, *Hayom*, 16 June 1967.

18. *Hayom*, 28 June, 1967.

19. *Eretz Israel*, Sept. 1973.

20. *Davar*, 20 Oct. 1969.

21. Yossi Beilin, *The Price of Unity*, Tel Aviv, Revivim, 1985, p. 141.

22. Bader expressed this stand in an article in *Hayom*, 9 June 1967; see also the resolution of the 13th Herut convention, *Eretz Israel*, Jan. 1977.

23. *Davar*, 13 Oct. 1969.

24. Lichtenstein, *The Herut Movement*, M.A. Thesis, Jerusalem, Hebrew University, 1974, p. 156.

25. Asher Arian, *The Choosing People*, Cleveland, The Press of Case-Western Reserve Univ., 1973 p. 35.

26. Interview with Dr. Elimelech Rimalt, 23 Dec. 1985.

27. The most important source concerning this event is an M.A. thesis on the subject by Yoram Lichtenstein (1973), as well as reports in the press by journalists who attended the convention.

28. *Yediot Ahronot*, 27 Sept. 1985.

29. *Ma'ariv*, 13 Jan. 1972.

30. *Ma'ariv*, 21 Dec. 1972.

31. *Ma'ariv*, 21 Dec. 1972.

32. *Yediot Ahronot*, 19 Jan. 1973.

33. *Ma'ariv*, 19 Jan. 1973.

34. *Ma'ariv*, 22 Dec. 1972.

35. *Ma'ariv*. 22 Dec. 1972.

36. Michal Shamir and Asher Arian, "The Ethnic Vote" in A. Arian, ed. *The Elections in Israel 1981*, Tel Aviv, Ramot publishing Co., Tel Aviv University, 1983, p. 96.

37. Gahal won 26 Knesset seats in 1969. The three parties that joined the Likud had six seats among them, the State List (Rafi) with 4, and the Free Center with 2. As a result, some maintain that the Likud gained only 7 seats in 1973 (a 4 percent increase) over 1969 (Arian [1975], 288). But at least two-thirds of the voters for the State List returned to the Alignment, and not all the voters for the Free Center voted for the Likud (ibid, 296). Hence, the Likud scored a 7 percent increase in 1973. They added another 3 percent in 1977. Thus, the crucial importance of the 1973 elections, even though it was not unti 1977 that the Likud attained power.

38. Asher Arian, *The Choosing People*. Cleveland, Ohio, The Case Western Reserve University, 1973.

39. Shamir and Arian, "The Ethnic Vote in Israel's 1981 Election," in A. Arian ed., *The Elections in Israel*, Jerusalem, Jerusalem Academic Press 1981, 1983, pp. 91–112.

40. Michal Shamir, "Realignment in the Israeli System," in M. Shamir and

A. Arian, eds., *The Elections in Israel 1984*, Jerusalem, Jerusalem Academic Press, 1986, pp. 292–293.

41. M. Rainer Lepsius, "From Fragmented Party Democracy to Government by Emergency Decrees and National Socialist Takeover in Germany," in Juan Linz and Arthur Stephan, eds., *The Breakdown of Democractic Regimes*. Baltimore Md., John Hopkins University Press, 1978, p. 60. A recent study found that most Israeli voters in three successive elections since 1973 switched parties at least once. Most of them moved right across the political spectrum. The study concluded that "in any given election, the partisan preferences of most voters are not strong enough to immunize them against the effects of campaign appeals." Furthermore, "several sets of voters are especially likely to be influenced by an electoral contest." Electoral studies recently conducted in other western European countries reached similar conclusions. This lends support to our contention that the role of parties is a crucial factor in explaining voters' behavior. See Alan S. Zuckerman, "The Flow of the Vote in Israel: A Reconsideration of Stability and Change," in A. Arian and M. Shamir, *The Elections in Israel 1988* (forthcoming).

42. My examination was based on data of the Central Bureau of Statistics in 30 electoral districts, with the majority of the inhabitants from established strata in 15 of them, in ten development towns and neighborhoods in which the inhabitants were new immigrants from the Oriental communities, and five areas inhabited by Orientals from the old Yishuv. These covered the years 1955–1973. Of the press reports special mention should be made of the examination of the 1955 election returns by Amitai Etzioni, *Ha'aretz*, 11 Aug. 1955, and by Shabtai Teveth, *Ha'aretz*, 12 Aug. 1955 and 19 Aug. 1955.

43. Asher Arian, "The Israeli Elections in 1977," in A. Arian, ed., *The Elections in Israel 1977*, Jerusalem, Jerusalem, Academic Press, 1980, p. 270.

44. Shamir and Arian, Elections in Israel, p. 96.

45. J. Nelson, *Migrants Labor Poverty and Instability in Developing Nations*, Cambridge Mass. Center for International Affairs, Harvard Univ., 1969, pp. 43–44.

46. Shamir, *Elections in 1984*, p. 292.

47. Shapiro, *An Elite without Successors*, Tel Aviv, Sifriat Poalim, 1984, pp. 134–135.

Epilogue

1. *Herut*, 10 Nov. 1950.

2. Katznelson, *Israel after Sinai Campaign*, 1957, Tel Aviv, Anach, pp. 155–156.

3. Seymour M. Lipset & Stein Rokkan (eds.). *Party Systems and Voter Alignment*, New York, Free Press, 1967, introduction.

4. Ian Budge, "Electoral Volatility; Issues, Effects and Basic Change in 23 Post-War Democracies, *Electoral Studies* 1(2) 1982, pp. 147–168; Michal Shamir, "Are Western Party-Systems Frozen: A Comparative Dynamic Analysis," *Comparative Political Studies* 17 (1) (1984), pp. 35–79.

5. A Summary of the literature on this subject appears in Shamir, 1986, pp. 267–270.

6. Amiram Gonen, "A Geographical Analysis of the Election in Jewish Urban Communities," in Dan Caspi, Abraham Diskin and Emanuel Guttman, eds., *The Roots of Begin's Success*, 1984, pp. 59–88.

7. Dan Sperber, *Rethinking Symbolism*, N.Y. Cambridge Univ. Press., 1975, p. 4.

Bibliography

Hebrew

Abba, Achimeir. *Revolutionary Zionism* (Tel Aviv, The Committee for the Publication of Achimeir's writings).

Achimeir, Yoseph and Emanuel Shatzky, Eds. 1978. *Behold the Sikarikin.* Rishon Le'Zion, Nitzanim. Achimeir Yoseph Ed. 1983. *The Black Prince: Yosef Katznelson and the National Movement in the 1930's,* Tel Aviv, The Jabotinsky Institute.

Ahronson, Shlomo and Dan Horowitz. "The Study of Controlled Reprisals: The Israeli Case." *State and Government* 1, (Summer 1971), 77–99.

Avneri, Arye. 1983. *David Levy,* Tel Aviv, Revivim.

Bader, Yochanan. 1978. *The Knesset and I.* Jerusalem, Idanim.

Begin, Menachem. 1978. *The Revolt.* Tel Aviv, Achiassaf.

Bela, Moshe, Ed. 1972. *The World of Jabotinsky.* Tel Aviv, Dfussim.

Beilin, Yossi. 1985. *The Price of Unity.* Tel Aviv, Revivim.

Bilsky-Ben-Hur, Raphaela. 1988. *Every Individual a King: The Social and Political Thoughts of Ze'ev Jabotinsky.* Tel Aviv, Dvir.

Book of Betar. 1973–1976, 2 volumes. Jerusalem, The Committee for the Publication of the Book of Betar.

Brener, Uri. 1978. Altalena: A Political and Military Study. Tel Aviv, Tabenkin Inst.

Eldad, Israel. 1975. *First Tithe.* Tel Aviv, Hadar.

Harkabi, Yehoshafat. 1986. *Fateful Decisions.* Tel Aviv, Am Oved.

Heller, Joseph. 1989. *Lehi: Ideology and Politics 1940-1949,* 2 volumes. Jerusalem, Keter Publishers.

Katz, Shmuel. 1981. *Neither Audacity Nor Grace.* Tel Aviv. Dvir.

Katznelson, Kalman. 1957. *Israel after Sinai Campaign.* Tel Aviv, Anach.

197

_____ , 1961. *The Decline of the Jabotinsky Movement*. Tel Aviv, Anach.

_____ , 1983. *Conquerors in Distress*. Tel Aviv, Anach.

Lenkin, Eliahu. 1974. *The Story of the Altalena Commander*. Tel Aviv, Hadar.

Livneh, Eliezer. 1959. *Aharon Aharonson: The Man and His Time*. Jerusalem, Mossad Bialik.

Mintz, Matityahu. 1976. *Ber Borochov—The First Circle, 1900–1906*. Tel Aviv, Tel Aviv University.

Nakdimon, Shlomo. 1978. *Altalena*. Jerusalem, Idanim.

Naor, Arye. 1986. *Government at War*. Tel Aviv, Lahav.

Niv, David. 1965–80. *Campaigns of the National Military Organization*. 6 volumes. Tel Aviv, Mossad Klausner.

Ofir, Yeshoshua. 1959–82. *Book of the National Worker*. 2 vol. Tel Aviv, The Executive of NWF.

Olmert, Mordechai, 1981. *My Road on the Public Road*. Tel Aviv, Or-Am.

Ornstein, Ya'akov, 1973. *In Chains*, Tel Aviv, Private publication.

Schechtmann, Joseph, 1959. *The Jabotinsky Story*, 3 volumes. Tel Aviv, Karni.

Shapiro, Yonathan, 1975. *The Historical Ahdut Ha'avodah*. Tel Aviv, Am Oved.

_____ , 1978. *Israeli Democracy*. Ramat Gan, Massada.

_____ , 1984. *An Elite without Successors*. Tel Aviv, Sifriat Poalim.

Shavit, Yaacob. 1978. *Revisionism in Zionism*. Tel Aviv, Hadar.

_____ , 1986. *The Mythology of the Right*. Beit Berl, Emda Library.

Teveth, Shabtai. 1982. *The Murder of Arlosoroff*, Jerusalem, Schoken Press.

Wallach, Yehuda, Ed. 1985. *We Were as Dreamers*. Ramat Gan, Massada.

Yevin-Robel, Ada. *The Purple Loom of Yair Stern's Life*. Tel Aviv, Hadar.

Yishai, David. 1980. *Between Blue White and Red*. Tel Aviv, The Blue-White Faction.

Zabotinsky, Eri. 1980. *My Father Ze'ev Zabotinsky*. Jerusalem, Steimatzsky.

Zabotinsky, Ze'ev. 1934. *The Idea of Betar*. Tel Aviv, Betar Headquarters

_____ , 1947–1953. 18 volumes, Jerusalem, Eri Zabotinsky.

English

Alexander, Robert J. 1979. *Juan Domingo Peron: A History*. Westview Press Boulder Co.

Arian, Asher. 1973. *The Choosing People*, Cleveland, Ohio, The Case Western Reserve University.

___ , "Were the 1973 Elections Critical?" in A. Arian, Ed., 1975. *The Elections in Israel 1973*, 287–305, Jerusalem, Jerusalem Academic Press.

_____ , "The Israeli Election in 1977," in A. Arian, Ed., 1980. *The Elections in Israel 1977*, 253-276, Jerusalem, Jerusalem Academic Press.

Baylis, Thomas A. 1974. *The Technical Intelligentsia and the East German Elite*. Berkeley Ca. University of California Press.

Bell, Daniel, Ed. 1953. *The Radical Right*. Doubleday, Garden City, N.Y.

Bendersky, Joseph. 1983. *Carl Schmidt: Theorist for the Reich*. Princeton Univ. Press, Princeton NJ.

Benes, Voclav and Norman J. Pound. 1970. *Poland*, N.Y. Praeger.

Brecher, Michael. 1975. *Decisions in Israeli's Foreign Policy*, Yale University Press.

Breully, John. 1985. *Nationalism and the State*. Chicago, Il., Univ. of Chicago Press.

Bromke, Adam. 1967. *Poland's Politics; Idealism vs. Realism*. Cambridge, Mass. Harvard Univ. Press.

Budge, Ian. "Electoral Volatility: Issues Effects and Basic Change in 23 Post-War Democracies," *Electoral Studies* (2) (1982), 147–168.

Cohen, Abner. 1974. *Two Dimensional Man*. Berkeley Ca., University of California Press.

Davies, Norman. 1982. *God's Playground*. 2 vols. New York, Columbia University Press.

_____ , 1984. *Heart of Europe*. NY. Oxford University Press.

De Felice, Renzo. 1977. *Interpretations of Fascism*. Cambridge Mass. Harvard Univ. Press.

Duverger, Maurice. 1955. *Political Parties*. New York, John Wiley & Sons.

Eisenstadt, S.N. 1983. *The Transformation of Israeli Society*. Westview, Boulder Co.

Fest, Joachim. 1982. *Hitler*. London, Penguin Books.

Firth, Raymond. *Symbols, Public and Private*. Ithaca NY, Cornell Univ. Press.

Germani, Gino. 1978. *Authoritarianism, Fascism and National Populism*. New Brunswick NJ, Transaction.

Gertz, Nurit. "The Few Against the Many" *Jerusalem Quarterly* 3, 1984, 94–104.

Gusfield, Joseph. 1963. *Symbolic Crusade* Champaign Il., Univ. of Illinois Press.

Hamilton, Richard. 1982. *Who Voted for the Nazis*, Princeton NJ, Princeton Univ. Press.

Kirkpatrick, Jeanne. 1971. *Leader and Vanguard in Mass Society: A Study of Peronist Argentina*, Cambridge Mass., M.I.T. Press.

Laqueur, Walter. 1972. *A History of Zionism*. N.Y., NY, Schocken Books.

_____ , Ed. 1976. *Fascism, A Research Guide*, Berkeley, Ca., Univ. of California Press.

Leach, Edmund. 1954. *Political System of Highland Burma*. Atlantic City, NJ. Humanities Press.

Lespius, Rainer M. "From Fragmented Party Democracy to Government by Emergency Decrees and National Socialist Takeover in Germany, in Juan Linz and Arthur Stephan Eds. 1978. *The Breakdown of Democracies*, 34–79. Baltimore Md. Johns Hopkins University Press.

Linz, Juan and Arthur Stephan, Eds. *The Breakdown of Democratic Regimes*, 1978. Baltimore Md. John Hopkins Univ. Press.

Lipset, M. Seymour. 1960. *Political Man*. Baltimore Md., John Hopkins Univ. Press.

_____ and Stein Rokkan, Eds. 1967. *Party Systems and Voter Alignment*. N.Y., Free Press.

Mannheim, Karl. *Essays in the Sociology of Knowledge*, 1952. London, Routledge and Kegan Paul.

Michels, Robert. 1956. *Political Parties*. N.Y. NY, Free Press.

Mills, C. Wright. 1956. *The Power Elite*. New York, Oxford University Press.

Mosse, George. 1975. *The Nationalization of the Masses*. N.Y. NY, Fertig Howard.

_____ , 1978. *Nazism: A Historical Perspective*. New Brunswick NJ. Transaction Pub.

_____ , 1980. *Masses and Man*. N.Y. NY, Fertig Howard.

Nelson, J. 1969. *Migrants Labor Poverty and Instability in Developing Nations.* Cambridge, Mass. Center for International Affairs, Harvard Univ.

O'Sullivan, Noel. 1983. *Fascism.* London, J.M. Dent & Sons Ltd.

Payne, Stanley C. 1980. *Fascism.* Madison, Wisc., Univ. of Wisconsin Press.

Plamenatz, John. "Two Types of Nationalism", in Eugene Kamenka Ed., 1976. *Nationalism: The Nature and Evolution of an Idea*, London, Arnold.

Putnam, Robert. 1976. *The Comparative Study of Political Elites.* Englewood Cliffs NJ, Prentice Hall.

Rock, David, Ed. 1975. *Argentina in the 20th Century.* Pittsburgh PA, Univ. of Pittsburgh Press.

Rotschild, Joseph. 1966. *Pilsudski's Coup d'etat.* N.Y. Columbia Univ. Press.

Schweitzer, Arthur. 1984. *The Age of Charisma.* Chicago Il, Nelson-Hal.

Shamir, Michal and Asher Arian. "The Ethnic Vote in Israel's 1981 Elections", in A. Arian Ed. 1983. *The Elections in Israel 1981*, Tel Aviv, Ramot Publishing Co., Tel Aviv University, 93–111.

_____ , Are Western Party Systems Frozen: A Comparative Dynamic Analysis," *Comparative Political Studies* 17 (1984), 35-79.

_____ , Realignment in the Israeli Party System, in Asher Arian and Michal Shamir Eds. *The Elections in Israel 1984*, 1986, 267-296. Tel Aviv, Ramot Publishing Co., Tel Aviv University.

Shapiro, Yonathan. "The End of the Dominant Party System," in A. Arian Ed., 1980. *The Elections in Israel 1977*, 23–38. Jerusalem, Jerusalem Academic Press.

_____ , 1976. *The Formative Years of the Israeli Labour Party.* London, Sage Publications.

Sofer, Sasson. 1988. *Begin: An Anatomy of Leadership.* Oxford, England, Blackwell.

Sperber, Dan. 1975. *Rethinking Symbolism.* N.Y. NY, Cambridge Univ. Press.

Sugar, Peter F., Ed. 1971. *Native Fascism in the Successor States*, Santa Barbara, Calif., A.B.C. Clio.

Wright, William E. 1971. *A Comparative Study of Party Organizations.* Columbus, Ohio, C.E. Merrill Pub.

Wynot, Edvard P., Jr. 1974. *Polish Politics in Transition: The Camp of National Unity and the Struggle for Power 1935–39.* Athens Georgia, Univ. of Georgia Press.

Archival (Hebrew)

National Workers' Federation Archives, Tel Aviv (NWF Archives).

Oral Documentation Center, Institute of Contemporary Jewry

The Hebrew University, Jerusalem (Oral Documentation)

Jabotinsky Archives (Metzudat Ze'ev: Herut Movement Headquarters in Israel (JA)

Dissertations and Master Essays

Ben-Eliezer, Uri. "Militarism Status and Politics: The Native-Born Generation and the Leadership in the Decade Preceding the Establishment of the State." Ph.D. Diss., Tel-Aviv University 1988.

Bergman, Dubi. "The Herut Movement from Underground to Political Party." (M.S. Thesis, University, Tel-Aviv University) 1978.

Lichtenstein, Yoram. "The Herut Movement: Structure and Internal Processes." M.A. Thesis, Hebrew University, Jerusalem 1974.

Newspapers (Hebrew)

Davar
Die-Tat (Yiddish)
Doar-Hayom
Eretz-Israel
Ha'aretz
Haboker
Hamashkif
Hamedina
Hayom
Herut
Kuntress
Ma'ariv
Yediot Ahronot

Index

Abdullah, King, 112
Abdullah, Prince, 14
Abramov, S.N., 142
Achimeir, Abba, 18, 43, 44, 48, 49
Agudat Israel, 68
Ahdut Ha'avodah (1919-1930), 43, 44
Ahdut Ha'avodah (1944-1968), 154, 155, 156
Ahronson, Shlomo, 154
Alignment, The. *See* Labor Alignment
Allon Plan, 159
Allon, Yigal, 158
Altalena, 66, 67, 80
Altman, Arye, Dr., 70, 71, 107, 108, 130
Amrami, Ya'akov, 83, 111, 125-126
Anti-Communist, 74
Anti-Fascist, 68
Anti-Liberal, 26
Anti-Semitic. *See* Anti-Semitism
Anti-Semitism, 17, 26, 31, 39, 56, 60
Anti-Socialist, 29, 51, 130
Arian, Asher, 164, 165
Arlosoroff, Chaim, 48

Bader, Yohanan, 26, 70, 73, 81, 94, 99, 125, 135, 138, 139, 143, 144, 158
Bareli, Meir, 153
Bar-Kochba, 40
Bar-Yehuda, Israel, 124

Begin, Menachem, 2, 9, 37, 38, 41, 53, 57-62, Chapters 3-8
Ben-Eliezer, Arye, 73, 114, 130, 139-40, 144
Ben-Gurion, David, 38, 52, 58, 66, 67, 102, 105, 115, 131, 135, 153, 154, 155, 158
Ben-Horin, Eliahu, 82
Ben-Meir, Yehuda, 101
Berman, Yitzhak, 101
Bernstein, Peretz, 135
Betar, 3, 7, 9, 10, 26-62, 64, 66, 67, 68, 72-75, 78, 85-86, 87, 97, 105, 107, 108, 109, 111, 112, 114, 119, 121, 125, 127, 131, 132, 137, 143, 146, 148, 158, 169, 171
Blue-and-White Faction, 132, 136, 144-7
Bolshevik, 44, 45
Bonaparte, Louis, 25, 45
Bonapartism, 25, 45
Bourgeois Parties, 68. *See also* Middle-Class Parties
Bourgeoisie, 15, 45, 152. *See also* Middle-Class
Bourguiba, Habib, 133
Brit Habiryonim, 43-49, 65

Cadre party, 128
Carlebach, Azriel, 77
Cavour, Conte di, 58
Charisma, 102, 108, 166
Chauvinism, 10, 31
Chief-Rabbi(s), 124-125

Poless, 123
Political discourse. *See* Discourse.
Political Socialization, 2, 3, 27, 157, 164, 169
Politics of the Piazza, 7, 171
Polish Military Organization, 32, 54, 73, 109, 112
Populism (Populist movement), 5, 6, 24,
Progressive party, 128, 141
Putsch, 24, 25, 27, 33, 45, 66, 67, 73, 86. *See also* coup

Rabin, Yitzhak, 164
Radical Right, Chapters 1-3; 63, 67, 68, 70, 71, 78, 86, 108, 109, 110, 111, 112
Rafi, 131, 132, 134, 135, 140, 141, 155, 156, 171
Raziel, David, 54, 55, 61
Raziel-Naor, Esther, 73
Realignment, 170
Reparation Agreement, 79-82, 105, 116
Revisionist (Movement Party), 9, 15, 17, 22-27, 29, 30, 37, 38, 41, 45-48, 60, 68, 70, 71, 72, 74, 75, 78, 106, 125. *See also* New-Zionist Organization
Rimalt, Elimelech, 160

Samuel, Herbert, 40
Sapir, Yosef, 160
Schectmann, Joseph, 23, 24, 61
Schnitzer, Shmuel, 162-163, 167
semi-Intelligentsia, 72
Shamir, Michal, 165, 167
Shamir, Ptachiya, 148, 161

Shostak, Eliezer, 71, 88-90, 93, 100-103, 109, 130, 136, 144
Sikarikin, 47
Sinai Campaign, 115, 128, 152, 154, 155
Six Day War, 8, 83, 141-143, 149, 152, 154-159, 163, 167, 170
Smigly, Edvard Rydz, 109-110
Social democracy, 11, 31
Socialism (Socialist movements, socialist parties), 5, 10, 11, 13, 15, 16, 18, 19, 20, 22, 40, 43-46, 50, 51, 52, 55, 56, 68, 76, 87, 88, 102, 129, 131, 133, 134, 142, 146, 147, 152, 159
Socialist-Zionist, 10, 11, 43, 44, 46, 48, 53, 55, 152
Solel Boneh, 44
Sorel, Georges, 5-6
Spanish Civil War, 46
Sperber, Dan, 171
Spiritual Dominance, *see* Dominant Party
status, 4, 6, 7, 21, 120, 165, 168, 171
status politics, 7, 118, 121, 169, 171; definition of, 6
status symbols, 6, 168, 171
Stricker, Robert, 15, 26
symbol(s), 2-7, 35, 46, 82, 102, 106, 112, 117, 118, 122, 142, 149, 151, 170-172
Symbolic discourse, 81, 82, 171, 172; definition of, 7
symbols of status. *See* status symbols
Szofman, Yosef, 127

Tamir, Shmuel, 82, 101, 132, 133, 136-140, 148
Tiar, Avraham, 147